You Lucky People

The Story of Travel – the world's most
delightful and devastating industry

Valère Tjolle

ISBN 979-8-616380-37-1

Cover illustration: Jon Birch
www.jonbirchartist.com

Design & typesetting: David Siddall Multimedia, UK
www.davidsiddall.com

Also available from Amazon as a Kindle eBook

Contents

For Eliza, James, Freddie,
Sophia, Thea and Naomi

You Lucky People is the story of one travel insider's fabulous journey – creating living experiences in the world's biggest industry.

It tells how fun in the sun has grown dramatically over the last 60 years to employ a billion people and cast its shadow and its riches all over our global heritage, making billionaires and bankrupts, desires and disappointments.

This is the story of the addictive industry of dreams that we all love.

Come for the ride…

CHAPTER 1

Falling in Love

In 1953, at the tender age of 8, I fell in love – twice. The lovely Janet Fairly-Clarke was the object of my warmly tender intentions in Country Dancing classes at my suburban primary school. But the travel industry became the real focus for my wild dreams of freedom and adventure. To be precise, I visited the Polytechnic Travel Agency. Here I acquired a full-colour promotional map of the Rhineland, one of a set published by the German National Tourist Office covering the whole of Germany like a jigsaw. Forget the 'Reveille', 'Tit Bits' the 'News of the World' 'Roy Rogers and Trigger' (my two lesser loves) these maps were the real stuff and I was in rapture. The thought of going to the Rhine, taking people there, being a part of the nascent industry of tourism really switched me on. I was like a novice drug-user dropping acid – the universe was exposed. I loved the whole idea, the new worlds that would open, the opportunities for escaping drab post-war Britain for amazingly colourful and exotic foreign parts enthralled me. Mr Colesley, the ex-soldier manager of the Polytechnic Travel Agency in Bristol's Zetland Road, became my guru.

Tourism was a major topic of conversation in our home too. My Dad, Fred Tjolle, was a train driver, secretary of his union branch and very popular with his mates. With a family in Belgium, he seemed the logical choice to organise a darts match for his fellow workers in Ostend – an enjoyable way for railway workers to use up their free passes. Well, one thing led to another and before you could say "Travel Industry" the old man swapped his two allotments, his push-bike and his overalls for a smart suit, a carnation and a taste for cigars, lobster and gin and tonic – at just 39 he became a tour operator.

I couldn't believe it – my dad – a travel boss! Most boys of my age would have been proud to have a train driver dad but mine had been elevated to stardom. My job was to provide him with his morning 20 'Players' cigarettes, his 'Sporting Life' and to make sure that he had his twist of leaf tea, his sugar and his little bottle of milk ready for action on the footplate. After a year or so cycling to work in his overalls, driving his steam train, cycling home, changing, and taking tours to Belgium, his guvnors gave Dad a year's leave of absence from The Great Western Railway. Our little suburban Victorian terraced home now became the international headquarters for the Jolly Party Continental Tours. Posters were liberally displayed in the windows advertising "(no) Tours to the Moon" (the printer's idea), and Dad talked famous comedian

Tommy Trinder (catch phrase 'You Lucky People" into endorsing his product – "You lucky people going on a Jolly tour!", he said in the ad's. Business, cash and cheques rolled in.

Then, as now, the travel business was about hype and escapism. My old man, like the many larger-than-life characters who followed, had found his métier. The public wanted an escape from boring Britain. Who better to provide it than someone demonstrating their own escape from a humdrum wage-earning life?

You've got to give it to the old man. He'd had no business training and he'd never worked in an office. The nearest he'd got to commerce was his love for gambling on the horses, an enthusiasm he shared with his Dad. Since a very early age, he'd spent time on racecourses, studying the form, associating with racing people and making well-considered bets. My Dad was a lucky gambler; a bet rescued a pre-honeymoon Belgian holiday with my mum when he was in his late teens in the thirties, and his Belgian connections provided a win serious enough to start the travel company. Apparently, a Belgian jockey friend had said to Dad in Ostend after Lavandin had won the Prix de Boulogne "Freddie, put your house on it for the English Derby". Freddie did. At nine to two he won a small fortune. Enough to start a business in fact.

And enough to convince my dad's friends (and my dad, unfortunately) of his star quality. They were certainly a celebrity-like pair, my parents. Dad was what they call a Man's Man, but he loved tailormade clothes, diamonds, gin and tonic, lobsters and caviar, spending money, being overgenerous and his daily carnation (always got from his friend in the flower market) people and pubs, women and, of course my mum.

Of course, she was beautiful, she was my mum. Described as a Green-Eyed Egyptian Bastard by my uncle (actually her eyes were grey, and she was Welsh) mum was tiny passionate and vivacious with a very strong helping of wild wilfulness and a very hot temper. Strange that she loved knitting and sewing and reading – but then at that time those were the only artistic pursuits easily available to the working classes.

And my mum was definitely working class. And a socialist. What else could you be if you were Welsh, born in the poverty and danger of the coal mining valleys, and if your dad had been thrown out of work by the mine owners because of his political beliefs. All this, and the fact that my mum, like many others, had been denied her county school scholarship because of poverty and had to work as a maid – coloured her beliefs and determination to succeed. Until her dying day she never had a good word to say for Winston Churchill – "the owner's bully-boy" "the warmonger" she called him.

My mum needed success more than anything for escape. She needed to escape the elephant who always turned up in the room – unbidden. My gran.

Not a nice little sweet gran like my mum would become, but a demanding determined strong rich self-made gran like the one who lived with us – or we lived with, more factually. The gran that bought the house and the telly out of her hard-saved earnings.

And wielded immense power because of her contacts. Originally a maid, gran had risen to prominence and a little fortune as a result of the sage advice, capabilities and trustworthiness that her upper-class employers admired. Her network of trusting ex-employers stretched from the Archbishop of Nigeria to the governor of Fiji. Naturally when, later, I needed an Italian teacher she produced Miss Marie Rogman – clearly a top spy fallen on hard times.

There was a blot on gran's copybook though – 'Charlie', actually Gustave Tjolle.

Wounded in the First World War 'Trench of Death' in Diksmuide, near to his home town, Belgian soldier Gustave Ivo Tjolle had been brought to Bath to recuperate in a posh mansion. Gran was working there and met him. One thing led to another, a few years and a lot of letters later found kindly, strong, romantic Belgian Gustave (Mr Charlie to those who knew him) living in Bristol with Annie and a baby on the way. The adored only child, Freddie, was born. Although she treated him abruptly, and with some disdain, gran truly loved Gustave (Umpah to me) and after he died in 1949 her heart was broken.

Nonetheless her fortunes, her hard work and her savings proceeded to grow, now all focused on her son.

So that was the family behind our travel business enterprise.

Within a year of Lavandin's notable victory the Jolly Party Continental Tours was rocking on to better and greater things. My Dad, as I said, had no business experience, but from a marketing point of view he was doing all the right things. He had created a branded product in a niche market – railway people with free passes and 'Privilege Tickets'. He had a database – never mind that it was just a big book in which names and addresses of enquirers and bookers were entered in his flowing copper plate longhand. He had a target market and a lot of goodwill from previous travellers. At least twice a year a mailshot was sent out – different coloured sheets of paper each with a different tour were collated, inserted in envelopes, addressed by hand and posted to the database – all the family joined in. The leaflets went out in January and September and the bookings came in February and October. Simple and very effective.

Jolly Party Continental Tours' holidays were certainly good value but costed to make a profit. The deal was simple – you got an 8-day (7-night) full board Belgium France and Holland tour staying in Ostend for £19 including the transfers to and from the hotel, half day excursions to Meli Park and Dunkirk, Bruges and Sluis, full day excursions to Brussels and Middleburg. The hotel cost £7 for 7 nights, the tours and transfers, operated by the local coach company cost £6, the old man put on a margin of £6 and got a gross margin of 32%. The customers booked in their droves and the money kept rolling in. Everybody loved it. The clients loved the tours. The suppliers loved the business. The old man loved the prestige and the money and the opportunities for enjoying himself. Magic.

Every Monday evening from May to September, Dad went out to have a drink or two. He'd make a little "Pub Tour" around Bristol. It came to be known in the family as "Tjolle Monday" and, although you'd never be quite sure where he was, you'd be pretty certain of the state in which the old man would return. All tours departed on Tuesday and he personally escorted them to Belgium so possibly he was saying goodbye to all his old friends in case he wasn't going to come back. Who knows? In any case, by Monday night he was always totally out of his head.

He never missed a Tuesday, though, and these followed their regular schedule too. The taxi came in the morning at about 8 (although he drove a train, my father never learnt to drive a car) and took him to Bristol's Temple Meads station. A superb breakfast on the train (tomato juice, eggs, bacon, sausages, mushrooms, fried potatoes, toast, marmalade, tea, coffee – the works) presumably settled his stomach and set him up for the day and at Paddington Station he got a taxi to Victoria. Passengers were met outside the Golden Arrow bar at Victoria Station, given their reservations, ticked off on the list and given a little red Jolly Party badge to wear, then despatched to meet at 2pm. Time for a few drinks and something to eat before joining the group for the journey to Dover and a couple more snifters on the train. All railway and ferry officials were kept in order and onside by the liberal dispensation of alcohol, bonhomie and the handshake transferring the folded ten bob or fifty franc note. On boarding the ferry, Dad would go straight to the First-Class Bar, where he'd hold court and quickly be joined by the ship's purser and ticket collectors, eager to enjoy the fun and collect their dues. Four hours or so later, on arrival at Ostend, the ship's purser would come to collect Dad to make sure he got off the front of the ship with the first privileged group. Coaches were waiting at the ferry terminal to take the passengers to the hotels, and once they were boarded, Dad would pop off for a drink or two before beginning his rounds.

The passengers stayed in a number of hotels in Ostend. Not very sophisticated by today's standards but certainly very good value. The £1 a night per person that the old man paid got a bed in a clean room (single or double) with linoleum floor and central heating and full board with packed lunches when on full day excursions. Breakfast was 'Continental' – weak tea or freshly-brewed coffee, rolls, butter and jam (eggs and bacon at a supplement). Three course lunches and dinners usually consisting of a home-made soup, or hors d'oevres, English-style main course, and a dessert. Packed lunches usually consisted of sandwiches, the inevitable hard-boiled egg or two and a bit of fruit.

Anyway, the old man liked making sure everybody was happy and having a drink with his mates. To make sure everybody was happy, he would visit the hotels immediately after the passengers had arrived, pay the bill for the accommodation and have a drink or two with the hotelier. Then, he'd go out and have a few drinks.

Our little company's big opportunity happened in 1958 when the World Exhibition was unveiled in Brussels. Amongst other exhibits, the Atomium was created – to this day the major architectural land-mark on Brussels' horizon. Expo 58 marked a surge in public interest and tourism to Belgium. Jolly Party Continental Tours, now offering a £10 weekend and a £20 week, was in the thick of it.

At the time the UK government had instituted strict currency controls but never mind the 'V' forms that were meant to reduce Brits spend abroad, Dad had the answer. Sterling (Dad's profit) was paid in the UK and stayed in the UK and the foreign currency content of the tour (the part that Dad had to pay his suppliers) was paid on the ferry to Belgium. Dad recruited his bank manager to assist and they spent their time from Dover to Ostend collecting Belgian francs from the clients which they stuffed into big holdalls. By the time they arrived in Ostend the holdalls were bulging and the passengers were ready to rock. Thirsty work.

Literally thousands of tourists were taken to Brussels by my Dad that year, railway groups, school groups, private groups and nurses' groups (this was his contribution to the local hospitals – he liked nurses my dad!). Everybody wanted to see this first of the high-tech world exhibitions and explore the exotic continent and Fred was the man to show them – "You lucky people!" Ostend, just two hours or so from Brussels was the base. We stopped at the Sandcarpet café – (with its work of art in sand) for refreshments, toilets and to collect commission on the passengers' spend. On to the Expo for the day and back to Ostend for the night's revels.

So, what was Ostend like in the 1950's, and why did we all love it? Like my Dad, since I was very small, I'd spent all my holidays in Belgium. Not at first in Ostend – far too upmarket and expensive – but in the villages of Diksmuide and Wareghem where my grandfather's family lived. Grandfather Gustave ("Charlie" to his friends) had been a wounded Belgian soldier invalided to the West of England during the First World War, had fathered my Dad and didn't want to go home. So, we all went there for holidays instead. It was another world. My first Belgian experiences were of staying in sleepy Flemish towns close to the French border – Wareghem or Diksmuide – with relatives.

What an experience for a kid in the late 40's and 50's. These people in the villages were simply different. Life was clearly tough but it was not the same sort of tough that we had. My mum had had to go out cleaning to supplement Dad's wages and she was good at it. In the Flemish villages where my family lived, they made cleaning into an art form. Gleaming stoves in the middle of tiny rooms, polished floors, and covered furniture – my great auntie had even won the Best Kept Cottage competition in Wareghem two years in a row! These people talked different, they looked different, their interests were different (who'd ever heard of cycle and pigeon racing in those days?) in both of these occupations my family were big – they even owned the bicycle shop and global cycling superstar Eddie Mercx was family too. They dressed different and in particular, they smelt different (a warm musky smell like malted butter biscuits that I remember to this day). My Dad liked pubs, so he often met old mates in one of the local cafés and they'd drink a "pintje" (a glass of beer – definitely not a pint) or ten, but visiting the café was seen as extravagant by my relatives so, often, Mum and Dad and Gran, my sister Marita and I would progress from house to house drinking a tiny glass of liqueur in each. Diksmuide and Wareghem were no more than an hour away from Ostend by car, but even if they'd had a car to take them, my Flemish relatives wouldn't have been interested in going there. Far too extravagant, but just right for us, the post-war "loadsamoney Brits".

I guess you'd describe Ostend itself ('Queen of the Belgian Coast') as a Belgian version of Bournemouth. Quite upmarket and genteel. Ostend had a posh, exclusive casino, a thermal bath, a Cathedral, a racecourse, a superb promenade complete with a pier and plenty of parked Porsches, a fishing harbour with restaurants, lots of cafés and a marketplace with bandstand. It had amazing ice cream shops, tearooms serving extraordinary cakes, a park with a lake and motorboats-to-hire, chips, tomates aux crevettes, grenadine, interesting looking people, strange sounds and something that felt and looked to me like freedom.

As I said, in these first few years of post-war tourism, my Dad brought small groups of railwaymen to Belgium to play darts with Ostend café teams. Now, I've always been prone to embarrassment, and these people, our customers, embarrassed me, even though I liked them – and, after all, they were our source of income and standing. The customers possessed a kind of tourism chauvinism which I've now come to understand is endemic and not only practised by the Brits.

The host country is always, in the tourists' eyes, less substantial than the country the tourists come from. From the Brits' point of view, "they" didn't know how to make tea or a good breakfast, their money was "funny" (the post-war Belgian coins were described as "washers"), "they" were all a bit "poofy", the local food and sauces were "messy", and the beer was "weak" and "gassy". The Brits, whatever their humble origins, also had a proprietorial air – after all we'd only recently rescued them from the Germans albeit with assistance from the Yanks. The Brits came on holiday with us because it was a good laugh, they could drink all day and night, they could use their strong pounds, it was cheap and they could brag to their mates when they got home. There were a few arguments and fights but generally the Belgians kept their mouths shut and served the beer with grace, after all, they wanted the money.

As British mass tourism to Ostend developed, the local small entrepreneurs spotted opportunities. Establishments like the Cosy Corner Café – "tea like mother makes it" sprang up. Guinness and Double Diamond signs became ubiquitous, a "British Ball" was instituted at the Casino, and at Jackie's marketplace café the band became adept at leading the audience singing "There'll always be an England" or "Inglin" as they sang it.

By 1958, Brits were coming to Ostend in their hordes. I was 13 and it was wonderful. I was helping in the business now and school was going badly – I don't think that there was much competition. I'd been pretty much exposed to all the benefits of tourism – flocks of envious tourists (some quite young, attractive and fanciable), nice things to eat and drink, status, cash in the pocket. The net effect was tourism ten, school nil. Winter evenings were to be spent stuffing envelopes, summers in Ostend-paradise-on-Earth, schoolwork fitted in between.

My next summer holiday started with my school's trip to Bavaria, by train via Ostend. Imagine my pride when a local hotelier boarded at Ostend with a specially prepared chicken dinner so I wouldn't get hungry on the overnight journey, even more street-cred. Bliss. The next morning, in the couchette cabin, as the sun rose, I looked out of the window while the train chuffed into fairyland. I was simply captivated by all the beauty. I saw green meadows studded with alpine flowers and crossed by little streams, deep valleys and soaring mountains, dinky chalets with geraniums popping out of every window box, clean cows (complete with bells) grazing in the fields, onion-domed churches, lederhosen-clad farmers, dirndl-draped farmers wives. I truly thought I was dreaming; I couldn't believe that such pristine picture-perfect beauty could exist.

Back to Ostend to work after my holidays (I was 14 by now after all), I spent the rest of the summer learning the basic lessons of tourism in a busy resort. First step was to learn to smoke and drink like the rest of the industry. Smoking was no problem – after all I'd been doing it since I was 8, I just had to choose a local brand that suited me. St Michel were very good, came in 25's without filter in a flash paper packet and were cheap plus they made me seem even more local for my customer interface. Drinking was a bit more difficult, even in Belgium a 14-year-old serious imbiber was a little frowned upon. I got over that problem by changing my age. From now on, in Belgium, I was a heavy smoking and serious drinking 17-year-old – quite part of the local tourism community.

It is a fundamental and unchanging tourism rule that tour operators can never make sustainable money by sending people on holiday. Tour operators simply do the basics, they create the holidays, do all the research, haggle with hotels and transportation companies. They then fight amongst each other to get the "Best deals for their clients" – to deliver the most product for the lowest prices. Effectively this means that he who has the slimmest and most dangerous margins, and/or he who has screwed his suppliers below the ground gets the most clients. The operator then writes and designs brochures and advertises his "Brilliant" holidays. A few telephone calls, a letter, a booking form and a cheque later, it's the tour operator's job to get the clients to the resort, to disburse the money that he's been looking after and to take responsibility for any screw-ups.

The action really begins when the ingenue tourist reaches the destination. Destinations, generally, have a limited season. That means a limited period of time in which to make the money that'll keep everybody happy for the rest of the year. Tourists are really welcome. They've done their part and shopped for the best tour, now they've exhausted (or left at home) their commercial perceptions with their inhibitions but they've brought their wallets and they want – and think they're entitled to – a great holiday which usually means spending as much as they can afford and often more.

So, what do tourists mean to a destination? Tourists simply mean money. At the beginning of their holiday, they're taken from their secure homes and delivered to a resort that they've probably never been to before. To spend! The tour operator probably talked to the tourists a couple of times before they booked, and a couple of times after. The total interchange can last for up to an hour – max. The destination hotel sees the tourist every day as does the resort rep (often a local). Local shopkeepers, bus drivers, guides, café owners and a multiplicity of local others have more of a long-term relationship with tourists than the tour operator ever does. All this is added to the fact that however self-reliant tourists are in their hometowns, when they are on holiday, they're dependent. Given all that available and unprotected money, and the need to make as much as possible before the season ends, it's understandable that tourists are screwed – often in more ways than one.

Successful destinations are efficient money-making machines in which every small entrepreneur – and I include tour operators' reps and guides in this category – play their well-rehearsed part. It's good for everybody, the tourist enjoys their stay and the local services make a wad of dough. The tour operator who thought he was in charge of the game – after all the tourists are "his" clients – has now fulfilled his purpose in the destination's evolutionary process. As far as the destination is concerned, he's delivered the tourists complete with money – job done. The balance between destination and tour operator would change over the succeeding years, but the basic process would always remain the same.

So, in Ostend, I went to the port each Tuesday with the transfer coaches to meet the clients (scanning the passenger lists first to see what I could glean from the Misses' names), meet Dad and take the clients to the hotels. There were frequent hotel overbookings in the high season and often I trooped around from hotel to hotel with a little group of tourists to find them beds. No threats of legal action, no complaints, the clients were pleased to get a nice clean bed and a continental holiday – after all, this was 1959!

Each week the clients were different but wherever they came from, whatever they wanted they got basically the same. As in every destination, all the operators do their excursions on the same day – just in case they need to consolidate and each summer week for the next three years went something like this:

Tuesday evening arrival. Make sure that they've all got beds. After dinner they'll all take a drink at their hotel, make sure they're all seen and chat them up a bit, particularly any attractive female young person. Maybe they'd like to go out for a drink, to one of the nightclubs perhaps.

Wednesday was free. This is their chance to have a really good look at Ostend and spend a little money also the chance for a local guide to sell them a night out or an extra excursion for cash (known as "Black" in the trade).

Thursday was yet another foreign country. A whole day trip to the market in Middleburg – a chance for the Dutch to get at the tourist money. The customers would all hop on to the coach at 8 complete with packed lunch – sandwiches, possibly a boiled egg and fruit – and relax to enjoy the day. The guide (often me) or driver's commentary would start on the outskirts of Ostend – hamming up the foreign accent and trotting out a few unimpressive facts (unimpressive unless you were a tourist of course). Down the coast, past Zeebrugge (the U Boat pen and the mole), Blankenberghe (pass) and the the casino and the millionaire's residences at Knokke. In no time at all we would be at Breskens, refreshment stop – free coffees and tips for the driver and guide. On to the romantic ferry (well I thought it was and I'm sure the clients did) to Flushing (Vlissingen to the locals) on the island of Walcheren. Main stop of the day was the market in Middleburg. Here, shopping and spending opportunities abound. Cheese, clogs, little Dutch dolls, Delft windmills, lace – plenty of things that would be worth nothing in two weeks and would be extremely collectible in fifty years. Eat your sandwiches with drinks at the recommended café (more freebies and tips for the crew) – afterwards you can take a picture with a nice big Dutch lady in National costume – for a fee of course. Personally, I loved the market for one thing – smoked eel, just peel the skin off and suck the flesh – magnificent. And the Dutch beer of course.

Back to Breskens for the afternoon entertainment. A big beerhall and a mechanical band, oompah marionettes playing real Dutch music, what could be better at teatime? The customers satisfied and our bellies and pockets full, we'd drive back along the coast to Ostend, dinner and the night-time entertainment. Good night out... tomorrow's just an afternoon tour. The White Horse Inn – "in t'Witte Paard", "au Cheval Blanc" provided a riotous night out for the clients. More oompah bands, you could have glasses, big glasses, big glass mugs or enormous steins of beer. These were expensive, even for the British and they had to be told that they didn't have to pay to get in, but they paid over the top for drinks ...what? They always enjoyed themselves, the more so because they'd been initiated into another quaint continental custom. If they'd gone upstairs into the Weinstube they could have had expensive wine too, but wine would have been a step too far.

My favourite day, Friday. Why? French cheese and white wine in Dunkirk and great big ham sandwiches and big, big hot Belgian waffles with cream at Meli Park – all free, and plenty of booze. So, we'd get the passengers on and usually I'd sit on the coach's engine to give a "commentary". We'd leave after lunch, down the Belgian coast past Mariakerke and Middelkerke to the border with France, stop for a drink at the border café – it's probably still got the same sign up "NO TOILETS WITHOUT CONSUMPTION" – and nip down to Dunkirk centre. Never the most appealing town in the world, but in those days many of our passengers had left there before – in a hurry, in 1940. So, it was interesting to point out the shell marks in the walls, and they liked coming back in a completely different guise. A few glasses of wine and some cheese and garlic sausage in a café, little walk around, another country done. It's off to Adinkerke.

Mr Florizoone is one of my tourism marketing heroes, one of the greats, if there was a tourism marketing hall of fame – and there should be – Mr Florizoone should be in its top ten of "Great Pioneers from whom everybody learnt". Mr Florizoone (sorry, Mr Florizoone's bees) made honey. Great honey, in fact. Mr Florizoone and his family put the honey into jars and sold it. Mr Florizoone's customers liked the honey, very much, as they should – it is very good honey as I said. So far so good, nice business. Now the basic principle of marketing development, one that should never be forgotten is... "Sell new products to your customers, sell your products to new customers". I don't suppose that he had a marketing degree, but like most of the post-war marketers, Mr Florizoone knew exactly what to do and he had panache and flair (and a wonderful product!). First, Mr Florizoone branded his product. "Meli Park, he called his establishment – French for honey "Miel" – geddit? I imagine Mr Florizoone in his new product department (Like Charlie's chocolate factory). Here, Mr Florizoone developed a range of honey products that defied belief. Honey with Royal Jelly, honey without, honey sweets, runny honey, firm honey, medicinal honey preparations, Royal Jelly tablets, and my personal favourites... chocolate honey and honey cake among many many more Florizoone-branded honey-derivated delicacies.

So, what about selling Mr Florizoone's honey-delicacies to new markets? This was Mr Florizoone's masterstroke. He created a park entirely devoted to honey and to the tastes of those that liked honey. – Meli Park, – Disneyland with a purpose and big-time attractions to draw the tourists... Lovely gardens, wonderful musical tableaux of classic fairytales, floodlit musical dancing fountains and an amazing variety of opportunities to buy an incredible array of honey products. The new markets came to him in their droves. I loved all of the honey-stuff and learnt that Cinderella is Puttefatte (in German), Ashputel (In Swedish), Cendrillon (in French) and Cenerentola (in Italian). I still love the honey.

Why was Mr Florizoone's coach park always full of coaches? Two basic reasons. He gave the customers a good deal – they loved the park and the honey, and he really looked after the coach drivers and guides. So, after Dunkirk, we'd show up at Meli Park for the rest of the afternoon. The customers were despatched to explore, we'd hive off to the "Chauffeurs Room" in the restaurant. We'd get a pot of quality coffee or a beer, a ham or cheese open sandwich (a thick slice of fresh bread with a thick slice of ham) and a waffle with icing sugar and fresh cream. These were called waffles plus we were in Belgium, but they bear absolutely no relationship with the things sold as "Belgian Waffles" nowadays. They were feather light, as big as two paperback books put together, sprinkled with icing sugar, and just warm enough for the cream that you spread to melt in each little recess. They melted in the mouth like sugary, creamy, delicious gossamer. See, Mr Florizoone always delivered quality – even when he was giving it away. Then we played mini-golf and had a beer or two.

And Mr Florizoone had learnt marketing from the bees too. He employed a gang of lads who smacked Melipark stickers on the backs of each car as they left to pollinate Europe with their honeyed message!

Early departure on Saturday for Brussels. All ready and set with the packed lunch, on to the coach and away up the motorway. Were there motorways in 1958? Hitler'd built it. Not much by today's standards but something really different at the time, and, renewed and upgraded, very effective in getting all those people to Brussels for the Expo 58. First stop, the Sandcarpet Café. Works of art in coloured sand plus coffee, tea and beer, then on to Brussels. Park the coach and walk them to the Grand Place "As you can see, the tower is not quite in the middle of the building... when the architect saw it, he jumped off the top" amazing what people will believe. More to the point it's time to walk to the highlight of the morning... the Manekin Pis. Little statue of a naked, cherubic little boy on the corner of a little street. Peeing. It's what people want to see, still. What an industry the Mannekin Pis has created. Photographs, models, a museum with its 250 costumes. Tourists buy Mannekin Pis corkscrews (yes, you can imagine where the corkscrew part is!), dolls, chocolate, biscuits, bottles, postcards the lot. You name it, the Mannekin Pis has endorsed it for over 400 years. "You wouldn't go to Paris without seeing the Mona Lisa, would you? Why go to Brussels without seeing the Mannekin Pis?" Guides with flags/umbrellas/whatever held high leading long lines of camera-clad people to the Mannekin Pis. It's what tourism's all about.

Lunch and a few beers, here's where I discovered Trappist Ale, and it's off for a quick tour, a panoramic view of Brussels and the Atomium before we're off again... to Ghent.

Now, to me, in those days, Ghent meant one thing... coffee in the Radskelder – the cellars of the belfry. I guess people wandered around, and I certainly told them about the wonderful sculpture of the "Merchants of Ghent" as we came into the city, but not much else, they liked to have their tea, you see. I'd have a wander in the very close vicinity and a drink. So, it took some 40 years, yes 40 years before I realised what a truly extraordinary city Ghent is. I guess that the customers we took there then never did. On to Ostend for dinner and a night out. Again.

Sunday was delightful always, and to be perfectly honest, a dream Sunday for me has still got to be a nice breakfast, a bit of a wander, lunch and then an afternoon in Bruges. We'd usually go to Sluis just over the border in Holland first, chance to shepherd the passengers into the "Chosen" souvenir shop to stock up on much-needed little dolls, lace and Delft, little musical windmills that lit up, snaps with traditional locals, buy some Advocaat or Cherry Brandy (real delicacies in those days), stroll down the canal, see the windmill, board the coach, off to Bruges – the first and only "Venice of the North". Chocolates? Not in those days – they're a massive moneymaking tourist economy gimmick that arrived really recently. Now try to count the chocolate shops in Bruges – maybe there are even more than Chinese-owned mask shops in Venice (another modern mass tourism phenomenon.)

The customers loved Bruges, they always did and they always will. Yes of course, it's a World Heritage site, yes of course it's got loads of churches, museums and wonderful art treasures, yes of course it's got stunning architecture created during its colourful rich historic past, but it's got much, much more than all that. In my view, Bruges has got nearly every trump in the tourism pack of cards and, over the years, it's played them all extraordinarily well.

The 2 to the 8 of Bruges tourism trumps are 'Special Interests'.

In the travel industry 'Special Interest Travel' is seen as a powerful magnet for tourists and a real money-spinner. Even to the extent that people are paid to sit around and create special interests where none exist, – think of darts festivals for instance – another example of a tourism consultant making money for his clients.

This is how it works... find a particular place where you only get gingham mice – sell trips to see them to the Gingham Mice Lovers brigades around the world. Niche product, niche market in today's jargon – the nicher the better! Result... the Gingham Mice fancier not only gets a trip for his money but also, they get to follow their addiction too... and they'll pay more for it. It all gets a bit dodgy when you make your own gingham mice – but hey-ho that's tourism for you – 'Quality tourism' it's called, quantity money it makes. Bruges has got lots of Special Interests, at least enough to count from 2 to 7 trumps. Just look at the list of potential clients – History buffs (you don't get more Middle-Aged-Important than Bruges), religious pilgrims (the Holy Blood in the church of the same name is said to liquify every 10 years), lace makers (a growth industry), beer drinkers (seriously, there's one café in Bruges with over 400 types of beer), architecture enthusiasts (Just look at the Step-Gables), art lovers (there's even a Michelangelo Madonna and Child here), antique hunters (Bruges' antique shops are stuffed with expensive old things and the flea markets are incredible), even chocoholics (believe me, now there are more chocolate shops per square metre in Bruges than anywhere else in the world), if there aren't Bruges chocolate-making courses for bored housewives in their hundreds now, you can bet your life there will be). Enough? Enough to ensure a steady flow of quality money, that's for sure.

The nine of tourism trumps is... visible history:

People like looking at history. Although learning about history in school is BORING! the general public love history facts and stories and they like to be where it happened. Often not to feel or look or indeed see, but to pick up stories and take Instagram and Facebook pictures, go home and retail/retell them to their friends. Also, one of the greatest facets of tourism is right there at the top of Dr Maslow's "Hierarchy of Needs" – self actualisation. This translates to the following statement "We went for a trip to Bruges, it's very historic you know – would you like to see the pictures we took – bet you didn't know we were into history did you – we loved it! Now all on Facebook to prove its veracity. This actualises the speaker in his or her own mind as a lover of all things historic. Lovely – one step up. Also, visible history, in particular the medieval sort that Bruges has, creates a fairytale atmosphere – just like the films – with knights and fair damsels and alchemists and witches and things. Except you're in it, that fairytale world, just where it all happened. As all the theme parks have discovered, fairytale worlds draw in the clients.

The ten of tourism trumps... Bruges is quaint, walkable and compact.

You can pack a great deal into half a day in Bruges. You can see the canals (can't miss them in fact), you can walk over romantic bridges, you can see boats in the water, you can see delightful outdoor cafés with colourful awnings, you can bump along cobbled streets. You can get it all in a very reasonable period of time without missing a lot of the superficial stuff. That's very satisfying to the tourist. "Been there, seen it, done it" and back onto the coach. Bruges "Drill-down" potential means that there can always be more, too, if you want to look deeper on a second or twenty-second visit.

The Jack of tourism trumps... there are a lot of things to do in Bruges.

This fulfils two very important tourism-industry needs – a) provide the tourist with a fully-satisfying visit – a real experience that they can go home and tell their friends about, and b) provide earning opportunities for the locals. So, in Bruges you can take a canal boat trip (with commentaries in numerous languages), you can tour by horse-drawn carriage where you'll get blanketed-up and trotted about, you can visit lace-making factories staffed with dinky old ladies who must have been damsels in those olden days – and who'll sell you lace with a fervour, you'll have opportunities to see and hear the Carillon bells. Enough. Until the next time.

The Queen of tourism trumps... There are plenty of things to buy.

Tourists, generally, want more than snaps as proof of their visit. They need souvenirs too. Yet another opportunity for self-actualisation here. So, you'll find the whole range of Bruges souvenir-tat readily available on each and every tourist-street corner. Plenty of Manneke Pis's for the "Bucket and Spade Brigade", nice bits of "Hand Made" lace for the ladylike ladies, mass-produced prints and watercolours for the artistically-leaning and Bruges chocolates for everyone. Now it's "Been there, seen it done it AND got the "T" shirt!"

The King of tourism trumps... close to lots of places.

Now, if Bruges were in the depths of Outer Siberia it would have very few tourists and a very small tourism industry. That may seem a crazy statement, but the availability of people-capable-of-spending is critical to the equation. There are places all over the world with just as much, perhaps more, potential than Bruges – they just haven't been able to hack it... yet. Prague is a classic example. It was always just as glorious, but inaccessible. As soon as it became "close" twelve million tourists a year. There are many, many more glorious destinations just waiting for the tourism spotlight to shine on them. Bruges was just lucky. The spotlight shone there first, and it's stayed... why? Because Bruges has played its ace trump very, very well.

The Ace of tourism trumps... looking after the tourism asset.

Managing the tourism asset is critical in the equation, there are so many people to be pleased and needs to be satisfied that it is very difficult to steer a course that provides a sustainable flow of tourists... and money! Even if you have all the trump cards, you can still screw it up – bigtime. Just imagine Bruges after the first 50 years of mass tourism. It could have a multi-national in every prime site. McDonalds, all the Starbucks, Holiday Inns and many more. Yes, they're there, but they're either outside of the city heart, or they're tasteful and attractive – and they're not there in force. Bruges could be full up with tourist coaches and open-top buses – resulting in traffic chaos. It's not; they're kept outside, and cars are provided with a big underground car park within walking distance of the centre. Why have the burghers of Bruges taken an up-market attitude to tourism development? Because they're not stupid, and they want up-market tourists providing up-market money for their own homegrown entrepreneurs. Many a tourist city could take a leaf out of Bruges' tourism development attitude.

So, the tourists get a quality experience, the locals get quality money and quality opportunities.

Back to Sunday afternoon 1958 and we're bowling along back to Ostend. "Sing Something Simple" is on the BBC radio and we're all joining in "Goodnight Irene, Goodnight". And it will be.

Sunday night in Ostend. Monday free and "Big Night Out", the whole process will start up again on Tuesday.

Just in time for the 1961 season, I got thrown out of school. At 16, complete with three "O" levels, a smattering of French, Flemish, German and Italian, a nice pointy Italian hairstyle, a sharp shiny mohair suit, winkle-picker shoes and a gold identity bracelet the world was my oyster. I was ready for action!

By now things had moved on a bit in our little business. An office had been rented, staff had been employed and Dad had got everybody nice bright red blazers to match with the little red badges that all the clients had to wear. New tours had been inaugurated. You could go to the Rhineland, Nice and Monte Carlo, Switzerland, Paris, or Amsterdam – all, naturally, via Ostend.

My tourist-life had filled up with characters too. Here are my tourism-industry archetypes:

The Hotelier:

Roland was 38, complete with a lovely blonde wife, three small sons, a big house, a Triumph TR2, a pretty – and wayward French mistress with her very own bordello – and the Grand Hotel Georges V in Vlaanderenstraat – Ostend.

At the tender age of 14 (oops 17) it was decided that I was to learn the trade by working for my Dad in Ostend, meeting the passengers, guiding the odd tour and generally making sure that everything was OK. Where was I to stay?

Somewhere pretty cool, I hoped – and where was cooler than in the attic of the Georges V, stamping ground of my mate and glamorous role-model Roland. So, from the summer of 1959, and each summer for the next few years, my continental residence had been a garret in the centre of Ostend – heart of the action! My nights were spent on the razzle or working in the hotel bar listening to the sounds of the street – in those days Elvis warbling 'Are You Lonesome Tonight' or Dalida belting out 'Bambino' or 'Quand tu dors près de moi' from all the cinemas. My days were spent on daytrips with the customers or drinking coffee with the hotel staff.

Getting up was my biggest problem, but that was solved by the hotel chef Ted – a dour Belgian who spoke perfect Yorkshire English and slaved away in a sweaty basement kitchen. Ted devised the multiple wake-up process. First, he'd knock on the door, five minutes later he'd throw me out of bed, after another five minutes he'd wake me up on the bedroom floor and so on.

Here I learnt how a tour hotel works and it's a pretty simple equation – captive audience + lots of spending money = a good life for all.

Roland used to charge my Dad a quid a night full board for each passenger. That quid had to pay for the room, continental breakfast (rolls, jam, butter, coffee or tea), three course lunch (soup, main course, pudding – or packed lunch on tour) and three course dinner. Even when a quid was a quid this was tight, the lease had to be paid, the laundry accomplished and the hotel cleaned and repaired. So how did Roland make the money to keep a mistress and a sports car? Extras.

So, you want 'English breakfast' (eggs, bacon. etc) – five bob. A Stella in the bar – five bob. A whisky and soda (illegal in Belgium then) – ten bob. Breakfast in bed – two and six, and so it went on. Holiday-makers buy the basics cheap; they then deliver themselves as a captive audience to everybody in the destination. Behind the walls of his hotel, Roland had a monopoly. Plus, this is where you first learn that the tour operation itself is pretty low in the holiday food chain – the holiday-makers actually expose themselves and their soft underbellies (purses) to the hotelier!

The guide:

Although I've met thousands of Sashas since, dinky little Sasha Ravinsky will always be my archetype guide. Sacha was certainly better educated and much more cultured than the rest of the motley mob of tourism hangers-on. To start with, he spoke half a dozen languages fluently, he had a real interest in music and history and came from a distinctly upmarket background. So why was this tubby, scruffy little 40-year-old waving his flag in the midst of definitely lower-class tourists who would take the piss out of him at every opportunity and call him "Slasher" to his face? Was he writing the definitive work about Kant, a great symphony or choreographing a supreme work of dance (surprisingly, he'd been a ballet dancer once) and just trying to support himself in the meantime? Well he should have been doing all of those and more, but he wasn't. He was earning his living and devoting his resources to being a poor, downtrodden tour guide. Desperately trying to make sure of his commission at the souvenir shops and living on free meals from the restaurants. Educated, emotional, somehow disenfranchised, part teacher, part joke, part philosopher, wholly disgruntled and downtrodden, Sasha administered to his groups with no deference whatsoever.

Yes, OK there were flash tour guides of that era, earning lots of dosh and getting their ends away with lots of their passengers. Even in the '50's, tales of randy Loadsamoney guides and couriers were hitting the tabloids with unremitting frequency – earnings of £500 a week and more were frequently reported. But these were mainly svelte geezers chaperoning American tourists "Doing" Europe with more money than sense – the real money and the amazing party for guides in the tourism industry came later.

The coach operator:

Coachies, whether drivers or owners, are the Sex Icons of the Tourism industry. Macho to a fault, they drive and run their vehicles with a certain panache that seems to beguile their female passengers with absolutely no respect for class, age or type. I've seen dour, prim, elderly schoolmistresses aching with passion directed at ugly, crude drivers. I've seen gorgeous, sophisticated women falling desperately for ineffably boring, louche uneducated coach proprietors. In what world is the feat of steering a coach with your beer-belly – hands in the air – a come on? When on a coach, lovely ladies seem to enter the world of the hen party, and the driver's the strip-off policeman!

In Ostend, Roger Ramoudt and his brothers were the kiddies. They owned Ramoudts Coaches, they brought the coaches to the party and they were going to drive them. Dark, sleek, moustachioed, and swaggering the five brothers could have been mistaken for bit-players in a Spaghetti Western. They'd leap into the saddles of their red-and-blue Leyland Tiger Cub Jonkheeres and whisk you away to foreign lands, today Adinkerke, tomorrow Cologne, and then... who knows?

Rather like the airline industry, the masochism of the coaching business has never failed to amaze me. You can buy a superb bit of printing gear for rather less than you can buy a coach and you can charge a much higher hourly rate for printing. There are no real seasons in printing, your machine is dead cheap to run compared with a coach – and it's not out in all weather and prone to client abuse and accidents. So, if you wanted to make money, why not get into print? Simple... you can't paint your printing press in flash colours with your own name on it, you can't drive it around and you can't pick up babes.

The local tourism oligarch:

OK, Ostend had been hosting foreign guests for centuries before the 1950's, but hitherto they'd all been posh... The "Mijnheers" and "Mijvrouws" of Europe's middle and upper classes had come to Ostend to try the thermal baths and bathe in the sea in the specially-constructed bathing machines. A little horseracing, a promenade along the prom, a turn in the casino was sufficient for their needs. And, although they spent plenty of money, there weren't very many ABC1's then. So, when the first waves of mass foreign tourism hit Ostend, the locals understood the game, but not the new players. At first.

Easter
Wishes

There were, of course, hotels and restaurants. Quite a few of them, in fact. They'd been used to catering for pre-war domestic tourists and during-war foreign tourists, mainly from Germany and mainly in uniform. The domestic market had dried up – they were too busy with re-construction to spend the little money they had, and the foreign uniformed tourists had been defeated and had gone home to reconstruct their own country. The only real market available was over the water – the triumphant Brits, eager to re-bond with their Belgian cousins they'd so recently liberated and to bask in a little hero-worship and sun-on-the-beach.

So, what do you need for (mass) tourism? Basically, accommodation and transportation and a bit of marketing; you're there. Tell the hoteliers that you can get them business, negotiate rates with a few coachies, rent some coaches yourself, brand the product, make friends with the embryo foreign tour operators to get their business and before you can say "Nello Maertens", you're the local tourism oligarch. You've called your company "Ostend Travel Service" so nobody has any doubts about where you are, who you are and what you do and you're in control of the game. For a surprisingly long time. The local tourism providers trust you because you're one of them, the foreign tour operators like you because a) you sort out their on-the-spot problems and b) you look after them very well.

Nello was young and attractive and quickly powerful. He established an office right in the centre of things beside the Cathedral, leased hotels and coaches, trained and uniformed guides and quickly captured and held the marketplace. Who wouldn't be impressed and/ or envious? There were to be Nellos all over the world – maybe he sold the franchise and training scheme!

The Tour Operator:

My Dad's first introduction to tourism came around 1928, when he was 10, taking his holidays with his Dad's family in Diksmuide. Never heard of Diksmuide? Well, it was pretty famous at one time. Slap bang in the middle of the First World War, Diksmuide was razed to the ground – the inhabitants mostly took off to the South of France and came back when the war was over to rebuild their village exactly as it was, complete with medieval market square. You couldn't tell the difference.

When the tourists arrived for battlefield tours, they could see the Trench of Death, Hills 60 and 62, the Ypres Salient, and various other notable sights. They didn't come in their thousands, but in a big enough trickle to provide some reasonable remuneration for the locals and the local lads. Here the old man saw that tourism existed – and that it could be a profitable occupation.

In the early 1950's, a few years after the Second World War, my Dad was working as a railway driver, one of the benefits of which occupation was a limited number of free continental rail passes. Seeing the potential (free travel + cheap accommodation), he organised a few of his colleagues to go to Belgium to play darts and have a good (and cheap) time. Calling his group the "Jolly" Party, they all went, they all played darts with Belgian teams for cups, they all enjoyed it. Dad made some money, he enjoyed himself, so he repeated the exercise, again and again. Pretty soon he had a business – and a market – railwaymen with free passes.

Working on the classic marketeer's formula (to expand, you sell your product to a new market, and you sell new products to your market), he expanded both his product range and he entered a new market. By 1956, new tours were being sold using Ostend as a bridgehead (Rhineland and South of France) and a new market entered – the general public. Advertisements were placed in the mass media.

Then came a stroke of luck. Dad met Tommy Trinder, a very well-liked comedian of the day. Dad liked Tommy, Tommy liked Dad, and he was kind enough to endorse the Jolly Party Continental Tours in the form of a photograph, which appeared in National Press advertising. Tommy's catch-line was "You Lucky People" – ideal as an announcement in a travel ad. As far as I know, Tommy did it as a kindly gesture, it was a very generous act, and certainly boosted business substantially. Jolly Party Continental Tours was on the road! And the old man became my archetype tour operator.

Like many, many after him, Tour Operator Tjolle followed a path that began with recognising the tourism opportunity, continued by being able to convince others to believe his vision, then promoting and marketing to create the necessary critical mass. He never went into a bar, hotel, restaurant, indeed any establishment, without leaving brochures, he nurtured his relations with the press, he grabbed any opportunity he saw to promote his brand. He just loved to deliver experiences that he enjoyed to others, but eventually, his enjoyment got the better of him and he went bust in 1967 because he hadn't paid Roland's bill…

The Birth of Mass Tourism

Well, there I was, as usual on a summer Tuesday lunchtime, sitting on Victoria Station, underneath the clock, by the Golden Arrow Bar, in my posh red Jolly Party blazer. Waiting for another bunch of customers to arrive. What would they be like this week? Then she hove into view. Red suit, pencil skirt, tight little buttoned jacket with a tiny fur collar, nearly shoulder length straight black hair, face like an Egyptian dolly, heavy make up around almond eyes. Tall and skinny. Looked like an exotic ballerina. WOW. I was introduced to her. "Chan', Anthia "Daisy" Day …off on holiday with her Mum – my Dad's secretary's sister. "That bloody Geoffrey (Dad's secretary's son)", I thought, "Got this lovely thing all to himself – he must have snapped her up by now"

By the time evening came, I'd dispensed with the Mum and had Chan to myself. The pre-programmed seduction process involved a lot of drinks in a lot of cafés and the result was usually the same. Drunk girl in my bed, horrendous next day. Anyway, it didn't work this time, either she had willpower like iron or she had a head for the drink or both. Any which way, Chan drank me under the table, but yes, she did come to my room where I found myself sleeping on the floor with her hand in mine. And, yes, the next day we both felt pretty bad.

Back in Bristol, I pursued Chan remorselessly, if drunkenly. Eventually, I managed to propose to her sober and eventually, she accepted. We were to be married a week before my 20th birthday.

"No way" or whatever the expression was then, was I to be allowed to marry while I didn't have a real job (real job = working for someone other than my Dad). All the cool dudes worked in Advertising in the 60's and so would I.

Walter Pearce Advertising was rather a Dickensian company, certainly for the hip 1960s. Based in a large Victorian house in a leafy, upmarket part of Bristol, WP's main business was regional dealer advertising for a farm machinery company and "Situations Vacant" for the local hospitals.

The company was divided into different one-, or two-man departments. The one 'Account Executive' backed up by Mr Ron (Walter Pearce's son) dealt with the client or two. The Media Buyer bought the space in the selected publications. The Art department (Mr Lucas and his friend) designed the ad. Copy was supplied by our copywriter. Printing blocks were ordered by the Production Department (Stuart from Newcastle) and sent to the papers. I worked in the Voucher department and helped check that the ad's appeared. To get a rise, I had to brave one of the two Pearce brothers "Mr Ron" or "Mr Brian". Usually Mr Brian, who was the gentler and most short-sighted (with perennial newsprint on his nose from close reading). Mr Brian would look up myopically from his paper at the request and nod. Often an extra five or ten shillings would appear in my pay-packet at the end of the week. Before long, I'd stepped up the ladder and was made "Classified Advertisement Executive" and got married on the breadline salary of seven pounds ten shillings a week, rather less than my Dad would spend on a round of drinks.

Anyway, I learnt a lot while I was at WP, when the advertising industry was rapidly changing from a short-sighted, black-nailed group of Ragged Trousered Philanthropists to a sharp-suited bunch of media-hypester Mad Men. I spent long hours on an IPA (Institute of Practitioners in Advertising) course at Bristol College of Commerce. Here I learnt soon-to-be-forgotten skills like what "Hot Lead" was made of, what a 'Compositor' did and upcoming trades like 'Media Buying' and 'PR'. I also had great times perfecting my skills at Three-Card Brag. A card game which involved my losing my lunch money in super-quick time.

I learnt all about the techniques of print and production and the ethics of advertising (yes, there were some once!). I made my contribution – titles on all the ad's I bought were to be in very hip bold lower case. But the job had enabled me to get married and now I was married, it was time to re-join my chosen profession and first love.

I always found Avonmouth rather homely. I'd walk from our basement flat in Clifton every morning to the bus stop in Hotwells, just by the River Avon. The bus ride down the picturesque Avon Gorge (always reminded me of the Rhineland, even if there wasn't much water in the river) took me to Avonmouth village, and James & Hodder, just by the entrance to the dock. Like a great many shipping agents, James & Hodder had to arrange for the repatriation of crews to their home ports as part of their service to the shipowners. Plus, at the time, it was fashionable for middle class Brits to cruise on dirty old banana boats so J&H had lots of people asking them how to do it. Hey Presto, James and Hodder Travel was born. And, as I knew more than most about the travel business, I'd become its Assistant Manager.

Short, barrel-chested, ebullient, colourful, rough and ready Hugh, the James & Hodder manager, left me to it from my first day when he swanned off to the bookies. He had other things on his mind – the fate of the favourite in the 2.30 currently his most pressing concern. So, I learnt a lot at J&H very quickly – I had to! I learnt to take bookings for package tours, to issue airline, rail and bus tickets – and how to account for them. I learnt to arrange and book itineraries (mainly for Greek seamen traveling home via the direct Orient Express, or through Italy and via Brindisi and Patras). And to write stroppy letters to tour operators after customers had had their holidays ruined. I got my second-level drinking certificate at travel cocktail parties and learnt to enjoy 'Educationals'. In short, I learnt how to be a travel agent!

For some reason my dissolute Belgian-Coast lifestyle had abated somewhat, so I was just about capable of holding my own in a business where no-one knew anything much. One minute I was arranging for groups of aggressively drunken Danish seamen to fly home to Copenhagen. The next minute, I was trolling around church halls with a portable cine-projector and reels of cruise films to show to potential customers (we were nothing but up-to-the-minute then!).

My boredom was abated by the company's best client, a local port agent who supplied stevedoring services – laborers who unloaded ships. How I envied the flamboyant Mr Pruett and vicariously enjoyed his lifestyle. He'd push off on holiday in his Bentley with his beautiful young wife and family and a pack of our travel vouchers in his glove compartment, I'd stay at home to relish the accounts as they arrived, with completed vouchers for us to pay on Mr Pruett's behalf. The vouchers and their accompanying invoices told a tale of lavish extravagance on trails from Paris's George V Hotel to the South of France and beyond. Champagne breakfasts, exotic meals, cash advances for gambling, they were all neatly annotated and invoiced and provided ample ammunition for my daydreams. Poor old Mr Pruett, his travelling cost him his company. When his extravagant use of J&H vouchers cost more than the stevedoring services he provided, they had his company to pay the bill.

But Mr Pruett was a traveller of the past. This was the very beginning of the package-tour era and unheard-of destinations were beginning to emerge. Cheap sun, cheap booze, cheap sex, cheap thrills, cheap holidays for the masses spawned a surge of activity to profit from the boom.

Tour Operators popped up all over the UK equipped with glossy brochures and telephone lines, reservations systems and 'key and lamp' telephone units that allowed reservations clerks to talk to two people at once. Lyons Tours came from Lancashire and took you to the Costa Brava for 19 guineas for a week. Cosmos, financed by a Swiss travel agency, started a massive European programme from a Surbiton front-room. Friendship Tours ("to be a friend is to have one" – Emerson!) and Pegasus took you to Holland. Apal-See Spain took you to, well, Spain. CIT took you to Italy, Wallace Arnold took you by coach, usually all the way. Lewis Leroy Holidays took you (Mr Leroy's "Voyageurs") everywhere with their big brochure. Then there was a clutch of others, Global Tours – owned by the powerful Great Universal Stores – Riviera Holidays, Lunn Poly, Frames, Blue Sky, WTA (the Workers Travel Association), Galleon Holidays, Universal Sky Tours, were all to have later incarnations. Railwaymen with free passes (my dad's marketplace) were also catered for by Martin Rook (queues all the way down Ebury Street as soon as the brochure came out) and Panorama Holidays in Brighton. The middle classes were dealt with by ultra-cool designer brochures (attractive on the travel agent's brochure rack) with a lot of white space, nice pictures, posh covers and good names, Wings – no picture – just lines on the front cover, Lord Brothers – ultra-cool matt white paper run and created by ultra-cool brothers and Horizon Holidays were top of my hip list. Thomas Cook looked on paternally.

They all looked so professional, the brochures, that is. Good enough to eat. Guaranteed sunshine and good nights out with the chance of a "pull", an ensuite shower and toilet, and the travel, all for a couple of week's wages? Amazing. The only thing that could spoil it was messy foreign food. The clients flooded in with cash-in-their-hands to grasp their places. Business boomed.

And, of course, I knew a little bit about it. I remembered Ted, the chef in the George V Ostend saying to me "Valere, every week they bring 40 people, not 35 or 45. Every week 40. And they pay. On the dot. Top prices. Wallace Arnold. Now, that's reliability". And my mate Eike drunkenly pushing me onto the hotel steps and telling me "I'm working for this company. They're going to be really BIG all over Europe – Cosmos, they're called. AND they're paying me top money" "Oh yes Ted, oh yes Eike, heard it all before – it'll pass. Even now both of those companies are still growing.

There had never been a travel industry before, apart from Thomas Cook and a few toffee-nosed agents. Where would all of these people creating and selling holidays have got their experience from? Well, the wartime pilots (one or two of those) knew about flying planes, the odd hotelier (one or two of those) knew how to look after the customers, and the London taxi drivers (hundreds of them) had the unique combination of transportation, negotiating skills, customer service and Chutzpah! Just imagine an industry dominated by taxi drivers and their mates. Yes – the booming travel business of the 1960's was.

And nobody got to work out just why these holidays (to Spain, principally) were quite so cheap. I'll let you into a secret. They were cheap for two reasons. The first, because tour operators are inherently gamblers, always willing to work on dangerously thin margins, they lived on customer's cash and adrenaline, not profit!

The second, and probably more important and sustainable, reason is that, since the 1960s, governments have seen tourism as a very attractive industry. High employment, loads of hard currency, spin-offs into other industries and good PR.

"Oh" thought officials in Franco's Spain "How can we get a slice of this cake – even a BIG slice of this LOVELY tourist cake?", "Why don't we give interest-free loans to build hotels and BIG tax incentives?" "Think about it, not only do we get a tourism boom with high employment and lots of hard currency, but also we get a building boom AND while our lovely foreign visitors are drinking our Sangría (and paying for it) they're not thinking about horrible politics or human rights or Dictator Franco are they?"

So, Spain fuelled the 1960s tourism boom with the tour operators and airlines piling in for all the fun of the fair.

And quietly, the World Bank was making a play on the tourism roulette wheel too. In 1966 its first investments were made in Tunisia, Morocco and Indonesia, within 10 years some $billions would have been invested and World Bank money will have built the Mayan Riviera, Agadir, Kenya Coast, Dominican Republic, the Gambia, Turkey's coast, Bali. Ironic or what?

Three tour operators utterly stood out from the crowd in the UK. Horizon Holidays had been operating rather upmarket inclusive air tours for years, their speciality – quality and service at a mid-market price. Horizon had a loyal middle-class client base and they were to build it significantly over the years. Clarkson's Holidays had been operating day trips to Holland for Women's' Institute groups and entered the package holiday market with a bang – then left it in the same way! The Travel Club (Upminster) gradually increased its database of happy customers over many years. The antelope, the hare and the tortoise, who got there in the end, but who had the most fun?

Everybody always loved Horizon. Apart from anything else, they were posh, they were reliable, they were there before anybody else AND there were never any complaints. Vladimir Raitz's Horizon Holidays had pioneered the air-inclusive tour with its inclusive tours from Southend Airport to Corsica in an ex RAF DC3 operated by BKS (Barnby, Keegan and Stevens). Two flights a week in 1953 operating two-week inclusive tours to the sun for less than £40. Cheap it may have been, but this was no typical package holiday and the passengers were certainly not mass-market.

Horizon were always professional tour operators operating for a professional market. They did it well, they didn't stint, they were well loved by their clients and the trade. The Marks and Sparks of the travel business. You could depend on Horizon. So why did they sell out to Court Line? Because, usually the big boys win – for a time!

By the time their first brochure hit the travel agencies all the holidays had been sold and year after year the Clarkson's phenomenon got bigger and better. The fuel for their success was cheap prices and lots of clients, ultimately tens of millions provided fodder for the Clarkson's machine. Clarkson's pressed all the right buttons at the right time and their enthusiastic young staff taught the whole industry how to do it. Practically nothing has changed in the package-tour business since then. Vertical integration? Clarkson's did it first. Time charter of airplanes? Clarkson's did it first. Mass marketing? Clarkson's did it first. Cripplingly low prices and 50p per person margins? Clarkson's did it first. Long haul cheap holidays? Clarkson's did it first. Build your own resort? Clarkson's did it first. High pressure excursion and insurance sales? Clarkson's did it first. Cruises? Clarkson's did it first, even the buzz-phrase of the 2000's – Dynamic Packaging (lots of profit from extras). Clarkson's did that first too!

Building on their stable base of Women's Institute air and coach trips to the Dutch Bulbfields – DC3s again! Clarkson's, led by Tom Gullick, launched their first full-colour package tour brochure to the travel trade. For a few years, it sold out as soon as it hit the counters. Then came the frenetic development of the company and its carryings. Court Line became Clarkson's holding group and we saw the Court Line fleets of airplanes and coaches (pink!), the Court Line hotels in the Med and the Caribbean, the Court Line-owned ground handlers (travel agent fixers in destinations), Even bills were computer-generated. What a phenomenon.

A colourful, attractive, fabulous, fast moving, acquisitive, groundbreaking organisation, to be true, but, at the end of the day, when Clarkson's went bust their only fundamental asset proved to be their staff (the only bit they couldn't mortgage). And Clarkson's staff were the legacy that the company left to the travel business after its demise in 1974. The Clarkson's' macho mind-set purveyed by ex-employees proved inescapable and unopposable. So, company after company followed the lemming-route, hoping to do it bigger and better and ultimately collapsing. The addictive mix of wafer-thin margins, high volume, low wages, mass marketing and vertical integration has made the travel business unsustainable to this day.

The Travel Club (Upminster) Ltd was a legend. Quality holidays, reasonable prices, good service since 1936. Diligently managed. Everything that a travel company could and should be. They always dealt direct with their customers. Harry Chandler, the boss, and his wife Rene were trade figures. There are a few companies just like the Travel Club in the industry, they hit it on the button every time and they made a profit, year after year after year. Everybody thought that they had some hidden extra. The fact is that they had something missing. Hubris? Greed? Avarice? Testosterone? Bullshit?

But the company that was to eclipse them all was quietly being created from the debris of lots of other failures. Captain Ted Langton's Universal Sky Tours was just one of the bits that the Canadian publishing company Thomsons bought to form Thomson Holidays (the base for today's biggest global tour operator TUI). Into the mix went lots of other bits and bobs – including brash Riviera Holidays, Lyons of Colne and if I'm not mistaken 4S Travel with its choice of acronyms – Sun, Sand, Sea and Sex (this was the 1960's after all!) or the names of the founders – Andy Sawicky, Lionel Steinberg and Sid Silver – all at the beginnings of their travel industry careers.

It's hard to believe now, but I had my 21st birthday and my first wedding anniversary at the beginning of 1966. Can't remember a party, can remember sitting with a pint on my birthday in the Royal Hotel next door to the office in Avonmouth. By the end of the year, I was out of it, Hugh had been given the sack (they'd found out that his gambling had been financed by the company), I hadn't been offered his job and I'd got myself another one in London. Wow.

Before I left J&H, I took part in a few trade perks. Educationals. Opportunities for young women and men in the travel business to learn more about the product they were selling, and each other. Opportunities to network involving traveling, drinking and all the other stuff that young men and women do together. Plus, build life-long bonds, enmities and rivalries.

Friendship Holidays ("*To be a friend is to have one*" – Emerson) offered me a few days educational in Valkenburg in Holland. I remember flying from Manston to Maastricht in an elderly Invicta (Stevens and Kennard of BKS airlines fame) DC4, in very choppy weather with lots of screams and howls every time we plummeted after hitting air pockets. I remember talking to the big and avuncular Jo Niemans the proprietor of Friendship in Maastricht. I remember fancying the guide. I remember drinking a lot of Dutch alcohol – and that was the total of my Valkenburg learning.

The educational to Southampton to see a Union Castle ship (gin and ginger ale, cruises to South Africa, a showing of "Goldfinger" and a drunken liaison with a travel clerkess from LEP travel were the sum educational total of this trip).

Finally, the visit to Rimini, on a SAM DC6B which involved a great deal of booze, six course Italian meals and memory loss. Then Rimini was the global mecca for mass tourism. The Lido of Europe with over 100,000 hotel beds. The stylish hedonistic beach party city magnet for Nordic blondes and longing Italians. Everyone conveniently forgot that Rimini was packed full of culture and history too – all they wanted was Roman orgies. Pity that I hadn't known just how much the area would mean to me in the future!

But they all came in handy in later years.

I was off to the West End of London and the high life – working for a Sicilian company at the very cutting edge of the travel industry. The Saintseal bosses told me that there had been 300 applicants for the job and that I was the youngest and they'd given me an interview because of the letter I'd sent and they'd given me the job because they liked me and thought I'd fit in.

I guess they must have liked me. I'd been interviewed for the job by Ron who was a sort of English consigliore to the Saintseal godfathers. Having sold Saintseal a Kalamazoo accounts system, they must have liked the cut of Ron's, very Home Counties, glib and had taken him on as a consultant. Anyway, I'd made a variety of claims in my letter of application, including having learnt Italian. This was quite true, as a 14-year-old loving all things Italian, particularly the haircuts and the suits, I'd spent some time learning Italian from my gran's friend, Miss Rogman. This was great. The only problems being that a) I wasn't a very good learner when distracted, b) I was completely distracted by the only other member of the class being a stunningly, gorgeously beautiful 19-year-old and c) Miss Rogman's principal teaching methods were conversations conducted entirely in Italian and sending me off to read the whole of Dante – the Paradiso, Purgatorio, Inferno AND Vita Nuovo, – story of my life.

None of which was up to the job when Ron, not being able to speak Italian himself, asked a lovely female member of Saintseal's staff to check my Italian language skills. Possibly she liked me, possibly she didn't like Ron. At least she didn't let the cat out of the bag and departed smiling.

So, I got this letter to confirm my appointment as "Domestic Travel Manager" at Saintseal Travel from Dr Fabbri. Even I knew that 'Dr' didn't mean a medic, it probably meant that he a was Swiss academic. Pretty far from the truth, in fact. Dr Fabbri was Sicilian, born in Tripoli, the ex-London representative of the Banco di Roma and the current representative of the Banco di Sicilia. So, a very smart, erudite, upmarket, cosmopolitan, international banker with a little bit of Sicilian spice and sharpness! Anyway, the letter confirmed my salary – at £1,200 pa pretty reasonable, my removal expenses – some £200, and my expenses – basically unlimited. In 1966 this was riches indeed for a 21-year-old.

Saintseal Travel, 122 Buckingham Palace Road, London SW1. What an education. What an opera. What a cast. I will always be grateful for the best, and the kindest, and the most colourful education in travel and tourism that anybody could possibly have had. For a tourism glamour-struck impressionable young man, Saintseal was simply all my dreams come true. Plus, they doubled my salary. Plus, they gave me unlimited expenses. I was in a heavenly job in a heavenly place with heavenly prospects.

Dr Fabbri and "Nanny' Olivares (at 24 a whole 3 years older than me, and a close-cropped, very Nordic Northern Italian) ran the company from twin desks on the 1st floor, overlooking Buckingham Palace Road and Gorringes departmental store opposite. 'Ran' meant Nanny screaming hoarsely on the telephone, at visitors, at Dr Fabbri beside him and at anyone who came in, in English, in Italian, in French, any other language that came to hand, or a combination of all. 'Ran' meant Dr Fabbri shouting back at Nanny when he cared to and negotiating with his variety of telephone callers using a larger variety of manipulative methods than Nanny's croaking shouts.

I was positioned downstairs at the back of the shop, within full hearing of the top volume tirades above. Frightening to a provincial newby, however sophisticated he thought he was. Anyway, I got used to it all after a while, not speaking the variety of languages in use, I didn't know what was going on anyway. If I had known, who knows what I'd have thought!

It was 1966 London. World Cup year in England. Saintseal had thought that, under the managership of Edmondo Fabbri (bit of synchronicity there?), Italy was an invincible football team. So much so that they'd booked out the newly built skyscraper London Hilton Hotel for Italians to stay when they came to see Italy winning the World Cup final. Unfortunately for Saintseal, Italy never got as far as London, having been kicked out of the World cup by North Korea in Liverpool.

Also, that Easter, thousands of Columba Easter cakes had been over-ordered by Saintseal – so we all had plenty to eat anyway.

It's my view that Italians have by far the most understanding of the tourism business of any race. First of all, they have a 2000-year-plus history of tourism, outbound and inbound. Let's face it, the Romans were the first European tourists and, the Grand Tour for European aristocrats consisted mainly of Italy. Secondly, Italians have an ability to entice and romance people into doing things and going places – obviously that's why they're such good lovers. Thirdly, they really understand how important food and hospitality is. Fourthly, when they say "Yes, you can book a double room for the 24th at 1,000 Euros, you know that the chances are high that, come hell or high water, they will deliver. And fifthly and possibly most importantly – they know how to bend the rules just sufficiently to make money without completely capsizing the boat.

Saintseal Travel were an Incoming Tour Operator (what's now known as a DMC, or Destination Management Company in the trade). And a Bucket Shop (cheapo, strictly illegal but tolerated air ticket agency). And, with my arrival, a Travel Agency – the 'Domestic' part of my title referred to the market rather than to the destination.

The incoming side was easy. Once a year Nanny booked some flights, packed his suitcase, stuffed a few thousand dollars in his wallet and a few thousand brochures into his briefcase and pushed off around the world. It's nice to have a network (in Nanny's case it was principally Italian Americans and Italian Italians) to do business with. And the business rolled in from the USA, South America and Italy and other marketplaces. All coming to London. Only the best was good enough. Great.

Additionally, Dr Fabbri's sharp intellect had worked out a little ruse with the UK government. At the time, manufacturing industries who exported were supported by the "Export Credit Guarantee Department", ensuring that exporters were not exposed to bad debts and therefore found easy 50-80% upfront finance for their operations. "We're exporters too" said Dr Fabbri. "We want ECGD cover as well". And he got it. Next stop Barclays Bank!

The bucket shop was a little more difficult, remember, in those days you couldn't just charter airplanes and sell seats. Licences had to be applied for, and if you were an ordinary Joe (not a state airline like BEA, BOAC or Alitalia), you simply didn't get them granted. NO, NO, NO. The only loophole was if you could book special flights for what was called "Common Interest Group Travel" or "Inclusive Tours" or "Student Travel". That's why esoteric organizations like "The Trowbridge Cage Birds Society" were formed – so that their members could get the benefit of buying special price seats on specially-chartered flights. Even in the case of "Inclusive Tours", the arrangement had to include the flight, hotel accommodation and transfers and the price had to be in excess of the comparable scheduled flight charge. In the case of "Student Travel", the flight organizers had to be a recognized student body and the passengers had to be "bona fide" students.

That's why STB (Student Travel Bureau), operated by Saintseal Travel, became the London office of CRUEI (Centro Italiano Relazioni Universitarie Estero) – an organization fully appropriate to arrange flights and issue student cards for students traveling to and from Italy. A counterpart organization in Italy handled the Italy/UK sectors. Consequently, British students and Italian chefs, waiters, churchgoers, nuns, office workers, firemen, priests – provided they said they were students – became able to buy tickets from London to Milan or Venice for about £8 and to Rome, Naples or Palermo for about £10 one way.

Costings were simple – if the flight was half full one way it broke even. Full one way it made 100%. Full both ways 300%. I bet today's low-cost carriers would go green with envy. It's no wonder there was a lot of dosh floating around Saintseal.

And, if the students etc., couldn't afford the flights, they could go by train. Weekly STB trains were organized from Victoria Station, with guides, at special group rates.

It was all so easy to sell. At the time you'd have to pay up to 4 times the prices on a scheduled flight, double on a train journey – so there was a price advantage. Most Italians in the UK were either practicing Catholics, or certainly knew a priest or two. All you had to do is to make all the UK Italian priests know about the flights and the prices. Job done. Queues in Saintseals (sorry CRUEI's) shop in Buckingham Palace Road, fistfuls of pound notes in their hot hands.

All these passengers fuelled the rest of Saintseal's business too. Even if they were real students, the incoming flight passengers needed things. Transfers, accommodation, meals etc., – all the things that Saintseal's incoming department did. Good. More profit.

And that was where I was meant to come in. Inclusive tours – more services to an already captive audience. More profit for Saintseal.

So, I worked away at the back of the shop with my new posh Italian speaking secretary/assistant Gillian. A motley variety of people worked behind the counter (mainly Italian-speaking) and between me and them was the till. The till was operated on a very simple system. Somebody gave you money, you issued a pink receipt (and often a ticket) and stuffed the money into the till. You wanted spending money for anything, and you took the money out of the till and put in a yellow 'Please Pay' slip. At the end of the day, it was simple to tot up. Receipts minus please pays = cash in till. Great. And great for me too. If I needed any money for expenses (unlimited, remember), I just took it out of the till and put in a please pay or two. My expenses were pretty high, they had to be otherwise I wouldn't have been doing my job properly and, I certainly wouldn't have been drinking enough!

Unfortunately, the please pays combined with my drinking were to be the fatal flaw in my relationship with Buckingham Palace Road.

Time to test the system – nice wodge of Saintseal's dosh in my pocket off to meet a new contact in the heart of the city.

Alan Davies was to be my drinking mate and much more. Based in Regent Street, as General Manager of Yugotours he was the hippest in the industry. Yugotours you may ask who they? One of the biggest on the scene.

The communist republic of Yugoslavia made up what is now Slovenia, Croatia, Macedonia, Bosnia, Serbia and Montenegro. Fabulous Adriatic seaside destinations all the way down to Dubrovnik and beyond and superb historic and lake and mountain destinations such as Lake Bled and Lake Ohrid.

In all Yugoslavia was a tantalising treasury of tourism. Plus, as a less than hardline commie state they had the advantages of a superb centrally run tourism industry without the annoying necessity to make a profit.

All the Yugoslavs wanted was to use their parastate-owned tourism facilities (hotels, buses, restaurants etc) to their best advantage, give their citizens holidays, and, maybe, get a bit of hard foreign currency.

The Yugoslav tourist facilities were brilliant, being part state-owned meant that they didn't have to bother about profit but concentrated on efficiency. So, all Yugotours holidays offered great value, low prices and top quality – all in sensational destinations. Of course, the key was tourism product creation, marketing and distribution, so having the whole process managed by quasi-state organisations worked a dream. All the hotels, restaurants and hospitality worked perfectly because everybody had both training and job security. The destinations were generally full because they were part-owned by the factories and organisations that were their customers.

And the whole was co-ordinated by the handful of professional Yugoslavian, vertically-integrated, partly state-owned travel agencies such as Putnik, Globtur and Compass.

So, when the Yugoslavs wanted a bit of hard currency, dollars or pounds, francs or DMarks they were in prime positions to get them. Offices in top locations in New York, Paris, London etc., sold great Yugotours holidays at low prices and the money rolled in. Yugotours was a real success! In fact, by 1980 Yugotours was the UK's fourth biggest tour operator and Yugoslavia the UK's second most popular destination after Spain.

Back at Saintseal, I was mainly having a good time.

John, a posh and attractive young sports car driving Brit from Godalming looked after the cash and worked up in the attic with Jean Pierre (even more British than John). Jean Pierre was company secretary and a fellow of the Royal Geographical Society. He spoke at least 12 languages fluently. JP's tour guide career had been impaired by his speech impediment because his major employment was on coaches with mixed-language groups. By the time JP had explained "Big Ben's" history in Spanish, French, Italian, German and (Yes!) Mandarin and had a few long stutters, the group was already at Buckingham Palace. Anyway, JP ultimately was a true and very kind friend to me, a real gentleman, but lost in the days when 4-hour boozy lunches were going out of fashion.

The second floor was where it all happened. My arch-rival Eugenio ran the student travel organisation STB with his cohorts. Eugenio was equal with me in Saintseal's hierarchy, had the deepest voice I'd ever heard, was wholly macho, paranoid about gays (in his view a decadent 1960s London phenomenon), and worked obsessively hard. Eugenio needed a holiday – in Italy preferably "Where there were no queers!".

Others floated in and out of the offices, a squad of smart young expensively-educated Italian girls worked for Eugenio, Dr Fabbri and Nanny PA-ing and networking – Gillian, who was much more English uptight but very kind, did for me as my assistant. Bob, an Italian whose accent was a combination of pure Golders Green and Milan swanned in and out with high level emissaries he'd just driven from the airport. Mr Levy, who ran the branch in Paris (just by the Place Vendôme) frequently flew over for lunch, where he taught me to mix olive oil with gorgonzola cheese. The counter, and the chartered trains, were staffed by friends and friends of friends doing it for the money, the fun and the chat.

The shop was always full and very noisy. Customers shouted at the part-time staff, gesticulated at tickets, shook their fists, waved their hands and involved anybody within hearing. The part-time staff shouted back.

It was all great fun, and then we'd go out for coffee, lunch or a drink or dinner. Coffee was taken next door at the Alpino, one of a very smart little chain of Italian restaurants – the coffee was always perfect. Lunch was taken at the Alpino – always delicious and expensive. Drinks were taken at the 'Bag of Nails' – next door to the Alpino. All the Italians liked a drink. I liked drinking. And, if we were still there working in the evening, Nanny would take us all to Tiberio – a posh restaurant in Curzon Street where I learnt to order courses one-by-one, after the previous had been consumed.

We were at the centre of things. Down the road was my arch enemy Andrea who worked for Chaim and who saw that his travel agency's (Anglo South American) prominence was now been threatened by this jerk from the sticks (me!). Andrea disguised his voice (not very well as it happened) and harassed me on the phone. He stuffed aggressive notes through my letter box and tried to stare me out when he saw me. But poor old spotty, diminutive Andrea couldn't do threat very well, it wasn't his thing. Unusual for a Venetian – who mainly seemed to have learnt the art of delivering blood-curdling threats from kindergarten. Maybe that was why Andrea was in London.

Further down the road were my mates at Wasteels (a Belgian Travel Agency populated by Italians and run by Benny). Wasteels had all the proper licences, IATA (International Air Transport Association) British Rail, the lot. This meant that they could compute fares and issue tickets at full commission direct to the public. In fact, most of their business came from other agencies like us, splitting the take. They did trains too and their speciality was Italians, the same as us. So, we were rivals. But we did our own charters so we were in control of the product and, because we generated our own incoming business, we were rather more upmarket. Plus, however technically perfect the Wasteels staff were, they were paid much less than we were. They were the travel agency sweat-shop, we were the tour operator whiz-kids. It's easy to imagine how much resentment this could cause – but, miraculously, it didn't. Wasteels had their queues of Italian workers, stretching for 100 yards or so towards Victoria Station keeping the ticket-writers busy. Enough energy was expended in fulfilling the customers' and the bosses' needs to waste more with petty rivalries.

We met just by Victoria Station in the Windsor Castle pub. Roy, very macho and camp as a row of pink tents drinking pints, Angelo a dapper, smart Venetian trying hard to quaff his half and me, attempting (usually unsuccessfully) not to finish my pint first. All in the local travel business – Angelo managing Wasteels air department, Roy managing Galleon Holidays (an old-established tour operator) and I working for Saintseal. The queer Brit, the hardworking Venetian, and the overpaid Englishman setting the world to rights almost every lunchtime.

And there was a world to set to rights. England had beaten Germany in the World Cup 4-2; Italy had been beaten by North Korea. It was lucky that Angelo had eschewed interest in football (being a Venetian after all) or he'd have got an even bigger ragging. Good ol' Harold Wilson was negotiating with Ian Smith about UDI (Unilateral Declaration of Independence for Rhodesia) on board HMS Tiger. From Angelo's point of view, it was just another example of all the Commonwealth's peoples being subjects – he, after all was a citizen (of Venice). Barclays Bank had introduced the Barclaycard (as Roy said, another opportunity for the lower classes to get into debt). Cassius Clay had beaten our lovable Henry Cooper – although Henry had nearly got him in trouble. And the Krays were in the news again. Closer to home, Laker Airways had just been formed. And American Airlines had just started Sabre (Semi-automated Booking and Reservations Environment) a computer system that would grow up to dominate the global travel industry.

We all knew Freddie, not in the personal sense, you understand. But, as the swashbuckling MD of British United Airways (based just down Buckingham Palace Road from Sainseal), we took a proprietorial interest in Freddie Laker and his doings. Freddie had been a paid-up member of the travel industry for a long time – indeed from even before it started. Ever heard of the Berlin Air Lift? This was the moment that provided the personnel, companies, money and airplanes needed for the birth of modern mass tourism.

In 1948, the USSR blockaded West Berlin which was then occupied by the Allies (France, USA, UK). As West Berlin was landlocked, there was only one thing for it – to supply this city of approximately 300,000 inhabitants by air. During the 14 months of the blockade, there was an aircraft landing in Berlin every couple of minutes. Naturally, the Allied forces didn't have quite enough aircraft or crews to maintain such an operation, even after the 2nd World War – so "Come in Commercial Airlines". Thousands of aircraft and crews cut their teeth on Berlin and the "Dakota" (Douglas DC3) was the workhorse. Dozens of budding entrepreneurs and fledgling airlines came into being to service the Berlin Air Lift and Freddie was one of them. And when it stopped, what were they all going to do? Wait for the air package holiday to take off of course!

Freddie's BUA was a mainly scheduled carrier providing a little competition for the state-owned BEA and BOAC. Laker Airways, which Freddie now started was not at all so upmarket. Whereas BUA had begun by operating ex-airlift Dakotas and DC4's they were now flying beautiful 2-year-old long haul VC10's and new short haul BAC 1-11's, Laker started with a couple of reliable prop-driven Bristol Britannias – old but economical. His idea was to take advantage of the package tour business by providing air transportation to tour opera-tors. A low margin and relatively risk-free business servicing a growing marketplace. How sensible. What a good idea. What a reasonable formula. No hubris? Little greed? No testosterone? No bullshit? How boring, so, just 5 years later Freddie's Skytrain was born, the first "No Frills" carrier. You could take your own sandwiches to New York on a flashy DC10 for less than £100 – now that was exciting – and doomed by the banks that had supported it.

So, I'd got my feet relatively under the table at Saintseal in 1966 and through the winter. Brixton, where we now lived (and my wife Chan worked), was easy to get to from Victoria. My city life revolved around SW1 (the Bag of Nails) and WC1 (The Marquess of Granby – mine host Ken Gamgee), with a few excursions to Soho for nights out at the Dolce Notte and the Dolce Vita night clubs. Time to relax and enjoy ourselves. The next spring, we decided to have a holiday. To Italy, of course. The flights were free, but I liked trains, so we got a Saintseal flight out to Italy, had agreed to meet Angelo (from Wasteels) in Venice and were to get the train back to London via Germany.

Nothing was ever going to prepare me for Venice "La Serenissima" was a dream, particularly in the company of a Venetian, passionately in love with his home city. We only had a day and a night, but, in that short time, I was completely captivated. No, I didn't miss the sensational architecture, the stunning vistas, the romance, the food, the wine and the music, the Rialto, St Marks, La Fenice and so much more. But, for me, Venice had one big plus. Venice was, and is, the world's enormous, living, thriving centre of excellence, school of practice and library of tourism and Angelo was my well-qualified guide.

So, you see a glass factory and think "Don't those glasses and those chandeliers look wonderful". We went to one of the glass factories in Murano (the one that Angelo had worked at) and met the salesmen, found out how they worked, how much they made, who they bribed, what hotels and tour companies they worked with – fascinating. The 25x4 principle of which only one 25% related to the actual glass.

So, you see a gondola serenely skiffing along a canal or a launch surfing imperiously over the waves and think "How delightful, no cars". We met the gondoliers and the launch captains – how can they possibly command such high fees? Because NOBODY else is allowed to do it.

So, you see those musicians at Florians playing little serenades to the café guests and think "What style". We meet the waiters and check what they get for tips in the winter and the summer.

You see, everybody who wants to can make tourism money. Tourism industry destination operatives can make a great deal of cash and even more in favours. Harvesting the tourism spend is a good life, if you know what you're doing.

You want to find out all there is to know about tourism. Then visit Venice with Angelo and keep your ears and eyes wide open. Venice is the BIG one and so it should be. After all, Venice is where modern-day tourism was born. Don't believe me? Let me take you back 900 years or so, to the 4th Crusade.

At the turn of the 13th century King Richard of England, and Philip of France (a couple of tour operators if ever I saw one) decided that it would be a good idea to have yet another crusade, so they sketched out their itinerary and requirements. Given the fact that they were looking to take a lot of people, they'd need a lot of boats to get to Constantinople (trains and planes not having been yet invented, and walking being too long). Where could they find all these boats? Venice, of course. Plus, Venice was en route for Constantinople for both the French and the British groups – and not too far for the peasants to walk to and the knights to ride to.

Next step pop off to Venice to arrange the hardware – well, a group of six tourism contractors from France and England went to see the Doge of Venice (Henry Dandolo) to make the arrangements.

As a result of the contractors' negotiations, this is what Henry Dandolo said – "We will build transports to carry four thousand five hundred horses, and nine thousand squires, and ships for four thousand five hundred knights, and twenty thousand sergeants of foot. And we will agree also to purvey food for these horses and people during nine months. This is what we undertake to do at the least, on condition that you pay us for each horse four marks, and for each man two marks"

Pretty reasonable package, eh?

In fact, the crusaders couldn't come up with all the dosh upfront, so the Doge arranged a "Travel Now, Pay Later" scheme, on the basis that the invaders would sack Constantinople and pay the Venetians for the travel arrangements out of the proceeds. The results you see today all over Venice.

Obviously, the inhabitants of Constantinople resisted this arrangement and the Crusaders didn't get as much as they needed to pay their debts, provide enough money to get home and the small fortunes that they had been promised. However, there were other opportunities for these brigands and less well-protected cities on the route home were subjected to Crusader robbing, raping and pillaging to fill up their and Venetian purses. An incredibly lucrative project for Venice.

It's hardly surprising, then, that the first general purpose travel agent – Agostino Contarini started up in Venice in the 15th century. Agostino offered, quite naturally, a tour to the same places the crusaders visited – the Holy Land (after all, the basic logistics had been put into place – hadn't they?). The "AC Tours" Holy Land package included:

Transportation, Accommodation, Two hot meals a day, A complete tour of the Holy Land, Guides, Fees, tolls and bribes, All for just 60 golden ducats per person

Back in London, I'd had a couple of "Near Misses" with Nanny and Dr Fabbri, generally starting with my going missing with a wodge of cash from the till and ending with my returning rather the worse for wear. The bosses were pretty incredulous, I guess that this sort of thing just didn't happen in Italy. Anyway, that's probably why they gave me the benefit of the doubt. That, and Chan asking elegantly for them to keep me on. But my days were numbered. Just before my departure, however, Saintseal became the proud owner of Pegasus Holidays.

Pegasus was a very small tour operator with a boss (Chris – an ex-naval officer) and a staff member or two. Its product was a limited range of beach holidays in Holland – well, that, in itself is a pretty limiting factor. Apart from hardy Dutch people there never was a big demand for holidays in Scheveningen, Noordwijk or Zandvoort – even if you could pronounce them. Big, modern, soul-less hotels, Dutch food (yuk), enormous empty beaches (why? one asks) and the bracing North Sea wind – not exactly what you'd call 'Holiday Paradise' and certainly not up to Tossa de Mar for 20 quid or so. Anyway, surprisingly enough, Pegasus had a business, unsurprisingly, they wanted to sell it and, surprisingly Nanny and Dr Fabbri wanted to buy. Maybe it was something about Nanny coming from Northern Italy and Dr Fabbri liking the 'Winged Horse' emblem – just like Ferrari's. Saintseal bought Pegasus and I was meant to help.

Of course, they weren't interested in Holland. They liked the name and the fact that it was an established company, but they also had their eyes on Court Line, Clarkson's Tours owners who, by now, had built up a clutch of resorts in the Caribbean and were (or would be!) under great financial pressure.

Pretty soon after the takeover, Pegasus had used Saintseal airline contacts and Italian/American connections to create a big programme of holidays to the Caribbean. And years later when it all went bust Nanny ended up owning and living in one of the Caribbean resorts and Ron (Saintseal's consigliere) set up Virgin Holidays for Richard Branson!

John Bloom had achieved fame and success and a great deal of money by selling washing machines. In the 1950s washing machines were expensive and John Bloom sold them cheap. The idea was that the more he had made, the less they would cost him and the less he could charge. Still not cheap enough? Offer a really cheap one then get your salesman to switch-sell to one a little more expensive. Obviously, the alternative of sevice-guarantees wasn't available in the 50's. Within seven years, John had run out of millions of people to buy his machines and had gone bust, but not before he'd started another get-rich-quick scheme. Cheap holidays for the masses. In Bulgaria. Just like Yugoslavia but cheaper and better.

Here's how it worked. The Bulgarian Black Sea coast was warm and sunny and littered with modern functional hotels. Why? Because Bulgaria was a communist country and part of the Soviet bloc. Communist organizations sent their best workers on holiday, not to Spain, naturally, because Spain cost hard currency. Holidaying at home, or near to it was better, and cheaper. Bulgaria was the workers' choice.

But Bulgaria wanted to buy nice, expensive western things and didn't have any nice expensive western money to buy them with. At that time there only two options – pay hard cash or barter – you get some Bulgarian wine and we get some jeans. Enter J. Bloom saying "You sell me hotel accommodation and food, I'll bring you millions of clients that you can proselytise at and, I'll give you loads (well, some) hard, very hard, western currency." Don't forget John Bloom was a salesman, so he wouldn't forget to sell the Bulgarians the "Benefits" rather than just the "Features". So, he'd have said " Our holidaymakers will Love Bulgaria and they'll have a wonderful time. So, they'll go home and tell all their friends how beautiful Bulgaria is, how good Bulgarian food is and how fantastic Bulgarian wine is. They'll love you all and they'll buy your food and wine and holidays. You'll be made – and popular!"

The Bulgarians fell for it, and soon the destination of Slunchev Bryag was "Sunny Beach", Zlatni Pyassatsi was "Golden Sands" and Drouzhba and Varna were Drouzhba and Varna. The state airline, the curiously named TABSO was contracted for flights from the UK. Holidaymakers in their thousands piled in at £59 for two weeks full board and all the yoghurt you could eat. Then Rolls Razor went bust.

As far as the Bulgarians were concerned, this was a disaster, they liked this game – hard currency for nothing that cost them anything, and good PR. It was great, and they didn't want it to stop. Luckily, the Royal Arsenal Co-operative Society came to the rescue and, with Balkantourist, the Bulgarian state-owned tourist organization, formed Balkan Holidays to satisfy the demand for Bulgarian holidays created by Mr Bloom.

Balkan Holidays was located in South Molton Street, W1. Not exactly a proletarian mecca in the heart of the posh West End, but at least comfortable. The first brochure was created with the unmistakable dancing Bulgars and the unbeatable lead-in £59 price on the cover. Obviously, they needed a travel specialist Independent Travel Manager. Obviously, by now I was being given my marching orders from Saintseal and needed a job. Jean Pierre (the Saintseal company secretary) knew Tim (a communist fellow-traveller and Balkan Holidays general manager) and the deal was done. The job was to be mine. No matter that I knew little about Bulgaria, Romania or the rest of Eastern Europe – I was the young professional and they liked me!

A politically-oriented company, run mainly by commies who did their marketing as much through their UK Marxist friends as through the media, they had a product that was extremely commercial, and in the heart of the West End, and in the vortex of political machinations, and with me as Independent Travel Manager. What could be more interesting?

The product was very simple. We'd charter weekly flights to Varna (for Golden Sands) and Bourgas (for Sunny Beach), we sold off some of the seats to other operators and kept the rest for ourselves. We also had access to the TABSO – (Bulgarian-Soviet Transport Aviation Corporation) scheduled prop-jet Ilyushin airliner which flew most days from Gatwick to Sofia with connections to other destinations in Bulgaria and onward. Further, there was a non-stop coach from Ostend all the way to Sofia and on to the resorts run by my friends from Ostend – the West Belgium Coach Company, it took around 72 hours straight – you don't have to believe it but it's true.

We had allocations at the hotels and on the flights and we put them on little cards, stuffed in slots on a carousel on top of a big desk in a back room – this was to be the reservations department. We all had key and lamp units, the tour operator's basic tool, where we could answer half a dozen calls at a time take reservations and put 'em on cards in the carousel.

The reservations department was managed by Barry (we thought he was gay because he cooked a lot, and never came in until 10) and staffed by Len (a red-haired Jewish Marxist balletomane who queued outside Covent Garden Opera House all night), Anna who was mid-European, yummy and engaged and Claire – a classic bright sixties beauty with an ever shorter daily miniskirt.

I dealt with anything too complicated to be handled by the reservations team like "I wanna go to Poland, Romania and Czechoslovakia in that order with a short stay in Paris – it's got to be done in a week, I don't like flying and I must take the dog". By the way, my budget's £15 for me and the wife" – fairly standard stuff in the travel industry.

The company was managed by the communist fellow-traveller Tim Howatson (Jean-Pierre's friend). And the overall boss in charge of direction and political connections was Moscow-educated Georgi Gotsev. Bald, chubby, mid-European Peter, the bookkeeper, lived up in the attic and complained all day that London wasn't like Vienna. Plus, he moaned at me for taking constant subs to fund my drinking.

Marketing was relatively simple. Once a year we produced a brochure (with the dancing Bulgars and the lead-in price, dates, destinations, etc) and I produced an independent one – with Poland, Romania and other points east. We booked ad's in the papers and sent brochures to travel agents – the usual stuff. Then we pushed off to rustle up the Marxist bookings through Marxist routes – i.e. very leftie union officials (there were lots then) and organizations proscribed by the Labour Party as being communist-infiltrated. My personal favourite was the Anglo-Bulgarian Friendship Society which specialized in folk dancing and political forment.

It was an intriguing atmosphere with good food and booze outside in chic South Molton Street. Political and trade machinations inside. Most afternoons Georgi had long, smoke-filled meetings with commie mates in the back room. This involved my "Organising" vast amounts of really strong coffee and coke – the Slivova (Plum Brandy) was provided by Georgi and the meetings usually finished late in the day. And it wasn't just the drinking that was damaging my marriage, I'd fallen in lust with Vivien, a delightful little long-haired commie who determined to cook me 'Cholent' in her Hampstead council flat.

Naturally, my finances were also suffered from the move – no "Please pays" at Balkan, but TABSO came to my rescue, providing me with a lovely stock of tickets to write and sell at whatever price I wanted. This could have been a goldmine. TABSO was a scheduled carrier, flying from London to Sophia direct, and a member of IATA (International Airline Transportation Association). As usual, in those times, the only airlines that were permitted to operate a route were the national carriers of the originating departure points. So, in the case of London-Sofia – British Airlines (BEA in 1968) and TABSO.

God knows how much British Airways charged for a standard economy return flight to Sofia – hundreds of pounds, probably, and as far as the regulators were concerned – so did TABSO. The only concession major carriers like BEA made was the ITX fare – a special tour-basing fare that had to be included in an inclusive tour arrangement (including flights and accommodation) and not sold separately. The ITX fare to Sophia was about £117.

TABSO had their own route network, based on Sofia, which included Greece and Cyprus – how many Greek and Greek-Cypriot restaurateurs were there within a ticket's swing of South Molton Street? Bloody hundreds! So, when funds dropped, I traipsed all over London selling tickets to Athens for £50 and drinking Retsina and Ouzo.

Throughout the trade, of course, I sold ITX tickets at ITX rates, but nobody bought apart from T Cook, down the road in Berkeley Street – the toffs of the travel trade. What a pity, thought I.

So, one lunchtime, I walked out of Balkan Holidays front door shouting "I'll be back after lunch" "No you won't" said Len "You'll be back sometime this afternoon, pissed as usual". Determined to prove Len wrong, I popped into the Marquis of Granby, went on a bender with Ken, the landlord and somehow woke up in Ostend the next day. Breakfasting at a café, I said to Ken "Beer?" "Why not" replied Ken, "If we don't practice, we'll never become alcoholics!".

Within a week of my return to London, Chan and I packed our bags and left. London had become far too dangerous – this was just one of a number of incidents involving large amounts of alcohol, a few drunken suicide attempts and at least one serious scar. I was a wreck At least we had family in the West Country where I was better known.

I'd had a rough ride in the big city, completely my own fault of course. Too much drink and lack of moral fibre. But I'd learnt a great deal, met some fascinating people and made a lot of friends. I was getting to understand how the nascent travel business really worked and who made it all happen – I still loved it.

CHAPTER 3

Holidays 2U

So, we made an ignominious departure from London in a hired estate car with our friend John (from Saintseal) at the wheel and all of our goods and chattels in the back. We'd managed to get a furnished flat in Bristol and fairly quickly, I got a job in Bath on a weekly wage of £22 – the going rate for a travel agency branch manager. The job wasn't spectacular but it paid the rent (or it would have done if it hadn't been earmarked for more colourful uses – like the local pubs and clubs). But, at least I was home.

It was certainly difficult not to feel at home in friendly, beautiful, faded, eccentric Georgian Bath and soon, we were lucky enough to manage to rent a tiny flat in the centre of the city. At £5 a week, it wasn't a fortune and it was on the third floor but it was close to the river and had views of the hills beyond, and the pleasure gardens beside the building. It even had a splendid address – 12 Georgian House, Duke Street.

As it happened, I was very lucky indeed and, it appears, blessed again by my Guardian Angel. There was a moment in time where things changed. Maybe I hadn't noticed, but I was faced by a decision that I couldn't avoid.

Everybody was worried about my drinking but only one person was worried enough to do something about it. Chan contacted the Samaritans because she thought that either she, or I would kill themselves, only I had form in that department, but she was so distressed about the situation that maybe it was her turn.

Anyway within a few days a man turned up on the doorstep. An alcoholic, like me and my father, but one who did not now drink. I spent my time with Joe curled in a foetal position full of self-pity while he pranced around full of life. The image is still with me.

It didn't stop me drinking, of course but it did put a very powerful image in my mind. So, when a week or so later, when I'd pawned my wedding ring to buy drink, and when I was standing at the bar in the Assize Courts Hotel in Bristol's Small Street, I decided to leave my half-drunk glass of lager on the bar and make a telephone call.

This, I thought maybe my only escape route. My wife was leaving me to return to London, we were being thrown out of our flat because the rent had not been paid, I'd been sacked from my job for drinking and stealing money for drink, my friends had deserted me, I was an embarrassment to my family. There was no way forward, I had to make a break for it.

I rang Joe, the non-drinking alcoholic. His wife answered. She told me to come and see her now. I was to get the bus to Bath Bus Station. I was to get another bus to the Bear pub. I was to walk past it without going in. Their house was close by.

I followed these instructions to the letter. The last drink I had stayed on the bar in the Assize Courts Hotel. I cannot express my gratitude for the kindness of Joe's family in the succeeding years, without their complete support and unconditional love and that of his friends I would almost certainly have failed and lost my tentative hold on reality and sobriety.

Not visiting pubs and clubs, it seemed, had many benefits. I had more time and, at least some money, And I was in Bath. So, what's so special about Bath, why did I find this city so incredibly, delightfully attractive?

In 1969, Bath was a sleepy little market town with some former glory and some hot baths (a geyser of near-boiling water streaming up from way below). It was friendly and a little eccentric, rather like the little old ladies and old gentlemen who, together with a fine quota of upmarket hippies and provincial-families-who'd-never-lived-anywhere-else formed the bulk of the local populace. All the Georgian architectural jewels had acquired a dull dirty brown coat over the years and the Roman Baths held a monthly "Roman Orgy" – for local families to think they were doing something naughty. There was a sedate ball each week in the Pump Rooms for local young men to meet local young women. Get the picture? Comfortable, provincial, faded, Bathchair boring. But, nonetheless, Bath was a happy and gentle place to be.

Beneath this unpretentious exterior was a very different picture. For over 3,000 years, Bath had regularly been a grade 1, class A international tourism destination until the end of the 19th century. When I saw the sunshine reflected off the golden stone in the central square of Abbey Churchyard, I knew Bath had something very special and she would attract and keep attracting tourists for millennia to come. Bath may have been sleeping when I arrived, but I felt sure that she would awake again to tourism glory.

Once upon a time, in our Celtic days, water was magical and its springs were guarded by Goddesses. The particular Goddess who lives in Bath is Sulis – the Goddess of healing and therapy and well-being, cursing and curing. It is said that Sulis presides over all hot springs and it is her presence that makes the springs hot and healing. She takes her name from the Gaelic "Suileath" meaning wise, all seeing and far sighted. It is said that she represents the depths all people must plumb in their journey to light, health and happiness.

Anyway, so the legend goes, in Celtic times, in the London area, there was a king called Ludhudibras and he had a son called Bladud.

Well, old king Lud was quite well off and he only wanted the best for his son so he sent him off to Athens to get a degree. Naturally, Bladud enjoyed himself plus he was a bright student – which would you fancy – staying at the centre of the Greek Empire where everything was happening – feasting and drinking and games, or coming home to boring old England where they only ate pork? But – 11 years later Bladud got ill so he had to come home. "My God" they said when he arrived – "You've got leprosy – you'll have to be shut up for the rest of your life" So Bladud was imprisoned.

Our story wouldn't be a story unless Bladud had escaped. And, of course, he did. Wandering about the land as a prince in disguise until he got hungry and needed a job. Now, the ancient Celts were very fond of a bit of bacon and pig farms were all the rage in 1500bc – always looking for extra staff. Bladud found a job as a swineherd on a pig farm in Swainswick, a few miles from soon-to-be-Bath. As was the custom, he was lodged with the family, which consisted of mother, father and blind but beautiful daughter (Grace, would you believe) who naturally fell in love with Bladud.

One day Bladud was herding his swine close to the steaming marshland habitat of the Goddess Sulis. Being exalted animals, the pigs took Bladud to the Goddess's location and he noticed that the pigs liked rolling in the hot mud. Not only do they like it but it appears to do wonders for their complexions. Thinks Bladud – "Maybe this mud will stop my fingers falling off" And, of course it did "Gosh", says Bladud, "Maybe this hot mud will make my beloved Grace see, too" And, of course, it did. Now both hale and healthy the couple marry and Bladud goes on to become king – and the father of King Lear – but that's another story.

What an endorsement for Sulis' powers. Bladud was a real example of plumbing the depths and coming back to life. And Bladud was happy and ready to bring all that Athenian feasting to Bath, which, of course, eventually, he did. It is said that Bladud established Bath as an early university town dedicated, of course, to Sulis.

The above story may or may not be factually true. What is certain, however, is that the Druids worshipped water and hot springs were extra magical. They would certainly have believed that Bath had a strong power and well worth a visit. Avebury, Stonehenge and Glastonbury plus dozens of other Celtic religious sites are all very close to Bath – within at most a hard day or two of walking. It is very easy to believe that many thousands of Celts visited Bath to make acquaintance with the Goddess and be cured and/or enlightened and that Bath, even in those days, was a significant tourism destination.

What we do know, for sure is that in the middle of the 1st century AD, the Romans arrived in Bath complete with their Goddess of

Wisdom – Minerva – expecting her to take over as she had in many other Roman conquests. As it happened, this was not to be, Minerva got together with Sulis and the result was Sulis Minerva. The Romans started building their great baths and temple at the sacred hot spring soon after the Conquest. They named their city Aquae Sulis and soon transformed the Celtic Druids' grove into one of the major therapeutic centres of the Roman world. Bath became the scene for feasts, orgies, baths and games and other big Roman social events. The Romans revered the spring just as the Celts had done and by the 3rd century AD its stunning temple and luxurious baths were attracting pilgrim tourists from throughout the Roman world. Eventually, though, the Romans pushed off and Bath's tourism figures dropped again for 400 years or so until the Saxons arrived.

The Druids had a temple for Sulis at the hot springs and the Romans had built a temple to Sulis Minerva. Naturally, the Saxons didn't want to be left out – in the Saxon Poem "The Ruin" they wrote 'Wondrous is this masonry, shattered by the Fates. The fortifications have given way, the buildings raised by giants are crumbling. The city fell to earth."

If there was power here – the Saxons wanted it too, so a grand monastery was built using as paving stones the Pagan sacrificial altar. As its lands increased, the monastery became rich and powerful, so powerful that the first king of all England (Edgar) was crowned on the site in 973. So, even though the baths had been ruined, Bath again became a pilgrimage site – now for Christian spiritual rather than Pagan physical health. And the tourists rolled in again – for another few hundred years.

Even the Norman conquest hampered Bath's tourism trade only for a short while. Although Bath was razed to the ground, it was soon sold to a Norman Doctor-Churchman-entrepreneur – John de Villula – for the substantial sum of £500 of silver. Instituted as the Bishop of Bath, de Villula set about recreating Bath in typical grand Norman style. A massive cathedral (at 100 metres long one of the largest in Europe) was built between the hot springs and the river. De Villula also extended the monastery which, by now, was widely renowned for its scholarship. Most importantly, de Villula combined Bath's spiritual attractions with its therapeutic ones by ordering the baths refitted and he built several treatment centres in the city – ready to attract both pilgrims and the health market. But, of course, the whole was eventually destroyed through neglect.

And the city languished for another few hundred years, until 1499, when Bishop Oliver King, on a visit from Wells, had a dream with a message. And the message -"Let an olive establish the Crown and let a King restore the Church". The message was understood by the bishop so he did what it said. The "Lantern of the West" – with its 52 glass windows, and the last of the English Perpendicular Gothic churches was built as the Bath Abbey – beside the Baths, of course. The Baths were restored and by the middle of the 17th century, Bath was firmly established again as a mid-level tourist destination. Modern visitors were keen on the spiritual stuff, and the water-therapy, but they needed something more – so land southeast of the Abbey was made into a bowling green (top sport in the 16th century) and east of the newly-refurbished King's Bath was made into five Real Tennis courts. Bath's tourism infrastructure was also increased with the addition of accommodation in the west of the city and even the Abbey Church House, Westgate House and St John's Hospital turned over rooms and alms-houses to visitors.

Then Bath hit the big time. King Charles II and his wife Catherine of Braganza visited to "Take the Water" – plus Charlie legalised gambling. Bath went straight into the premier league. Quickly adding gambling to the pilgrimage/therapy/sports mix Bath could now attract even more visitors and use the Royal endorsement.

By 1703 when Queen Anne visited, Bath already had the therapy, the religion, the gambling and the multiple royal endorsements – major tourism draw cards. Now, what the city needed was more infrastructure and massive promotion. Beau Nash was your man.

Into the 'decayed' country town that was Bath at the start of the 18th century, walked the wigged adventurer and dandy Richard 'Beau' Nash. A drop-out from Oxford University, the army and the law, Beau Nash earned his money as a gambler and socialite. With Queen Anne's visit to Bath, Beau Nash saw his chance to make a fortune and gain influential friends. Quickly, Beau Nash arranged the finances, the contacts, the builders, the architects and, most importantly the entertainments and the social calendar to create a top-level destination.

Bath was to make the very most of its assets – its baths, its Celtic history, its golden stone, its proximity to London, its gambling and sports and its royal credibility. Bath was to create new assets – wonderful architecture, pleasure gardens, great balls and entertainment and a comprehensive social calendar. So, when "Tout le Monde" visited Bath – everybody else would have to come. If you wanted to meet anybody, a visit to Bath would be a social imperative, reasoned Beau Nash. Bath was ready to become 18th century upmarket Disneyland and much more.

Just imagine what Bath was like at the peak of its tourism success. All the "Great and the Good" were there (and the not-so-great and the not-so-good). Why? They were attracted by an integrally-coordinated tourism destination vision. Fantastic architecture in shimmering golden stone, amazing balls and entertainments in glorious surroundings, sublime hospitality and service, the best of food and accommodation, fabulous pleasure gardens, unique spa-therapy with naturally healing hot water and mud, Celtic and Druid esoteric connections – and a social calendar that meant that you missed not one moment of pleasure nor one opportunity to meet someone interesting or notable. Plus, fancy a little pleasure on the darker side, a little nefarious connection? It was all possible in Beau Nash's Bath, gambling houses, upmarket brothels, all kinds of mind-altering substances, escorts of all types – you name your fantasy and it would be fulfilled. Bath simply provided the total 18th century resort experience. It's no wonder that Bath's population grew tenfold (from 3,000 to 30,000 inhabitants) in 100 years and Bath rivalled London as the 18th century place to be seen.

In the end, Bath was usurped for the tourism crown by the pleasure-loving Prince Regent's Brighton and then by rather primmer Victoria's reign, Bath became again a quiet country town.

The Druids, the Romans, the Normans, the Saxons, the Georgians and the New Elizabethans have all flocked in their turn to Bath and, for a hundred years at a time at least, Bath revelled in tourism's economic glory. Why? Bath's major tourism attractions are simply its (supposedly healing) hot waters, its religious significance and its proximity to power centres. To a greater or lesser extent each succeeding tourism inflow has been augmented by extra facilities, by better infrastructure and by effective marketing. Only the Romans and Beau Nash had really exploited Bath's assets and when I arrived, the city, and its Goddess Sulis, was waiting for the next big tourism inflow.

Bath has always had something else, of course. There is the indefinable magic that grips you when you visit the city, faded, but still atmospheric. Perhaps it's something esoteric, something that we can't quite fathom. Go to Venice or Rome, Athens or Cairo, Bruges or Barcelona, Amsterdam or Dubrovnik, Cochin or Bangkok, Istanbul or Zanzibar, Prague or Paris, Ochrid or Ostend– the same magic is there too. Maybe it's the tourism destinations' Goddess you can feel.

Here I was in quiet, comfortable, friendly town that disguised its beauty and power perfectly. Bath was a top-class tourist town with no tourists. For me it was paradise!

In my busted state, I didn't think that I could get another job in the travel industry, so I got a job selling vacuum cleaners from door to door. That lasted a week.

Having failed again I responded to an ad for encyclopaedia salesmen. I was interviewed brusquely by an enthusiastic, foul-mouthed, tall, gangly Irishman called Olly. "Why did you leave your last job?" said Olly "Because they said I was incompetent" said I. "Well you can't be fucking incompetent at fucking everything can you" Said Olly "Remember you judge yourself by what you think you're capable of doing – others judge you by what you've already done – Emerson". "You can start tomorrow".

It was dead easy to make money selling encyclopaedias if you followed the rules. Wander round a shopping centre with a clipboard. You're looking for a young female parent with a male baby from 6 months to 2 years old. Pounce. "I'm doing a survey for an educational supplier on parents with babies, do you think that I could interview you and your husband at home please. "Yes" was usually the response. Sort out time and date (today). Make sure husband will be at home. Check the age of the baby and its name. At the end of the day, check the addresses, you're looking for new council estates (yes there were some in 1969) and new private estates. Get 10 appointments. That evening does six appointments, that means deliver the script memorised word for word. You'll get 3 sales (worth £10 each to you). Work 5 days a week and you'll make £150 a week. Good money. But make sure you say the script word for word, make sure that you go for the specific target audience – or you'll lose it. I didn't do too badly.

Eventually, I became a team leader which meant that I got commission on my team members' sales. It was my first sales-people management job. And what it taught me is that bright, self-centred people can be a problem. They frequently couldn't understand that adding their own "Spin" did not work. They often knew better. "10-year-old boys are better than ones from 6 months to 2 years" Bullshit. "Lots of people think girls need it more" Bullshit. "I don't say the script exactly because my own words are better" Bullshit. And every other excuse you could find. It was amazing. You'd get naive 17-year olds who did what they were told for the first week and made money. After that they knew better and didn't make money. Week after week after week after week…

And I found a guru. Would you believe Dale Carnegie of "How to Win Friends and Influence People" fame? This book taught me everything I needed to know about selling and I put it into practice. I realised that from then on, my sales technique would be harnessed simply in identifying and fulfilling needs, whether it was only to put a point of view or make a massive sale. I was a salesman!

Nine months to the day after I'd stopped drinking, I'd become a very proud father. Adam changed my way of thinking. Finally, I'd arrived and had a family to be responsible for. A new job was called for, with a secure wage, not just commission payments, like the encyclopaedia selling. I managed to get a job selling rental contracts for telephone answering machines with a company called Shipton Telstor. Travelling all over the West Country suited me, I loved the holiday resorts and the small businesses that I sold telephone answering machines to.

But the travel business called again and by 1971, I found myself behind a desk staring at the phone in an ex-antiques shop in Clifton, trying to remember just what to do. My old friend Stephen, the antique dealer, had provided me with the shop, and the desk, and the phone in the belief that I could produce some business and some profit with which to pay him some rent. Practically the only sales lead I had was my mate John (who'd driven us back from London). John worked in the London office for a very interesting company called "$5 a day tours" based in the USA and a subsidiary of a major USA guide book company "Europe on $5 a day" run by the then-famous Arthur Frommer.

$5 a day tours' London office was in Belgravia, and their basic function was to contract and organise Frommer's programme of London Theatre trips. The company brought thousands of tourists to London from all over the USA to enjoy London and its theatres on these inclusive tours. Included in the price were the flights, transfers, hotel accommodation, a sightseeing tour or two, and theatre tickets.

And it was cheap – hence the thousands of tourists! Why was it cheap? Bulk buying and the usual travel business machismo. The London office's job was to contract the London ground arrangements cheap and to look after the passengers. A tall, brash Dutch American – Hans – was in charge, and John worked for him. Hans was a travel business philosopher – "Problems, I love them, they're the only reason we're in the travel business – without them everybody would book their own trips". And Hans was a great contractor, he prided himself on the top hotels he could get for very little money. The flights were cheap too – booked on what were called C-BIT fares (Contract Bulk Inclusive Tour) on scheduled flights. At least the USA was then the land of free enterprise and the clients were getting serious value.

My idea was to sell $5 a day customers staying in London an upmarket tour to the West Country – that we (now called Unicorn Travel) would organise. The American tourists would enjoy a superb 3-day trip, visiting Marlborough, Bath, Wells, Glastonbury, Salisbury and, of course Avebury and Stonehenge, seeing stately homes and staying at a nice hotel in Bath. £12.50 including all meals (not bad, eh?). We employed very posh guides (mainly Stephen's upmarket mates) and the customers got a great deal. But we weren't making enough money – yet, so we tried to sell a stake in Unicorn to Sparkes Coaches, the coach company who we'd contracted to carry our passengers, and I found myself working for them as well.

In 1971, the Traffic Commissioners controlled the Bus and Coach Industry. In today's era of free competition, the situation would be scandalous. Then, if a coach company wanted to advertise and operate any route or trip, they had to apply for permission. And when they applied, their application was objected to by all the potential competition.

If you wanted to operate a trip to, say, Paris for a weekend, anybody who was licensed to operate Paris coach trips would object on the grounds of diminution of their business, even the Railway companies, who had transport licences, and potentially the airlines, would object. This, of course benefited nobody, not the travelling public, not the tourism industry, not the innovative, efficient coach tour operator. Only the licensed coach tour operator had the necessaries to operate tours – and only if they wanted to and at a price that they wanted.

Coach companies regarded licences as capital, they bought companies for licences, they bought licences from companies. Their focus was the licence, not the business which, of course had become stagnant as a result of this anti-competitive bureaucracy.

Like many coach companies, Sparkes was champing at the bit. They had a nice fleet of coaches, a number of contracts to take children to school and workers to work at knock-down rates and a couple of licences. And in my view, one big success – Sparkes had designed a series of inclusive Sunday day trips which they sold to the big companies whose workers they took to work. You could choose a day trip to Dartmouth and Totnes, including breakfast, a cream tea and a river cruise, or a visit to London's Petticoat Lane, with breakfast, a tour of London and a cream tea at Windsor amongst other opportunities. These tours sold in bulk – they had to, the only way they could be operated under the current legislation was to "Closed User Groups" in other words employees only had to hire a full coach. But they did. My last act at Sparkes was to get them a load more business for day trips by visiting their local big companies and doing some determined selling.

Roger and John, the owners, were very kind to me, but eventually they hit hard times and I had to go. God knows where I found the money but I rented office accommodation in Bristol's posh Park Street to sell Sparkes-style coach day trips to big companies. Plus, a new product – a weekend to the Belgian Beer Festival in Wieze (a brewery) – back to the Belgian Coast again. Unicorn Travel was in business.

I recruited an operations manager (Roland, a schoolfriend and ex-coach driver), a sales manager (Gordon – an ex-boss), an admin manager (Blandine – a friend's French wife) and an accounts manager (Phyllis), all we needed was a takeover to make the business really cool. So, we merged with a Bucket Shop. Very with it! John ran it together with a very sexy operations manager called Jenny.

OK, so what's a bucket shop? In the 1970's airlines' prices were regulated. They had to sell their tickets at the prices that had been authorised – and no less. That's great, everybody knows where they are, don't they? But, if an airline had bad load factors (not enough passengers) on a route, the temptation to 'Dump' tickets at any price was severe. And, in my experience, there wasn't an airline flying that didn't surrender to the temptation.

Let's face it, a flight seat is a more perishable commodity than fruit or veg. The minute the flight's departed, the seat is worth precisely nothing. So, where did the airlines dump specially discounted tickets? Bucket Shops, of course, the top rung of which were usually called "Consolidators". Every airline had its pet consolidator or two or three. Usually the same nationality as the airline, the consolidator could buy tickets at discounts up to 90% if the time was right or the route was bad. The consolidator would then pass on the tickets to his or her contacts down the Bucket Shop route.

The customer usually got a ticket with the full fare on it and paid, maybe, less than half that fare. Bucket Shops were shady and often located in colourful areas like London's Soho – but they were great fun and patronised by "People in the Know".

My favourite Bucket Shop/Consolidators were Odyssey. Based in Kensington High Street in a smart big first floor office suite Dotty and Peter and their staff juggled calls on their key and lamp units, selling tickets and buying tickets. It was a fascinating atmosphere and they certainly looked like they were making money until they disappeared without trace. Which most bucket shops did.

Our first travel trauma happened in September. We'd managed to get 300 people to book on our first trip to the Wieze Beer Festival. Great. And we'd applied for a licence. Great. And we'd been refused. Not so great. The upshot was that we had to deal with a coach operator that had a licence to go to Wieze. And who could name his price because he had the licence. In the event, we dealt with a company from out in the sticks, who, obviously had a pick up out in the sticks, the pick-up time was midnight – out in the sticks. Great for rival coach operators who took to pushing our passengers into the ditches in the dark. Anyway, we got them all there, more or less intact.

But where was "There"? Well, the Beer Festival itself is held in a village called Wieze, right in the heart of Belgium, but with no hotel accommodation of course (villages generally don't). So, we had to get some accommodation that was cheap and good. Brussels was very good but not at all cheap, Ostend was good but not cheap, Blankenberghe, down the coast from Ostend was not so good (at that time the hotels catered more for schoolkids with multiple-bedded rooms) but very cheap. So, it was Blankenberghe then. We used a variety of hotels for our 300 passengers.

The trip could have gone all right, even after the battles at the pick-up point, if we'd managed to complete the rooming lists in time and get them to the hotels some time prior to the passengers arriving – (the hotels didn't have telex machines, unfortunately – at that time the only way to transmit messages). As it happened, this wasn't possible, and I had to try to get to the hotels with the rooming lists, at least an hour or so before the rooms were needed.

The taxi I got from Calais didn't want to travel very fast and so, in fact, I arrived after the passengers. It was a very sad sight driving around Blankenberghe and seeing small disconsolate groups sitting on their suitcases in the streets. It was lucky that it was a fine day. It was unlucky that I had to give substantial refunds to the passengers.

So, we decided that coaches were a problem and planes were reliable. It was so lucky that we'd merged with the bucket shop who, specialised in flights and had connections with airlines. We put our transportation arrangements out to contract with a variety of airlines. Yes, you did need a licence if you advertised, but, of course, we didn't – we dealt with closed groups – this, at least, we'd learnt.

God, it was wonderful to see the times on the quotations. Like "Depart BRS 07.00Z(Zulu or GMT in the trade) arrival LBG 09.15". They looked so impressive and certain. And the prices were OK too. On the surface at least, everything seemed so much more controllable.

It's good to deal with someone who knows what they're doing isn't it? Invicta certainly did, they'd been around since the travel business was a baby – they knew all about it. Plus, they had their own airport – Manston in Kent an ex RAF airport with a big runway. Just a hop, skip and jump from the continent. After all they'd done lots of high-density operations in the past including big bulbfields operations for people like Friendship and Clarkson's. Ideal, of course for Wieze. Coach to Manston, flight to Ostend, coach to Wieze etc., etc. Flights, of course were much more reliable than British coaches all the way! Weren't they?

Sorted. OK, off to Belgium to sort out the ground arrangements with Willy. Willy was a typical Belgian in the travel business. Big and moustachioed, well-dressed and avuncular, a good eater and drinker, and, naturally a linguist with at least Flemish, French, German, Italian, Spanish and English to his credit. Willy was a Mister Fixit for foreign tour operators. There's a Willy or two in every destination.

The form was as follows. You told Willy you were coming. Willy arranged a room for you (complimentary of course) and, the next day, Willy took you out for lunch, naturally at a seafront restaurant selling the very best seafood. "Just a little for me", he'd say, "I'll only have a snack", there followed a long conversation about Willy's "Snack" with the restaurant owner. "Maybe I'll have a little something before the snack", Willy would say. "I think you should have the prawns grilled in garlic to start; I'll have a couple too". And so, the meal would start. "A little taster, compliments of the owner" "Ooh, our prawns in garlic and parsley! Could we have some more bread?" "I see you've got the Dover Sole meuniere and frites, I'm only having a snack, a little bit of turbot, so, I think I could manage a few of your frites – they'll bring another tray anyway" "And dessert?" "A 'Dame Blanche'? (Vanilla ice-cream with hot chocolate sauce) "That's too big for me. I think just a little Creme Caramel".

We'd discuss business over coffee. A little bit of haggling and the meal and the deal would be done. So, Willy would get on and book the hotels and the coaches that were necessary for our trips to Wieze. Ostend hotels this time, they were a bit more expensive but well worth it after the Blankenberghe disaster.

The Wieze Beer Festival was a great bit of marketing. For many years, the Belgian Coast was busy in July and August. If the weather was good, you'd get people in June and September too, but it was hardly high season and couldn't command very good rates. In September, there was a lot of availability, and in October, the place was empty.

The Belgians are famous for their beers. They make a lot of beer and a lot of different types of beer. I know a café or two that have more than 300 different types of beer on their menus. That's because the Belgians drink a lot of beer, and they like it. When I say drink a lot, I mean drink a lot, I don't mean get drunk a lot. The Belgians drink beer because they enjoy beer, not because they like to get drunk. I found that quite interesting.

In Munich, every October, there's an event called the "Oktober-fest". It's a beer festival and it attracts tourists from all over the world to eat sausages and grilled chicken and pork and drink beer and sing and dance. There's a fairground too, with a big wheel, and visitors have a great time.

"So, why not have a Beer Festival in Belgium, just like the German one but with Belgian Beer, not German? And sausages and chicken and pork, and a fairground, and singing and dancing? Lots of tourists will come and we'd fill the hotels on the coast. We could do it at Wieze, which is a village and a brewery, and they've got a field that we could have the festival in. The British would love it – they like drinking beer like us." Said the Belgians.

And the Wieze Beer Festival was successful from the start if you counted the money and the numbers. But the Belgian mistake was inherent in the belief that the British "Like drinking beer like us". The sort of British people that came on cheap coach tours to Wieze, often just wanted to get drunk and frequently cause an affray. Thousands of people were attracted to the image of everybody enjoying themselves and having a good time but disappointed by the event itself.

At the time of Wieze, you'd find wandering British drunks all over Belgium who'd forgotten the hotel, street, town they were staying in.

While we were operating tours there (interestingly enough I'd just stopped drinking) we never brought back the same number as we took and spent much time pouring oil over troubled waters. Week after week after week, I'd listen to the battle stories from the guides "I was just helping her out of the coach and put my hand out for a tip – she was sick in it!" "They (the passengers) threw out all the TV's from the rooms – and they certainly aren't pop stars!" "The club wouldn't let them in unless they had ties on so they cut up the curtains in the rooms" "He nicked a glass ashtray put it in his pocket and then went on the slide – it smashed and there was blood everywhere" etc., etc., etc. It didn't stop us taking thousands and thousands of people there though, until the brewery decided to close it down.

Anyway, beer festival time 1972 was great. We managed to get thousands of passengers to book. We managed to get them all, more or less, to Manston Airport. We managed to get them all to Ostend and to Wieze. The only problem came on the final day, most of the customers didn't like one of the hotels so they took unilateral action and the hotelier had followed them to the airport to get back all his cutlery, linen and curtains that they'd stolen and already checked in as baggage.

For flights, we did deals with everybody. But in particular, we dealt with Invicta, who had a great deal of history. They were owned and run by Keegan and Stevens, the people who flew the first package tour (to Corsica for Vladimir Raitz's Horizon). And – they'd flown me from Manston to Maastricht in their DC4 in 1964. Now they were flying big 146 seat jet-prop Vickers Vanguards.

We were always after "Empty legs" where the flights for the inbound passengers were pre-sold leaving the outbound passengers flights available. In other words, a group from Paris had booked flights to London on Friday night, and back from London on Sunday evening. For a UK airline to operate these flights, they had to fly out empty on Friday to pick up the French and back empty on Sunday after they'd dropped them off. Leaving two sectors empty.

And we got an empty leg, but the other way around – we got the leg from Paris to London. No problem, after all I knew about incoming travel when I'd worked for Saintseal in London. All we had to do was to set up ground arrangements in London and find a French group to fill the flight. So, off to Paris I popped to see the British Tourist Authority who, I hoped, would help me find a French co-operator.

This trip resulted in a co-operation with a company called 'Sepi Voyages' who dealt exclusively with 'Comités d'Entreprise'. Fascinating.

Sepi dealt with groups only from works committees. Apparently, every French company who employed over 50 staff had to start a works committee (Comité d'Enterprise') AND provide it with money for good works for employees – including trips. What an opportunity for a tour operator – I stored this in my mind very successfully.

The weekend trip to London was a sell-out. It should have been, at 100 French Francs (about £10) including hotel and transfers – it was a steal. We paid really low prices for the hotel accommodation, rock-bottom prices for the transfers and almost nothing for the flights. Everybody even made a little bit of money. Naturally Sepi wanted more of this good thing. Naturally, so did we.

By now, I'd got over a set of bad experiences walking around Paris looking for hotels and I'd come to love the city. Almost every week Blandine, and I would take the night ferry from Victoria Station, have some dinner on board and arrive at Paris Gare du Nord after early breakfast the next morning. Time now to get to the Place Vendôme to have coffee with the posh lads (Jim and James) at the British Tourist Authority when it was so posh as to be almost the British Embassy.

Then lunch in Les Halles (an important occasion involving at least four courses) with Jacques and Pierre from Sepi. They loved Blandine, she was so French and tough. But it was Sepi who taught me how to do business in France. Never give an inch! And, when I did, Sepi were all over me. To them all was fair in love and war and business. Back in the evening (after early dinner of course!) on the Night Ferry again.

I'd fallen in love with Paris years ago. When I was 14, my favourite author was Georges Simenon, I was besotted with his stories and I so wanted to visit the Paris of Maigret which I knew inch by inch from his books. My dad thought that my going to Paris was a good idea too and so did Harry, the owner of the Hotel Winston in Ostend. Harry was an elderly gourmet and he wanted to go to Paris to eat, Dad said that I could go with him. "Pas de problème" said Harry, my son Georges can look after the hotel and Valere can come with me at the end of the season.

The trip with Harry had started well, at least we stayed in the Rue Rochequart in the Pigalle, a well-known Maigret haunt. And then it went downhill. All Harry wanted to do was to eat rich meals on his list of restaurants. All I wanted to do was to smoke Gauloises cigarettes, drink and look cool. The combination of hours and hours of strange food in crowded smelly restaurants and French cigarettes made me feel perpetually sick. But, luckily, the experience didn't put me off Paris.

The thing about Paris is that it's another tourism Goddess city and tourists will always visit. Who first populated Paris? The Celts. Where's the Notre Dame placed – right on the ancient Celtic centre of power.

Paris has visual history in abundance. Stand in the Notre Dame and you can feel the power of this incredible place. Walk across the Isle de la Cité and you can visualise those accursed Capet kings organising their massacre of the Templars. Visit the Louvre and you can imagine Leonardo bringing his Mona Lisa there. Look at the Place des Vosges and you can see the horse-drawn carriages driving round this exquisite architecture.

Years later, it was at the Notre Dame was where it hit me. To be honest, I was looking for a bit of peace and quiet – the last thing you should look for in a major tourist attraction. It was crammed with people taking photographs to take home with them. Legally "stealing" a bit of the place to examine and hoard in their sitting rooms. And I was sad. To really feel the place, you need to sit and see and hear. So, the tourists lost, the pictures couldn't give them anything they needed.

Now, taking advantage of an opportunity was one thing, setting up an opportunity to take advantage of is something a little bit more complicated, as I was to find out. It was easy enough to arrange the flights: Luton/Paris/Luton on Friday afternoon/evening, Luton/Paris/Luton on Sunday afternoon/evening. And, it was easy enough to arrange the hotel accommodation in London, and Sepi took care of the accommodation in Paris. Keeping the price low was critical and that meant that we had to have a 75% load factor to break even. At these prices it shouldn't be difficult, should it? It was difficult. We could sell as many Paris-London weekends as we wanted, but London-Paris? Not a chance. Even for a tenner a weekend, would you believe it?

We were good at getting business, but often it wasn't as easy as it looked to operate, Take the France v Wales rugby match of 1972. I'd given my friend Joe's son, Ben a job to help out in the office. Although he was only 17 at the time, Ben was to look after the passengers and go with the trip to make sure that everything was OK. After all, Ben was a real rugby enthusiast and a great player so I felt he would do a good job. There shouldn't have been a problem. Anyway, Sepi wasere looking after the tickets and all the ground arrangements (including the hotels) so there was little to do except make sure that the customers got what they were entitled to.

As it happened, the group were entitled to tickets to the match after all, that was their principal reason for flying to Paris. Sepi had ordered tickets, but there was some mix up on the day. The new stadium was smaller than the old one and there were fewer tickets it appeared. Not enough for all of our group of 300 Welsh rugby supporters. Luckily I was on the end of a telex machine, so when I got the message, I replied "Can't they find a café with a TV? This didn't go down particularly well. Plus, of course, you don't know precisely who's on the other end, do you? So, when I slagged Sepi off for messing it up, I got an abusive message from them.

Of course, the group was drunk. That didn't help. In the end, they went around Paris causing a commotion and then we brought them home. Wales had lost. I learnt never again to do a sports group of any type.

The profitable stars of our business show were the day trips. Isn't it silly how something small turns out to be something big so simply? One day, I was visiting a big factory, Fry's the chocolate people. The idea was that they should offer their employees the opportunity to go on a Sunday day trip to London which we would organise. The trip would include a full cooked breakfast en route (egg, bacon, sausage, beans, toast, marmalade and tea or coffee), a visit to the Petticoat Lane Market, a guided tour of London, a visit to Windsor, a cream tea and a visit to a pub to round off the day – all for £3. Not bad eh? Fry's would offer this trip to their employees through their sports and social club. And my contact, the social organiser, said to me "Do you think that you could print something for me to hand out so that people can book easily?" Naturally, I agreed. So, I knocked him up a few hundred leaflets, he handed them out and got a hundred or so people to go on the trip.

What a good idea. I could now print leaflets for every contact who wanted to organise a trip. They'd distribute the leaflets and take the bookings. It made life much easier, no longer did I have to depend on my customers to describe the trips, I could do it better, and more factually. It was a much more effective sales method.

Gordon was great, he'd been my boss when I was selling telephone answering machines. Gordon loved driving around in his car and selling things, so I sent him off to see companies and sell day trips to Petticoat Lane and to Dartmouth. His results were OK, but not fantastic, we got hundreds rather than the thousands of passengers we needed to pay the bills.

Then, one day, Invicta approached me with an interesting offer. They had availability for a cheap charter flight. The flight could go out to Cologne early in the morning and back in the evening. The price was cheap and we could do a day trip. I did a few figures, it looked expensive – £14.50 for a day. The trip would include the flight from Bristol, a coach and steamer trip of the Rhine valley and lunch plus a wine-tasting. I wasn't sure that it would work but was persuaded by Invicta that it was worth a try. I put an ad in the local paper and by lunchtime it was sold out – 146 reservations had been made.

Naturally more day trips followed. A day to Venice cost just £16.50 and included breakfast on the flight, a vaporetto trip through the canals to St Mark's Square, a guided tour of Venice, lunch by the Rialto Bridge and, naturally a visit to a glass factory. A day trip to Nice and

Monte Carlo for £16.50 included a drive down the Corniche and lunch in Nice. Finally, a day trip to Switzerland included a flight to Basle a visit to the Lakeland and, of course, lunch. They were superb days out and attracted a devoted clientele who travelled again and again.

But the company wasn't in very good financial shape. Basically, our overheads were too high and week after week, the Paris operation with Sepi was draining resources. Stephen the antique dealer was now my partner. One bad omen was that our friendly bank manager took to wandering around at night to see what was in Stephen's window. Mr Collins the banker was a nice avuncular man, and would be very comforting in our interviews, but clearly wasn't very hopeful about my business acumen. "I think about you, you know, Tjolle" he'd say "I think about where you're going to go on your day trips next. Would it be Egypt – a quick trip there and a walk around the pyramids? But you'll have to put some money in the account before the 17th or I'm in the hot seat – I'll have to report it you know." And he'd lean back in his seat behind his big desk in his big office, look at the ceiling and say, "How are the kids by the way?"

On the whole, life wasn't too bad, though. If we had day trip flights operating, I'd get up early and drive round to where Ben had slept the night before. I'd get him out of bed and drive on to the airport for 7am ish. I'd frequently pick up my dad on the way and he would act as a guide on the trip as well as Ben. The passengers would be checking in at the Dan Air desk, they'd fly off to their destination and I'd often stay for a cup of coffee with Edwin, the Dan Air station manager, before going off to start work at the office.

Invigorated by the Berlin Airlift at which they were major players, 'Dan Dare', as Dan Air were known by all and sundry in the trade, was a pretty relaxed airline. By 1972 they were operating a small fleet of Comet 4b's, very, very thirsty British airplanes – apparently with enough power to land on just one of their four engines. Although they had some scheduled business – the reason they had an office at Bristol – their main business was tour charter flights and big operations like the 'Hajj' which they operated from Berlin – and made a great deal of money from this intensive flying programme.

My big event of 1972 was the birth of my second son Robin, who I mistakenly registered as Edward Robin. It was a welcome break to come back to Bath on a summer afternoon, make some tea in our little flat and take it down to the Parade Gardens below, to drink with my little family whilst listening to the band.

By 1973, things had got very difficult and I knew something had to be done. The Paris trips had been draining us of money week by week. We'd got in very deep with the airline and owed them quite a lot of money. They clearly didn't want to lose the money, but, just as much, they didn't want to lose the business. We had to talk.

Naturally, Invicta were prepared to do a deal. It's a common practice in the travel business for a supplier to take over a client so they'd keep the business rather than lose it. So, finally, we got to an arrangement that looked reasonably sensible. Invicta would write off their debt and put in an amount of cash so that other creditors would get 25% of their debts. Invicta would take over our company. This was subject to the agreement of the majority of the creditors.

Then Invicta suspended their operations. Apparently, they were in financial trouble too! Eventually they were taken over by European Ferries a big ferry and port company, so the deal was on again. We quickly re-arranged our flying programme, consolidating flights so that we could have the best load-factors and wrote to the creditors and the passengers. We were in business.

Tuesday 10th April was a beautiful spring day, a superb day for a day excursion to Switzerland, which is where our passengers were going. Ben and my dad were on the flight and I was at the Avon Rubber Company at Melksham when I got the call. Jim, Invicta's operations manager was on the telephone "OP's come down, don't worry Val, she's a tough old bird" Jim was referring to G-AXOP, the airplane carrying a full load of 139 passengers and 6 crew to Basle that day, including my Dad and Ben. Numb, I drove back to the office in Bristol.

There was already a group of reporters and cameramen outside the office, I made my way through them and leapt up the stone stairs to the first floor. I rang Chan to tell her as much as I could. All we could do all day and night was to answer the constantly-ringing telephones. After initial optimism about numbers of survivors, as the day drew on, the picture slowly became terribly clear – the majority of the passengers and crew had been killed. As far as who, precisely, had survived, we simply didn't know yet and so could give little succour to distraught friends and relatives of passengers. The press pestered, wanting details of survivors and people to interview. The telex machine chattered away with questions and condolences.

The situation was harrowing, it was the biggest disaster to affect the Bristol area since the last war. The passengers were mainly from Women's Institutes and mothers' groups from Mendip villages, the crash tore into the heart of the little countryside communities. The grief was palpable.

Stephen arrived in the evening, sitting himself in the corner, unable to do anything, but tacitly offer his support. Through the night we answered the telephones, able to offer little to the panic-stricken callers. Acting like automatons, we couldn't afford yet to come to terms with the immensity of the situation.

Miraculously, I heard that my father and Ben had survived. Apparently, they'd both been sitting in the back of the plane when it hit a mountainside in a heavy snowstorm. The tail section had broken off in the impact, the majority of the casualties were in the front section. 108 of the 139 passengers had been killed and 4 of the 6 crew.

There was now a mass of organisational work to be done, to assist those that had been affected by the crash. An operations centre was set up in the beautiful Mendip village of Axbridge, at the heart of the affected communities, and I went to work there to help. There was much work to be done, the survivors had to be flown home, undertakers had been commissioned to organise the repatriation of the remains and relatives needed to visit survivors still in Switzerland.

The RAF flew the majority of the survivors who were prepared to fly back to Lyneham, where their PR Officer organised a press conference. The remainder of the survivors made their way back overland. Then I attended the funerals in the little country villages. The disaster had affected thousands of people, the sorrow and anguish of this traumatic event would never go away. I had no means to deal with this event, so enormous and unpredictable. There would be no closure. I had to go back to work.

The final day trip in the series was to Venice from Bournemouth. Ben's father, my friend Joe, had decided that he'd take Ben's place on the flight to support me. We were to go together with the group.

British people are amazing – they never seem to panic. When the inflatable gangways pushed out onto the tarmac and we were ordered to evacuate the aircraft people chatted amongst themselves. "I thought I could smell petrol, dear" said one old lady. Anyway, it appeared that there had been a bomb threat by telephone, and as soon as the plane had been searched, we were cleared to go.

What an amazing outing. Arriving at Marco Polo airport on a glorious early summer day, we took a vaporetto ride to St Mark's Square, time for coffee before our guided walking tour. Lunch was arranged, just by the Rialto Bridge, watching the gondolas go by – how romantic can you get? Then we went to St Mark's square again to visit the Trevisan Glass Factory.

It's pretty easy to lose your passengers in Venice. No buses parked outside, lots of crowds around. So, before we went into the glass factory, Joe organised a passenger-count. St Marks is neatly divided into painted squares, so, when each passenger was counted, they had to move forward one square. Simple – and it worked.

Looking out of the window onto St Mark's square, I noticed all the pigeons suddenly take off in a cloud. Minutes later, the square became silent as the people moved too. A whirlwind was on the way, it passed through St Marks in a torrent of rain and squall, and it was gone. The people and the pigeons returned and St Marks was back to normal.

Now time to take coffee with the Trevisans. The passengers had had a good time and bought some nice things. "Now Signori, we need to talk about the commission" said the younger Trevisan "We don't pay commission" said Joe, while I sharply kicked his foot. The Trevisans paid us nearly £150. Not bad for a couple of hours guiding. That evening, we watched the thunderstorms over Venice as we flew home.

I was now working for Invicta and, after commuting daily to their offices in Piccadilly, trying to reorganise the daytrips programme, we settled on setting up an office in Bath. Our new programme was launched from two floors in Georgian Milsom Street where we had a lot of fun but didn't do much business.

We were now Faircourt Tours – an off-the shelf company with proper financing, a Commercial Manager (me) and a few staff. Day trips by air was a concept that could really work – we thought! Unfortunately, now we were owned by the airline, the seamless operation had to make profit after their appropriate operating costs – not like the old days where you could do a deal on a quick telephone call. Boring!

It was 1974 and I was really treading water, Invicta offered me the opportunity of a transfer to their base in Kent, but I didn't really want to leave Bath and was made redundant and the offices closed.

I simply didn't know what to do but Joe again came to my support – he encouraged me to stay in the travel business and he rolled up his sleeves to help. In the event, we decided to set up a company together, after evenings spent discussing possible names and activities, we settled on calling the company Land Travel because that's what it would specialise in – travel by land not air!

I had a great deal of support from the ex-Faircourt staff, three months free work with no salary in fact! And they helped me set up the company in Joe's sitting room. Next we recruited a printer (Joe's son in law Martin) and he introduced us to a local accountant – David and a designer Hilary. We were to concentrate on operating Sunday day trips by coach to Petticoat Lane. The trips were to be sold to groups from the sports and social clubs of companies North and West of London.

Joe and I drove around together getting coach companies, restaurants and guides organised to deal with our clients. We planned the tour of London. We set up our sales and accounts systems and got nice little leaflets printed. Then, every day, we got on the telephone together, sharing the one telephone on the dining room table.

Within six weeks, we were taking between 10 and 20 coachloads to London every Sunday from all over the North of England. The day trips were going well, people loved them, we had absolutely no complaints, and, unusually for a tour operator, we had loads of letters of compliment – which we put up on the wall. Now to do something a bit more complicated! We arranged weekend trips to take place in the autumn – to Paris and to the Wieze Beer Festival, would you believe?

Joe's dining room became a little cramped for all this activity so we started looking around for proper office premises. We found the ideal offices slap bang in the heart of Bath, the 1st, 2nd and 3rd floors of a café in the Abbey Churchyard. Right opposite the Pump Room, the Abbey itself and the Roman Baths.

It was 1974, the train drivers were on strike, UK unemployment was over 500,000, and Court Line folded.

Court Line was, and is, the travel industry in a nutshell. Hitherto Whizz Kids. Now bust. Dead and gone for ever but leaving a legacy of doom in the travel industry in the form of its ex-employees...

And Court Line left another little legacy too – a law bringing in a surcharge on every new air holiday booked, to build up a trust fund (the Air Travel Reserve Fund) so that holiday money would, in future, be protected. Fat chance.

So. How and why? What happened? Basically, Court Line was a shipbuilding and transportation company operating 11 BAC 1-11's and 2 wide-bodied Tristars, and some very smart coaches. Court Line provided flights for Clarkson's and had over-exposed itself to them, Clarkson's then had 25% of the UK inclusive tour market. Clarkson's was on the point of going bust (they were losing money hand over fist), which would mean that they couldn't pay Court Line what they owed them (millions and millions of pounds) and it looked like Court Line would lose the Clarkson's business too.

So, what do you do when you're overexposed to your major client who hasn't got any money? Well, Court Line managed to get Shipping and Industrial Holdings, who owned Clarkson's, to give them the loss-making company together with £6million. "Phew" I bet the executives of Court Line thought "We've managed to pull it off, not only have we ensured our future business but we've got a cool £6m to boot.

You know, however much in debt they are, tour operators have usually got quite a bit of money in the bank. Plus, everybody likes an operator. The operator owns the customers after all, the operator directs where the customer is going to spend money. The operator has the power. When Court Line looked at the bank balance and the list of hotels and resorts that wanted Clarkson's business at almost any cost, they must have thought they were on to a good thing.

What would be the next most sensible thing for Court Line to do? Evaluate Clarkson's and make sure that it was profitably managed? Or think that they'd come up with a brilliant new idea to make easy money and play it for all it was worth?

You've guessed it. Court Line bought OSL who owned Wings, an upmarket operator who just had lines on their brochure cover not scantily-dressed beach babes. Court Line bought ATLAS and then Horizon Midlands. One assumes for all the lovely, lovely cash they had in the bank. In February 1974, obviously fed up with acquiring companies for their life-blood, Court Line attempted to get at the life-blood direct without bothering about the company by acquiring the passengers and goodwill of Horizon (Vladimir Raitz's pioneer of package holidays) and Four S Travel (not only a pioneer, but also a suggestive play on words). Obviously, it didn't work for a number of reasons:

Reason 1:

Clarkson's, the biggest of them all, probably never, ever, made real money. Owned by a medium-sized old-established group of shipping brokers, at the beginning they were probably content to operate tours and give a few people jobs just so they could look at the bank balance. And borrow a bit when they needed it. When the company got bigger, it would have excused itself by saying it was searching for critical mass – in other words "Jam Tomorrow" After all, it was dominating the UK travel industry and that had to be worth something. And, of course, there was the safety net – the company could always be sold for something (i.e. all those customers pounds in the bank could be sold at a discount).

Reason 2:

You may buy the company but you can't be sure you can buy the customers and they, after all, are what you want. Holiday buyers are notoriously fickle, you have to have an absolutely cast-iron Unique Selling Proposition to make them stay.

Reason 3:

Tour operators actually like being tour operators. Most of them like the freedom and power they enjoy. If they're making a profit too, there is no reason for them to sell, whatever they say. The only way to get a good, profitable tour operation is to pay way, way unsustainably over the odds.

Reason 4:

You can't buy a tour operator in a vacuum. You really have to know what you're buying and what's going on around your target company. Let's face it, the travel business is made up of not-so-hungry people who buy companies and hungry people who are prepared to steal them, your business, your passengers – anything they can get.

Anyway, as they say, in death there is life and in destruction there is creation. The 'Angel' who incubated it all was Harry! Harry (Goodman) was very, very hungry in 1974. So, he laid in wait in his executive jet and when he saw the writing on the wall, he pounced. Teams of contractors were jetted out to resorts to buy Clarkson's/Court Line hotel contracts, teams of salespeople were brought in to get travel agents to switch-sell. Court Line's business was being dismembered before it had hit the ground. And Intasun, Harry's company made an enormous leap into Clarkson's' place in the trade, in more ways than one!

But remember the tale – tour operators like Clarkson's are holiday bubbles from the start – the bigger they get the louder they bang when they finally, inevitably, implode. In the end the precarious logic that holds them together runs out of cash and credit and their ideas and executives are blown around the industry like germs ready to infect the whole industry. We'll hear more about Harry later...

CHAPTER 4

Success at Last

The reason for Land Travel's success was very simple. At the time, most tour operators put together a series of tours and then set out to sell them to whoever. Most tour operators produced a colour brochure a year or so in advance of the holidays and sent it out in the post. Boring.

Well, ol' Dale Carnegie (the sales guru who wrote "How to Win Friends and Influence People") had certainly affected me, and Land Travel was set up along classic Carnegie lines (identifying people's needs and fulfilling them). So, we'd done something quite different from the other tour operators (we thought!).

We'd identified a market (Sports & Social Clubs in large companies) and their needs (Jolly times together) and created a series of tours specifically to fulfil that specific market's needs – great fun day trips and weekends away. We did fabulous-value Sunday coach day trips to London and coach weekends to Paris and the Wieze Beer Festival. – everybody could enjoy themselves together in the comfort of their coach "It's like real telly" said one of our first passengers.

We also had a simple marketing method, although we'd sent some 400 brochures out – the traditional way – we hadn't had one response. So we (that's Joe and I) prepared ourselves with scripts and got on our one telephone to the 400 potential clients (organizers at Sports and Social Clubs) to see if we could persuade them to organize groups on our trips. It wasn't that difficult, we followed up the sales by sending big batches of leaflets overprinted with the organizers name and the name of the specific club. Just like the man at Fry's had asked. All the organizer had to do was to give out the leaflets and collect the bookings and the money and send it to us. We had everything set up already.

For the club members the initial trip offering was a "steal" – a Sunday "Charabanc" coach day trip to London's Petticoat Lane market from about a 200 mile radius North or West, a full fried breakfast (eggs, bacon, sausages, fried bread, toast, tea or coffee) en route, plus a full guided tour of London (St Paul's Cathedral, Tower Bridge, Piccadilly Circus, the Thames – the lot!), plus a cream tea at Windsor or Woburn in the afternoon. All for from £3 to £3.50 a head. For every coachload the organizer booked, he or she got a couple of free trips – that gave the organizer the necessary incentive and commitment.

My mathematics were simple. I thought that if Joe and I sold to 30 social organizers each week, they'd get an average of 10 passengers each

– a total of about 300 passengers a week – 6 coach loads. As it happened, the majority of the organizers got at least one coach load each.

Although it seems unbelievably low-tech today, it was pretty state-of-the-art in 1974. We'd built up a database of potential clients from researching the market, and we telephoned them to offer our trips. The key factor was the need of our clients for the experiences we offered, and in that, we were a little bit of social history.

We dealt with organizers in electronic manufacturers like Plessey, vast buildings with hundreds or thousands of ladies working at work benches. We dealt with all the potteries – more thousands of working women. We dealt with the mines.

We dealt with big post offices. We dealt with factories and tax offices and local governments and car manufacturers. We dealt with shoe-makers in Northampton, engineering manufacturers in the Midlands, mills and carpet makers in the North of England.

It appeared that in 1974, people liked their workmates sufficiently to go on a day trip or weekend away with them – and they enjoyed it. After all, they'd always done it. Hitherto factory groups went to Weston Super Mare or Blackpool for the day. We'd just introduced a few new destinations and a bit of upmarket and a large helping of pzazz.

It wasn't just about good value – it was more about experiences that people didn't think that they could afford or were entitled to. Tours to Belgium's Wieze Beer Festival for clubs had happened before. But they used low grade hotels and B&B's along the Belgian Coast. This was good for the hotels because they became full and they also had an opportunity to complain about drunken British tourists. It was not so good for the tourists because the accommodation wasn't so hot. The tourists didn't complain, they probably couldn't remember anyway.

Looking around for something a bit better (or cheaper, or easier to book) than Belgian coast boarding houses, we wrote to lots of hotels within striking distance of Wieze and stumbled on a very interesting phenomenon – Antwerp. Tourists went to the Belgian coast, they went to Bruges and Brussels and to Ghent, some even went to the Ardennes. But they didn't go to Antwerp. Antwerp? Even I'd never been there, I knew where it was, I knew what it was (capital of East Flanders), but what it looked like, I'd no idea.

Until the four-star Eurotel wrote to me stating the magic number 325, Belgian francs that is, per person per night that was less than £5 at the time, including full breakfast buffet. Bloody hell! That was cheaper than a Belgian coast boarding house, and the Eurotel's rooms were with shower/bath and toilet, no night walks down lino-ed corridors. And the hotel was EMPTY at weekends. Why?

The answer was very simple too. A bunch of European hotel groups had done their sums at the same time (they always do!) and they all came up with the same answer and built at the same time. Antwerp used to have a reasonable occupation level (say 80% – 8 rooms out of 10 full) with a couple of hotels in use. Then a bunch of international hoteliers built a few big hotels and a local building company decided not to be left out of the act – and built a few more. Result 20% occupancy level (2 rooms in 10 full) for a few years until all the marketing kicked in and the smell of all those hotels leaking blood brought all the sharks – thank God.

I made hay while the sun shone. We could now sell a whole weekend trip including the coach travel, the ferry crossing, the hotel accommodation (unbelievably four star, all rooms with TV, Minibar and full bathroom) breakfast buffet the guide service AND our profit for less than the rack rate the hotel said it was charging for the room alone. Dream on you poor punters (wash my mouth out with soap and water – I promise I'll never use the 'P' word again) stopping in grimy, lino-floored, shared toilets Belgian Coast B&B's.

The hotels were actually losing money – the breakfast and the room cleaning cost more than we were paying. But the people who did the deals with us (the hotel general managers or sales managers) didn't care. They only had to report to their bosses on their occupancy levels, not their profitability. Plus they hoped that our customers would spend money in their bars. Fat chance – these were 4-star hotels for businessmen and charged 4 star prices for 4 star ale, not our customers' cup of tea at all! But the hotels loved us. Full rooms told the story every manager wanted to tell.

And Antwerp actually was simply stunning, even more so for the lack of tourists. The city has fabulous architecture from the superb 20th century railway station to the gorgeous 17th century merchants' houses. You could stroll along wonderful shopping streets, eat great food, enjoy a delightful cathedral with its outside evening concerts of dreamy carillon music. Above all, Antwerp is a city with bottle as its colourful history demonstrates. Plus the Wieze Beer Festival!

By the time we'd moved into those offices in the Abbey Church-yard, we'd become a real business and we had a list of things we needed, including staff and an accountant to sort out the books.

And we were able to understand and create a formula with a sustainable competitive advantage or two.

Firstly because we had created our own database of organisers at companies' sports and social clubs, we had unique access to our market by telephone and mail rather than through any intermediary.

Secondly in buying the different services for our trips we were fulfilling a number of needs – business hotels were empty at weekends then, coaches too in the 'shoulder season' and our tour managers (who we usually took from Bath) often had weekday jobs and liked money and fun at weekends.

Thirdly, we never bought in a sellers' market, in effect we hired coaches, booked hotel rooms and ferry crossings only when they were really cheap – and we could even then negotiate the price down.

Fourthly, we were fulfilling the genuine needs of our customers for low cost, high quality fun experiences in a less than sophisticated era.

Finally, we maintained a strict control and management regime. We knew where every penny went and exactly how much we'd made immediately each trip was concluded.

More than anything, the money, the power, the success, what our operation brought everybody was fun. We gave fantastic value, our customers loved us, everybody had fun and none of it would have been possible without our guides and the coach company's drivers. We simply provided the background to their days, weekends and weeks of pure theatre with the drivers and guides the stars and the passengers the "extras", We never ceased to marvel at these weekly events which provided us with colourful entertainment, vicarious pleasure and real insights into life-with-all-its-warts-and-wonders!

The Wieze Beer Festival was a real phenomenon, but it was the basis for our business philosophy.

Naturally, we expanded this weekend concept to other destinations – Paris, Amsterdam, the Dutch Bulbfields, the Rhineland.

It was a very simple and very effective formula. In all these destinations we used superb business-style accommodation which was empty at weekends, bulk-bought from ferry companies and coach operators. Negotiated like hell for the very lowest prices. Sold by telephone to group organisers at big companies and organisations, followed up with personalised colour leaflets. We sold bare bones weekends at rock bottom prices and then added two special ingredients – exciting excursions and tour managers. The excursions added a lot of pzazz to the trip provided massive revenue and cost almost nothing and the tour managers made sure everything worked well – and sold more excursions to create more profit and bring back lots of cash.

To do all this, we trained and built up a great team of young, tough, mainly female contractors to buy all these services cheap. We trained and built up a great team of young, hard-working telesales people and we trained and built up a great team of young, resourceful tour managers.

And above all, we trained our clients! Our groups came from everywhere – car makers, carpet makers, bankers, insurance people, union members, policemen and women, tax inspectors, piemakers, hospital workers, nurses and doctors, store staff,

They all had one thing in common – the need to have a great time cheap – together. A bunch of experiences that were the essence of fun and escapism.

For about £29 our groups got luxury coach travel from their chosen local departure point – usually the place they worked, the ferry crossing to Europe and a night's hotel accommodation in a business-style three or four star hotel and a tour manager to make their trip superfun and interest-packed. Incredibly good value.

To make the most of the time available the outward journey was always overnight. Groups left all points south of Scotland on Friday afternoons or evenings arriving in their destination on Saturday late mornings usually at the right time to check into their nice hotel.

Of course, the tour managers travelled with the groups primarily to make sure that check in was OK and everything was efficient and that everybody was happy. But he or she was also there to make money for themselves – and us – and to make sure that everybody made the most of their limited time abroad.

This all added up to extra, good value experiences – excursions, evening meals and parties plus visits to selected shops. So, for instance, in Amsterdam there was a walking tour of the Red Light district, a coach tour of the city, a special meal in the Sea Palace restaurant and a visit to a diamond factory. In the Rhineland, tours and Rhine Wine tastings and a Rhine Steamer cruise. In Paris a posh dinner, a guided tour of the Illuminations and a River Seine cruise on a Bateau Mouche. All these excursions were charged extra. But we charged lower prices than anybody. Why? For three major reasons – unlike destination excursion companies – our clients knew and trusted us – we had a relationship; we used our own coach for the excursions so it cost us no more money; our tour managers were paid by results and provided the commentaries so they wanted the biggest audience possible and finally we were tough negotiators with restaurants and other providers. The results – fantastic numbers of excursion participants, fabulous excursion profits; rich tour managers – making enough money in one weekend to last them a month or more and last, but not least, very very happy clients.

After all, for the normal cost of a bed in a similar hotel they were getting a whole package including the transport and assistance. Superb value.

Naturally we expanded the list of destinations and the variety of tours but the formula remained the same: Overnight travel outwards, quality hotel accommodation, good value, high profit excursions and friendly, knowledgeable tour managers.

Next steps were longer holiday-style one-week tours to old fashioned famous destinations such as Lido di Jesolo and Rimini in Italy, Lloret de Mar in Spain and Zell am Zee in Austria.

Pretty much everything was done in the off season – winter, spring and autumn weekends and holidays. And to take advantage of the seasonal empty-hotel opportunities we organised our own shopping and beer festivals.

Sounds like a lot of fun? It was. At our height we were carrying over 100,000 passengers a year and employing over 500 staff and pretty much everybody was having a whale of a time.

Usually there was a great deal of money floating about – much of it in cash. Our holiday destinations had teams selling and operating excursions and were taking hundreds of thousands of pounds. Plus everybody was after our business so their generosity was pretty much unlimited – after all we were in the hospitality business.

Everybody made good money and had a great time. Of course there were excesses – after all we were young and loaded – the world was our oyster – and it got even better as we expanded.

We realised how important bright people were so we gave them lots of unhampered opportunities.

We realised how important good working conditions were so we made them fun and totally informal.

We realised how important it was to try new things and take risks so we constantly set up new initiatives – Limeberry, for instance, was a product company with its own warehouse selling all kinds of good value stuff to our social organiser contacts for their club members with our leaflet promotions. We sourced, bought in bulk and sold cutlery, pots and pans, glassware, even rocking horses (modelled by my son Robin). We bought, designed and re-invigorated a local tourist magazine called 'This month in Bath'. We started a property development company buying and 'doing up' old buildings and selling them. With a contact, a director of the British Tourism Authority we started a cottage rental company and bought, leased and rented cottages in the West Country. Far before its time (unfortunately!), we even financed a home delivery grocery company, we even bought a debt collection company!

We realised how important it was to be in control of key issues so we also established our own print & design company.

We realised how important it was to be warm and welcoming so we let staff go, get experience in other jobs and come back home!

We realised how important it was to give young people, boys and girls lots of power and responsibility, to let them make mistakes and support them and we saw how much better and tougher the girls were.

But above all, we realised the importance and the power of interpretation, describing and adding value to things. In other words telling stories about places and giving our clients more to marvel at – in other words identifying and fulfilling needs...

There were a bunch of needs! The major drive, of course, was the need of our customers to experience something really different to take them out of themselves – at ridiculously affordable prices, in the safety of their friends' company, managed and in a bit of control, but still with the excitement of the potential of strange and memorable happenings above all lots of fun in foreign, exotic places.

Then there was the need of the social organiser in the client's place of work. At that time every organisation had a social organiser. Usually it was a voluntary position but often it was a fully paid job. The social organiser's function was to spread harmony and communication by organising events for the workers. Christmas parties, sports days, theatre visits, bingo nights, days out – these and many other functions were where the good oganiser shone. Why not offer the staff brilliantly inexpensive weekends away and holidays too? Naturally we gave the organiser free seats on the trip and naturally we brought the organiser to the party with extra free fun weekends especially for them. So fun all round.

At the height of our marketing success we would bring over a thousand social organisers on a free mass outing to Europe. For me it was a fascinating insight into all of human life. Promotional weekends were simply sensational.

At one level they were a simple PR and communications exercise – after all we rarely met our clients physically as all our business was conducted by telephone and mail. This was a chance to meet and press the flesh and enhance our knowledge of each other.

A number of conditions caused all the weekends, and particularly the promotional weekends, to be extra full-on.

Firstly, the fact that groups arrived in exotic continental Europe early in the morning having had little or no sleep and after having had usually more than a modicum of alcohol instilled a shaky level of latent hysteria in everybody. Given the right events, nice accommodation plenty of jollity, kindness and efficiency – everybody could be hysterically happy.

Given the wrong events, delays, cold service, rude drivers, rubbish accommodation, disengagement and sour notes – everybody could be hysterically mad.

The oil that was poured on potentially troubled waters was that of our tour managers. They could simply make or break any tour. We recruited and trained hundreds of them. Recruited is probably the wrong word –

we never had to advertise, everybody came to work for us through word of mouth. Tour managers were always friends of friends.

Why did they do it? Simply because they loved it! And our customers loved them.

Packing off up to a hundred fully-fledged tour managers every week and up to 20 or so trainees on 'dry run' training experiences – all fully briefed and with emergency money was a major logistical exercise in itself. But off they went week after week to have exciting adventures taking a bunch of clients (new friends) to the continent. A few days later they would return (usually) with their pockets full of money to spend and (always) a repertoire of war stories to recount.

Promotional weekends were only available to bona fide organisers. The idea was that they would go home afterwards and organise a whole coachload (or more) to come on a trip.

Promotional weekends were usually free and obviously very prestigious, they also allowed tour managers to meet and bond with organisers so they vied for the opportunity of participating. Also, they were even more fun than usual. Just imagine over 1000 people off on a free weekend to Europe with drinking and dancing and singing and great meals and great hotels and great fun. Quite – you're thinking all kinds of fun, aren't you? And you are right.

The first night social event was always a revelation to me. There would usually be around 50 staff – all quite young, extrovert and attractive – telesales staff and managers and tour managers. Happy, energetic, well turned out, adventurous and well-fed and watered – everybody was relaxed and excited enough to bond at lots of different levels. Over-the-top great fun for all and thank goodness marginally less outrageous and full-on than a Stag or Hen weekend – just!

My speciality was usually to do a Can Can – arms linked with a dozen or so lovely female and male staff standing on top of a bar!

Exhausting weekends and really educational.

But what were the 'ordinary' weekends like? Not much different! One of our specialities Shopping, Beer and Chocolate weekends went something like this...

Remember my family came from Belgium? What the Belgians don't know about beer and chocolate and shopping could be written on a very small chocolate wrapper with a big pen!

Naturally Belgium was the venue, and every weekend in the praline chocolate season (yes there is one!) we took dozens of coaches with dozens of tour managers and thousands of passengers to stay in Belgium's glorious cities.

We used posh hotels on Saturday nights; pretty much all the hotels were top four- and five-star – Holiday Inns, Novotels, Sheratons, Hiltons – the lot.

The coach would roll up at the hotel in the late morning/early afternoon and discharge its group with its tour manager.

Remember, everybody had been travelling since early the night before and usually drinking for that time too. Let's say that they were almost always somewhat tired and emotional. Quick group check-in, wash and brush-up and back to the hotel reception for an optional guided tour of Brussels. This was the first opportunity for the group to get a revelatory experience and the tour manager to make real money. Let's say that a guided tour bought locally with a local guide could cost £20, we'd do a better one for £15. And we had big advantages – we paid no more for the coach and we knew our audience intimately by now, plus the tour manager's knowledge and language were superb. So probably all the group would take it – £750 takings 25% for the guide meant nearly £200 in his or her back pocket when this was a good wage for the week. Brilliant – and the weekend had only just started.

Our clients were a mixed bunch, pretty much nice people but the occasional group of hooligans. We used posh hotels in Brussels, like the five star just-built Royal Windsor by the Grande Place (now the luxury Warwick Hotel) they would not serve guests in the bar without ties. No problem for our hooligans – each room had lovely curtains so with a rip and a tear our hooligans had lovely ties.

On to the chocolate and beer festival in the massive hall in the centre of my family's hometown – Diksmuide – the 'medieval' Boterhal (Diksmuide is famous for its butter too). This was neither an ancient festival nor an ancient city although they both looked the part.

Once the stunningly beautiful and awesomely tranquil medieval town of Diksmuide was famous for its nuns in their ancient Beguinage and its superb butters. Then the First World War happened all around it and the town was smashed to the ground by the opposing forces. Nothing left – I know, my grandfather was one of the casualties, fighting in the 'Trench of Death' he narrowly avoided annihilation, but that's another story.

Diksmuide's inhabitants packed what they could and beat it – to Aix en Provence as it happened, waited until the coast was clear and then went home. To what? Nothing was standing, so they rolled their sleeves up and rebuilt their hometown – exactly as it was. Step gables, cobbled square, town hall, Beguinage, Boterhal – the lot. The only difference you can see now are the dates above the doors – whereas they were, say, 1678 they became 1923. But to all intents and purposes – from the outside Diksmuide was again a medieval town – and home.

The beer festival was another matter. We'd started our business with the Wieze Beer Festival. Great, but we had to pay entrance fees. Why not have our own where we wouldn't have to pay? We popped off to

Diksmuide to talk to our nice avuncular friend Mr Van Nevel (also known as Mr Belly Button) who had made chocolates for us in the past. "Why don't we have a beer festival in Diksmuide, we'll bring you lots of British groups who will spend lots of money?" we said. "Yes" said Mr Van Nevel. So there it was – our own beer festival in my family home. It was to be held in the massive medieval-looking Boterhal. All of the entrepreneurs in the town would get a chance to sell stuff, the organisation, strong-arm management would be down to the football club players and the beer-selling was down to their wives. We would provide thousands of British revellers. Job done.

And the great thing about it was that not only was it ours, it was better than Wieze in one main respect – at Weize there was one beer available to drink (Wieze Beer) at Diksmuide there were dozens.

Plus of course, as the festival was ours, we had pride of place everywhere.

So Saturday night was singing and drinking and dancing, oompah bands in the 'ancient' Boterhal, plenty of great Belgian food, and, of course brilliant Belgian chocolates & terrific fun! And plenty of purchases to provide us, and our tour managers, with plenty of commissions.

And Sunday morning was a great breakfast buffet feast in the first-class hotel before a visit to Bruges and an (optional extra) walking and canal boat tour. More money for the tour managers and us, but above all great value and experiences for our customers – after all these tours were finely researched and enacted and superb value.

Bruges is truly wonderful and very, very lucky. The city is an authentic gem of 16th and 17th century architecture and art of then, one of the richest, most powerful and most colourful cities in the world.

Connected to the sea by the Zwyn causeway and riddled with canals for easy transport, it was one of Europe's great centres of commerce and trade. And when it was powerful Flanders was important, not just for trade but also for politics and the arts. The Flemish painters, sculptors, architects, scientists, writers and philosophers were the world's best. All this incredible activity pulled the world's great artists and writers, rich and famous, good and great (and not so good and great) and powerful people to this rich mecca. And then it all stopped. The Zwyn silted up and everybody pushed off to Antwerp and the herring port that was called Amsterdam. And Bruges became fossilized – the perfect tourism destination. All show, all beauty – no activity to get in the way of visitors.

When we arrived on a Sunday, Bruges was the perfect stop – for sightseeing and shopping. Maybe the best chocolates in the world (at our partner commission-paying chocolate factory of course). Some of the world's greatest beers and beautiful hand-made Bruges lace.

And Bruges provided an extra highlight. Over the border to Holland and back. Full of duty-free bargains, Sluis is just a few km from Bruges. Duty-free shopping. Cigarettes, tobacco, whisky, gin, licquers, wine and beer – all so cheap you could save so much you could pay for your weekend twice over. Plus you were on a coach so there were plenty of places to stash your hooch!

And then off to to the port for the ferry crossing, a few drinks with happy passengers and home. Time that night for the Tour Managers to work out exactly how much money (lots!) they had taken and prepare their accounts to take to the office to claim their share.

There were lots of weekends that followed the same formula – travel out overnight on Friday, fab hotel on Saturday, return on Sunday afternoon/evening, different trips had different excursions on the Saturday. So, in Germany groups stayed in Cologne, did a Rhine cruise and had a wine tasting (more big commission) on Saturday afternoon and went to a wine festival Saturday night. In Paris groups enjoyed four-star hotels on the outskirts and a 'Bateau Mouche' cruise, dinner and illuminations tour in the evening. And in Holland they enjoyed great hotels near Amsterdam, a visit to the bulbfields, a cheese and clog experience, a diamond factory tour and a visit to Amsterdam's Red Light district.

All these tours generated lots of enjoyment and fun for the partici-pants, lots of business for hotels and coach companies, lots of jobs and vast amounts of excursion revenue for us and our tour managers.

There were, of course fabulous honeypots on each and every tour that provided our customers with great deals and us with lots and lots of money.

Most of them operated on the 4-times-25 formula – a deal that was established in that great doyenne of the tourism industry – Venice. The formula allocated parts of the 100% that the customer paid – 25% the cost of the article, 25% overheads 25% staff commission and 25% for the person or company that introduced the customer.

In Belgium it was chocolates; in Germany wine; in Holland tulips, cheese, china and clogs; in France perfume; at borders duty-free goods and in Venice, of course glass (and now masks!). Just imagine 1,000 people spending £20 a head average on Belgian chocs each week – 25% soon mounts up.

So why not expand a bit? By this time I had developed a bit of a business philosophy.

Bit further? Bit more fun? Few more excursion opportunities? Where could we get amazing value in the 1980s?

The travel and tourism industry is strange – the truth is that it always destroys what it loved. So, in the 1960s and 1970s everyone loved the Spanish and Italian beaches and Austrian lakes. No more – by the 1980s they were in the process of becoming passé. Simply because 'New' is a powerful marketing term and saving a few quid is a travel industry mantra. Turkey, Egypt, The Gambia, Thailand had gained the notice of the big European tour operators and rock-bottom prices combined with weak currencies had filled their hearts with greed. So they were a bit further? Who cared, since 1947 until today airline fuel is cheap as chips and nobody pays taxes on it. Forget the good old places they thought – we're going to make lots of money!

Lovely unfashionable destinations meant an opportunity for us.

In Italy I chose Rimini (which had been the venue for my first familiarization trip) and Lido di Jesolo, close to Venice. In Spain – Lloret de Mar and in Austria Zell am See and in Yugoslavia – Istrian Porec.

We organised 1-week holidays by overnight coach on full board at knock-down prices but with loads of fabulous great value excursions.

By far the most successful were the Austrian and Italian destinations. After all, you could do a superb (and very lucrative) optional day excursion to Venice from all of them. From Rimini you could visit Rome and the mountaintop republic of San Marino too. From Zell am Zee you could see all the Sound of Music country – including Innsbruck and Salzburg plus the Grossglockner scenic mountain road. And every destination had a 'three markets tour' for our groups it was fun, fun, fun – for our tour managers and us it was money, money, money. These three destinations were so successful that we established our own local offices where the managers were making massive commissions.

And, why not air as well as coach? Re-enter my friend Angelo who I used to drink with in the 1960s and took us on our first Venice experience. These days Angelo was an important pillar of the regular travel industry – he was managing director of one of the most respected travel agencies going – Barry Aikman travel in posh Knightsbridge – London. His problem was that the elegant, classy Mr Aikman wanted to sell his business and retire and he wanted top dollar. Angelo couldn't afford it so he was looking for an opportunity. He took a look at our business, saw the opportunities and liked them. I already had a company – Carefree Cottages Ltd – for the foreign visitors, so it was the work of a moment to establish a trading name – Carefree Holidays was born. It took a little longer to find premises but quite quickly we were able to buy the lease of 122 Knightsbridge from a friendly travel trekking company who were in difficult times because Afghanistan and Iran were closed to them. Their business was the Hippy Trail which had been basically cut off.

Anyway 122 Knightsbridge was a great address, a nice small shop with offices and it was dirt cheap. I sold Angelo 24% of the company, he became Managing Director and we were in business.

Angelo had brought a lot of very lucrative conference organising for global companies with him. They were often very complex with delegates flying from all over the world – with Angelo organising complicated deals with airlines – but not quite our market.

Actually, it took a long time to find out what our market was. We tried the obvious things – air holidays to our coach destinations, winter holidays to Malta, special group air quotations and nothing really sold through our system to our group market. And then we discovered weekends to New York.

And what a discovery! At that time it was possible to get rooms for groups in big mid-class Midtown hotels like the Pennsylvania (famous for its telephone number Glenn Miller's hit 'Pennsylvania 6-5000'). We bought flights in the market from the new Virgin Atlantic and from Delta Airlines. And we got great low prices which meant that we could do an amazing lead-in price of £299!

And the time differences helped our itineraries – going to New York late on Friday morning meant that you arrived early on Friday afternoon leaving the rest of the day free to enjoy the 'City that Never Sleeps'. Leaving on Sunday evening you have all night to get home.

All this meant a full weekend in the world's glitziest destination with time to buy super-exciting optional excursions. Helicopter rides around Manhattan, guided tours of the city including its major glorious sights, dinner in 'Little Italy', a Staten Island ferry ride, visit to Greenwich Village – pretty much everything you would want to have a great time plus shopping opportunities galore from discount designer outlets to fabulous stores like Saks Fifth Avenue to Tiffanys and great departmental stores like Macy's.

This whirl of a weekend sold again and again, thousands of our clients got wonderful value, wonderful experience and wonderful fun.

All this activity didn't just happen by itself – customers simply didn't come to our door.

No. It was the outbound telesales team that more than anybody created the business. The team and the well-oiled machine that supported them.

The fact is that pretty much every member of the sales team was brilliant. At their height there were forty or fifty young people in one room – a room totally full of energy. Many would be sitting as they talked conspiratorially to their group organisers, many would be standing, others would be standing on their chairs and a few would even be standing on their desks. Why? To generate more and more energy. To get the energy levels as high as possible morning meetings would be held on the roof complete with shouting and songs. During the day, trainers would be crouching and supporting individuals as they talked to clients. We even organised firewalks and meditation classes to get the clearest, most powerful energy, fun and laughs into each and every call.

The sales management team were totally professional and supportive and the training was brilliant – what would you expect if you paid sales trainers £1000 each a day? And many sales staff earned more than their managers – that was the object of the exercise.

Print could be quite expensive and if you wanted it when you wanted it, it often cost more. It seemed sensible to create our own print company. It was designed entirely to fulfil our own needs. Short-run print work so that we could promote specifc trips through our customers, each getting their own individual promotional material. When we had an opportunity to buy another, much bigger printing company – naturally we did. I thought that my printing training would come in handy one day. What did come in handy was all the heavy machinery we'd bought with the company getting more valuable every year. All we had to do was to revalue our assets every year to make a substantial profit.

By the early 1980s we'd got a sizeable (and profitable) design and print group – Beau Nash Studio. Now the sales ground was prepared by our own design and print businesses. Super artists and experienced printers with state-of-the-art equipment and machinery. In all, we were a very sophisticated, vertically-integrated marketing organisation, built up over a few years from nothing – just energy, integrity and superb team spirit had created the Land Travel group over a short 10 years.

Land Travel in the 1980s was like a modern-day tech start-up. Lots of business, lots of intellect, lots of drive, lots of youngsters, lots of modern marketing techniques, lots of optimism, lots of turnover but not lots and lots of profit!

The team had made it happen and it naturally attracted more like-minded souls to the group.

Like-minded souls? Who were these people? You may ask.

We were very privileged to have strong links with our local university's business school – now one of top business schools in the world. Our relationship started by our giving students work experience – they always enjoyed the experience so much that they stayed. So the university decided to investigate how we were operating and their specialist in business psychology wrote a report.

The results were very interesting. The bit I remember is that they said we had an 'Earring Mentality'. What? This was meant to mean that we tended to employ young people that were somewhat exhibitionist, maybe a little camp and certainly had difficulties finding a work-home in more formal regimented offices. So these young earring mentality people came, we liked them, they liked us and we gave them lots of responsibility and lots of power and quite a lot of money very quickly. Most truly loved it, a few ran away screaming.

My earring mentality was reflected in my new and lasting relationship with Pam. Celtic, cool and beautiful, she was to drag me out of my self-pity again and again. Our snatched moments were to fill me with energy and self-confidence.

Now the company was successful, iconoclastic, clever, tough and quite cocky, added to which most of us had been written off at one time or the other in the past and we just loved getting our own back.

There was always some new project on the go – over a weekend we decided to create a free local weekly newspaper using a newly-created and trained telesales team (we had our own print and design company, of course). The launch took place in just seven days. It cost us a vast amount of money which luckily we got back on its sale. However the benefits were enormous – more great salespeople and a new project was born, doing something we knew how to do – selling holidays to free newspapers all over the country.

Another initiative to bring foreign tourists to the UK resulted in our creating a property and renovation company to purchase houses all over the West of England, renovate and do holiday lets.

And then came 1984. I had taken my eye off the ball. There was yet another recession in the UK. Our business was down, we'd become lazy, more formal and softer than suited us and we'd got a board of directors who expected director-style lives. Like they wanted to make the decisions. The outcome – the draft accounts showed that we lost £500,000 in a year. Shit! I had an interesting interview with David our accountant and apart from telling me (in a nice way) that if I didn't like the heat I should stay out of the kitchen he told me that the best thing we could do was to keep the draft accounts draft until we could turn a profit – if not, then that was it – the end.

I thought that I had to take responsibility and do three things – forecast our next year's takings accurately (meaning to me, pessimistically); cut the overhead costs accordingly; change the whole bureaucracy to have a hungrier and less lazy group of people.

I knew from now on we had to fight every battle. So in one day, unhappily, I sacked 23 people including all the other directors. I sold off Carefree Travel. I raised all of our charges (fighting with each and every client to do so). I then created a new accounts and finance department from clerks and empowered them to talk to all of our creditors to reduce our bills.

Result – a more vigorous company that that turned a £500,000 loss into a £100,000 profit in a year. Now we could publish our accounts!

Thus we became a revitalised and even less formal company. More energetic, tougher and with a new vision. Phew!

Shortly we were able to move into much bigger premises and dramatically to increase our business.

We got a tough, capable woman to run sales – Elke; a triumvirate of young women in charge of marketing – Sylvia, Katherine and Diana and a tough managing director whose main responsibility was cash and contracting – Theresa.

So, the root of the change and our dynamism – girl power.

And our girl power was rather more macho than its male alternative. The vast majority of our staff were female, from the top down and we were perfectly prepared to give them as much responsibility as they wanted and usually much more. Anything to avoid a boring life.

At the time I was very lucky indeed – I was incredibly privileged to live such a lifestyle. Cigars, ballet, opera, horse racing, cars, properties and travel.

And in 1980 our third son had been born – Alexis who was to add his golden hair, bright blue eyes and angelic demeanour to our family.

How did we make money? You may imagine that as a travel company the difference between what our customers paid for their holiday and what we spent on it represented our profit. You'd be wrong.

By now we had worked out just where our profits lay. In effect our customers payment for their tour was actually just an initial payment. Like the budget airlines today, we recognised that once we had a connection with our customers they could spend much, much more. For instance on their trip they would need to buy things – souvenirs, duty-free goods, consumables, excursions and meals. Not only were we their guides and advisors but we knew exactly where they were and where they were going. So we provided everything they needed for a fascinating and fulfilling weekend or week away – at good value prices. You could say that our customers were our captive audience and that we did everything we could to fulfil their desires – at reasonable charges!

It worked like this: the tour payment probably made a little bit of gross profit – say 5%, meals and visits to tourist attractions made, say, 50%, just coach excursions made 100% (after all, we'd hired the coach for the whole weekend!) and commissions from duty-free shops, diamond factories, vineyards, etc., topped up our profits.

So provided we kept our customers very, very happy and sold them lots and lots of events we made loads of money.

And now on to more interesting things...

CHAPTER 5

Even More Success, Decline and Fall

By this time I was able to indulge my two big passions after travel.

Remember my dad and his days on the racecourse? And the money that he won on Lavandin to start his business? I was also part of the family horse racing tradition, but I didn't gamble much – certainly since the time in my teens when I believed that a drink or three made me lucky. Duh.

But I do love horses, particularly racehorses. And a friend offered to sell me one, or two. The first was called Lorgan Prince and he was a well-bred steeplechaser, but he hadn't done much. A quite unknown young rider, a friend of my friend, had just arrived from New Zealand. Mark Tod was totally brilliant as time would tell – as he became the world's pre-eminent three-day eventer. Now Sir Mark Tod he has been voted "Rider of the 20th Century". Then he was a brilliant young man but unknown on the racecourses of the United Kingdom. The idea was this – Mark would ride Lorgan Prince in hunts to qualify him, then in a few point-to-point races (largely amateur races, but with bookmakers). We would win a little money (there was no big money at point-to-points) and Lorgan Prince would get a bit of experience. Finally, with the experience, the qualification and the brilliant unknown jockey we would enter Lorgan Prince in a big hunter chase at the biggest race-course in the country and we would make a fortune. Nobody would see it coming so the betting odds would be wonderful! Great!

Lorgan Prince was to go to be trained at a very posh stables: those of Captain Tim Forster at Wantage on the Marlborough Downs. Tim had over a thousand winners to his credit so we now had nearly all our ducks in a row.

The horse was to be owned in partnership but the jockey would wear my colours – which we now had to choose and register. What would they be?

I chose black, yellow and red. Very easy to see when the horse was running, and the colours of the Belgian flag.

All set then for gambling riches? Not quite set, my racing partner Simon wanted to inject another horse into the deal – a young filly called Somerford Glory. Simon was married to an old friend of mine and neither of us had yet realised that Simon was a rogue.

Of course we had to have a racehorse trainer for Somerford Glory too and we decided on Robert Baker who had taken a lease on one of the greatest yards and most fabulous gallops in the country – at Manton near Marlborough and in the rolling hills surrounded by Avebury and Stonehenge's ancient sites. He was to look after Somerford Glory who he described as a "rabbit".

I, of course knew better than Robert. I liked little Somerford Glory – her dad had been Hittite Glory an incredible sprinter, and through her mum she was related to Lavandin – the very horse that my dad had won all that money on!

As it happened, Lorgan Prince was not the success we hoped for and Simon had borrowed a lot of money from me which he secured with his half of the partnership.

Result I came to own two horses that had won nothing and I was paying training fees, food and board to two trainers. Eek.

Anyway there was a solution to both problems. It appeared that Lorgan Prince had bad legs so the consensus was that he should be fired. No not sacked – his legs were fired with a piece of red-hot metal in the belief that the scars would eventually make his legs stronger.

Robert Baker had a more inventive solution – another horse! This one was called Charles Stuart and I could lease him to avoid the cost of purchase and I would just have to pay Robert's not insubstantial training fees. But he was going to win definitely. He had been run into the ground by his previous owners in order to win a small race so all we had to do was to be kind to him and he would win for us. And eventually he did at an evening meeting at Wolverhampton, I still love the pictures of me leading him into the winner's enclosure. I was there with Robert and his wife and we jumped up and down with joy. I was so elated that on the drive back I was caught by the police speeding at 120 miles per hour. Ahem.

But the big plan with Charles Stuart was Belgium! Ostend race-course – the Hippodrome Wellington.

I had a lot of experience with Ostend racecourse

My dad had taken me there of course when I was a kid and I remembered it as small and pretty and posh.

Anyway, one day I mentioned to Robert that I fancied taking a weekend with my wife to see the Grand Prix Prince Rose – Ostend's BIG race. I thought that it may be a bit of fun and I longed to see Ostend again, well actually I longed to see a particular restaurant in Ostend harbour again.

To me there is nothing as good as my top number 1 favourite meal and only one place that I know I can get it. The meal? It starts with Tomates aux Crevettes (big fat sweet tomatoes stuffed full of real mayonnaise and salty brown North Sea shrimps shelled by old ladies on their laps while sitting on their front steps) followed by a massive North Sea sole cooked in butter (Meunière) on the bone with a liberal helping of perfect golden Belgian chips. This would be followed by a 'Dame Blanche' (home-made vanilla ice-cream, with a topping of freshly made warm chocolate sauce with sliced hazelnuts). Simple perfection.

Although Robert had married the daughter of champion trainer and well-known sporting man, Ryan Price, he was not the sort of man to talk about gambling or give you a tip. So I was, to say the least, surprised when he told me that Castle Keep would certainly win this prestigious group 1 race in Ostend.

The day dawned and we hopped off to Ostend and checked in at the top hotel, a stroll from the racecourse. I was buoyed by the fact that the horse in question was trained by John Dunlop – one of England's brilliant trainers, owned by the Duchess of Norfolk and ridden by soon to be champion jockey Willy Carson. Also Robert had been Dunlop's assistant for years and he would have known the horse well.

Gambling on races in England is easy. You see the odds offered for each horse on the bookmaker's boards, go up to your chosen bookmaker (the one that offers the best odds on your horse) with your money in your hand, he takes it and gives you a slip to confirm your bet. In less than ten seconds the deed is done. In Ostend it is different – individual bookmakers will limit the amount of your bet to reduce their exposure. So, to get any sort of large bet on you need to visit lots of bookmakers in the betting hall. So, it's a rush to see enough bookmakers and added to the stress is the fact that as you're putting your bets on the odds are going down – very frustrating! Anyway, I got as much money as I could on Castle Keep and we went into the best enclosure (quite snobby in Belgium and reserved for those paying the highest entrance fees). We took up our usual places on any racecourse – just by the winning post – to watch the race.

As the race progressed, Willy Carson had been niggling Castle Keep on and as they turned the bend and came towards us and the winning post they were a few lengths clear of the field. Wondering why everybody around us was so quiet, we could hold back our enthusiasm no longer and screamed "get your ass up Willy" and Willy and Castle Keep duly obliged. Pity I'd forgotten that it is bad form in Belgium to shout in the posh enclosure. We had disgraced ourselves in Ostend! But it certainly didn't stop us from collecting our winnings from the 20-or-so bookmakers that had taken our bets – and organising a crate or two of champagne to take back to Robert.

So good memories of Ostend. A few months later it was time for real triumph. We were off back to Ostend with Charles Stuart to win a big race. Imagine – my horse winning in my colours at my dad's favourite racecourse in the land of my forefathers – what could be better?

And we had great expectations, as had the Belgian public according to the local press. "Charles Stuart to win the big race" they all shouted.

We checked out the horse and the young jockey in the pre-parade ring, strolled seriously into the parade ring in a group and talked together conspiratorially and seemingly knowledgeably in the parade ring as owners and trainers do. Naturally we then had a substantial bet – as big a one as Belgian bookmakers would allow – and got to our positions near the winning post. Now we were set to cheer Charles Stuart to victory just as we had Castle Keep.

But of course it was not to be. The race was won by a rank outsider whose odds had dropped dramatically in the few minutes prior to the off. Someone had made a great deal of money that day but it was certainly not us. Sad for a few minutes we grabbed ourselves together before I realised we were in Ostend and I could look forward to my very favourite meal. Victory in Ostend? Another time, maybe!

By then I'd met Peter Hopkins, another travel industry racehorse owner and the man that provided what was to be the route to my big-time success and failure.

Even though he was a tough competitor in my group travel market-place, I liked Peter very much and still do. Pete was Welsh and proud of it, had lived in the same street as my mum in a mining village as a child, had built up the biggest school travel company in Europe from scratch, was by far the biggest winter sports tour operator in the UK and shared my passion for travel, opera and racing (he had 13 horses, I had 3. He was also a brilliant Elvis impersonator and lived a totally full-on big-hearted lifestyle.

We all liked to keep up appearances but my God Peter was extraordinarily good at it.

He operated Schools Abroad from a beautifully-restored historical ex-convent in West Sussex. I remember my first – rather agressive meeting there after I had refused to allow them to advertise their group tours in my magazine. They threatened all kinds of legal action, but we kept on talking and realised that we had more things in common than we had in contention.

Anyway, in my view Peter was and is a star. His lifestyle was as starry as his big, expanding business. The great thing about big-time school travel is that they book and pay a year in advance so you always had squillions in the bank and in those days interest rates were high – therefore providing the operator with a guaranteed income. In Peter's case this meant a life of luxury – a mansion as a home in the UK and a palatial pad in France where he spoke fluent French. But above all Peter was a great sportsman, at one time he owned all of the top 10 jumping racehorses in the UK, had the very best box at Cheltenham with amazing views over the course and everybody liked him from the royal family, to other top racehorse owners to all the bookmakers on all the UK racecourses. One day, as our friendship developed, we went to elegant upmarket Sandown Park racecourse together. We were hardly inside the course when dozens greeted him with bits of inside information, stories and the latest news, in confidence, of course. Peter was a 'face'. Why? Because Peter was a big-time gambler. Peter would bet on a fly on the window, it was said. And gambling was in Peter's nature. He loved danger, he loved fun and above all he loved to win and lose. Obviously Peter enjoyed the racecourse most, but he loved gambling on anything. One weekend when he was in his Antigua home, he took a night out playing poker, lost a million pounds, flew back to the UK and won it back on the racecourse.

The fact is, too, that running any kind of tour operation is, in itself, a really big gamble. There are so many things that can affect business existentially. Currency exchange rates, load factors, legislation, accidents, political strife in a destination, and, in recent years terrorist attacks and government advisories against travel to certain countries – they all can swing the pendulum in the wrong direction. Of course, you can manage your business to attempt to avoid these risks but, at the end of the day, any one if these risks could wipe you out. It is amazing just how few travel businesses collapse nowadays.

By this time I was happily living Peter's sort of lifestyle too. Just half a dozen years from the incorporation of the constituent parts of the Land Travel group, in my mid thirties, I was lucky to be living the dream. My kids were at private school, we were living in a superb historic house, we'd bought a chateau in Normandy, every winter we were in the Caribbean, spring in Greece and summer in the South of France. We had our own reserved seats at the Royal Opera House and with my horse-racing connections, I was proud to have been sponsored into the Royal Enclosure at Ascot. It was the champagne lifestyle without the champagne!

And in India without the meat. I'd always wanted to see Kashmir and walk through the flowers by Lake Dal – so off I went. Well not to Kashmir as it turned out, a war had started, but India anyway. Off I went to Himachel Pradesh in search of whatever you go in search of – a change of view, maybe. I had booked with a nice young lady in London and she had arranged for me to meet a man called Vijay Thakur in Delhi, get a train to Chandigar, the rack railway to Simla and then a car (with a driver) to Manali then to Rajastan by train, back to Delhi and home, by which time I planned to have achieved a bit of self-discovery. Great.

Getting to Delhi was the easy bit. VJ was fantastic and had dispensed with the need for an hotel by deciding that I could have dinner in his house before he would take me in the early hours to New Delhi Railway

Station for my late night/early morning train trip to Chandigarh. Well, the dinner part was fantastic and is even now etched indelibly in my memory. VJ brought me to his house and ushered me into his main room, all around it were sitting elderly Indians, mainly women. I had the table for one in the centre. The food was brought in for me only and the audience were prepared to watch me eat.

Food? There was everything, totally delicious spicy and hot, gentle and cool and this was just the odour. I really wanted to eat. But how? There was nothing to eat with. Now I realised the joke was on me. I had to eat with my fingers for the first time in front of a chatty watching crowd who were obviously talking about my ineptitude. Anyway the meal was truly delicious, even though I provided the evening's self-conscious entertainment.

Later that night I got a taxi to the station for the night train to Chandigarh. At the station there were massive crowds talking, walking, sleeping on the pavement. People everywhere. It was a task in itself to find my train and my berth. My travelling companion had already installed himself. Big, sleek and in his silk pajamas, he was lounging on the top berth as he gustily tucked into his curry – with fingers! Anyway, we didn't talk for the whole of the journey, unusual for India, I was to learn.

I had time to explore Chandigarh, the 'New' town in the Indian bit of the Punjab. Built by Le Corbusier, Chandigarh was astonishing. After independence in 1947 Chandigarh was Nehru's dream city, built for a population of 100,000 now with over a million inhabitants, it is a bit of a challenge. I felt claustrophobic with the crowds but really enjoyed two of its claims to fame. The Rock Garden was stunning, built entirely out of junk it shows just how much fun you can have from garbage. But the memory of Chandigarh's Rose Garden affects me to this day.

And then I was to have a real travel experience. I was to be on my way to Simla via the rack railway from Kalka. Of course the rack railway, a relic of the British Raj, was amazing and the views were quite stunning as the old train picked its way through the hills. But I was distracted by the massive bang as soon as the train arrived at the station. The big bang was the sound of hundreds of porters leaping on the train, forcing their way inside and grabbing bags willy-nilly. Determination paid as one grapped mine. Of course it later turned up at my hotel.

Clarke's Hotel was another relic of the British Raj. Built like a big bungalow, it embodied all the smells and atmosphere of a Victorian British Hill Station, where imperial wives and children were sent to enjoy some gracious peace and coolness away from the heat of the plains. And Clarke's is right in the centre of things in bustling Simla abounding with shops and markets, cinemas and cafés where little had changed for many decades.

Checked in and brushed up, I needed to have a chat with my new guide and companion who had turned up to greet me. Sanjay was great, young and enthusiastic, he'd come all the way from Chandigarh for me to make the most of my visit to Simla.

I remember my question-and-answer session to this day. In particular my questions about Sanjay's religious beliefs – he was a Hindu. "How does it work, Sanjay" said I. "Well, sir I worship idols". I don't know why but it threw me back right into the Old Testament and wild ritual dances, human sacrifices and all that stuff. Now I knew that I was somewhere exotic.

Nervously I carried on with the journey. Next stop Dharamsala via the Kullu Valley – Valley of the Gods.

Sanjay left me in Simla. My new companion was Raj, the proud driver of a white Ambassador taxi. Ambassadors were everywhere in India, based on the 1960s Morris Oxford, their chief advantage was that they were very low-tech, in other words repairable by hand. Obviously, Raj had a little trouble with his throat because he proceeded to cough and splutter all the way through the mountains around precarious hairpin bends.

Eventually we stopped. I needed to see an important spiritual shrine, obviously. Off I walked up a hill into the mist over hundreds and hundreds of plastic bags and associated filth. A wrinkled old crone barred my way and pointed at her feet. My God, I thought, another beggar. I offered her money. She refused and screamed at me gesticulating at her feet again – obviously crazy. I walked on – looking back I saw a family, one by one. kissing the old lady's feet. How crass could I have been?

Not learning from this lesson, back in the car we drove on to the sound of Raj's coughing and spitting. But the scenery became extraordinary and the atmosphere strange and wonderful as we entered the truly enchanted Kullu Valley – the Valley of the Gods. Stop, I shouted to Raj as I noticed a group of pretty little Indian kids. They looked wonderful, colourful, animated, noisy. I just had to film them. I jumped out and followed the kids, filming all the time. As they stopped at their classroom I was confronted by a tall angry man. "What the bloody hell do you think you're doing. Who gave you permission to be here?" he said.

An interesting start to a friendship, you may think. In any case, angry Navdeep and I talked a little; I got a tour of the premises, an introduction to his wife Simran and an invitation to return. We kept in contact and this meeting was to lead to more than I could have imagined.

That afternoon after much coughing and spluttering we arrived at Dharamsala via the laughingly-named McCleod Ganj. Checked into the old hotel. Went for a walk. Very, very Buddhist. Well, I suppose it would be as it is the home-in-exile to the Dalai Lama. And a very strange place.

That night as I walked down the hotel corridor to my room, I spotted a suit of armour outside my door. Natty, I thought, then I realised that the suit of armour was actually a fully armed soldier stationed there all night to guard me. From what? Maybe the monkeys who banged on my window all night. The guards certainly couldn't defend me against the freak storm, lightning, thunder and tornado that kept me awake until the calm misty dawn.

What a pity I was too late to get an audience with the Dalai Lama himself but work and the UK called.

Well, that was the first of many trips that I made to India, a place that never fails to charm me.

The backwaters in Kerala, with its water lilies and washing ladies was the first place that I wept for the sheer beauty of the surroundings. Gujarat amazed me for its amazing and delicate vegetarian thalis. Rajasthan for its glorious materials – and my misfortunes there – (getting dysentry in 45-degree heat and losing my suitcase full of the glorious materials!). And Maharashtra – maybe the sub-continent's amazingly undiscovered tourism opportunity. But above all Bombay, which epitomises India's glorious in-your-face reality-crack. The fissure between the heartbreakingly sublime and the ballbreakingly stupid which is the constant in any Indian endeavour.

And I'm an addict to India's astonishing written legacy from RK Narayan through VS Naipal, Salman Rushdie, Rohinton Mistry and the rest. It's what makes me cry with joy at India's sublime beauty and art and music. It's what makes me cry at Indian's brutality, bribery, cruelty and crass, mindless stupidity. India is my lesson in human frailty.

And Kullu? When I went back I found out more. It was a magical visit. Flying through a mountain storm in an old Indian Airlines plane had freaked me out and I'd started smoking again (my driver's local bidis instead of the Cuban cigars I'd given up years ago).

This time I arrived at Simran and Navdeep's home and we sat and talked. Refusing the brandy (now over 15 years since I stopped) I accepted the local joint. Simran cooked as we talked. Navdeep blamed it on the apples. They had been the Kullu Valley's cash crop and had made many fortunes. But now it was the 1980s and there were many cash crops richer than apples. These had brought unwelcome visitors to Manali. Italians who had offered heroin for marijuana had been locked up for weeks in the temple before being shown out of the district. But they would come back, the writing was on the wall.

Navdeep's answer – education, hence the school.

And one little fact that still makes me chuckle. Rajneesh had just died. He was the Indian guru who got global fame (and 17 Rolls-Royces) from preaching that the way to heaven was paved by sex.

As it happened Navdeep's guru was Rajneesh's too. What did he say? I asked "He went a little overboard on the Tantra" said Navdeep.

Back in the UK – little did I know that Peter had a plan to propel himself into millionaire-dom and out of the risk arena.

After a year or two of doing little deals together, having nice meals, going racing and generally sussing each other out, Peter told me he had a plan and I was involved in it. Basically we'd all sell our companies for lots of money but we'd keep managing them and there would be lots of fun ahead. It was pretty much as simple as that; Peter's forte was never detail and managing the information was his way of keeping both control and flexibility.

Anyway, he did tell me that his initial deal had pretty much been done – buying a stock-market listed company and reversing his company and his brother-in-law's – both school travel companies – into it.

It was at this stage in the 1980s that I truly realised the power of public relations combined with greed.

The Wolverhampton Steam Laundry plc, (WSL for short) a London Stock Exchange company with nothing at all in the bank acquired the assets of Schools Abroad together with those of a company that ran flights to Italy (just like the one I'd worked for in the 1960s) and another school travel company. The owners got paid with WSL shares, so they (that is, Peter and his brother in law) owned WSL plc.

Travel wasn't WSL's business but nothing really was. The company was established in the 1890s and for a short period of time was the largest employer of women in Wolverhampton and the worst payer. By the late 1960s the business was finished but the stock exchange quote was still there – WSL was a classic 'shell company' and a friend of Peter's had taken control of it.

What did WSL pay for these aquisitions? Paper! They issued share capital to the people who were selling their companies (Peter and his friends) so that everybody had a stake in the enlarged entity. Peter and his friends now became directors of WSL.

And WSL, as a result of good financial PR and great timing was a force to be reckoned with. On its launch on the stock exchange the city valued the company at no less than £25 million. For a small bag of travel companies with very little in assets it was an extraordinary fortune, a massive windfall for Peter and his friends. And I was not to be left out, we were already talking about Land Travel being bought by WSL and about me being a part of the management.

Then the whole process became extraordinary. The Granada Television Group made an approach to buy WSL as part of its strategy to move further into the leisure business. In the event, Granada paid around £45 million for WSL. Personally, I was very pleased as the Granada Finance Director had already written to me indicating his, and his directors', wish to purchase us; it was only a question of time.

So, Granada purchased WSL in 1986 and, no doubt all involved were instant paper millionaires. Paper, because as is usual in these situations, Granada had swapped their shares for WSL shares plus some cash, so the WSL shareholders were not yet in a position to cash in totally.

The Granada Financial Director was as good as his word, so pretty quickly we began to discuss the principles of the formula for sale of Land Travel.

A meeting was set at Granada's top solicitors' offices for everything to be negotiated and agreed. Fascinating. By then I had met another top solicitors and agreed a fee of £30,000 for the few days' work. They had examined the contract that Granada's solicitors had proposed. Together with the man who was working for me – a partner with the glitzy transatlantic showbiz solicitors Simon Olswang – and my own financial advisor – David Shaw who by then had supported me through thick and thin for 12 years – off we went to London to talk until we had a definitive signed agreement. We were to sit around a table until it was done, at least a whole day and night – maybe more! Just like a big-time poker game – no wonder Peter was in his element.

And Peter was in his element in more ways than one – his interest was in getting an agreement so he was advising and cajoling both sides. The way it worked was that we were all sat down around one table but there were other rooms available for private discussions.

David – by now my financial advisor – and I went through the draft agreement paragraph by paragraph. By now we had all annotated and indexed our personal agreements and knew pretty much what we wanted – also, more importantly, we thought we knew pretty much what they wanted.

By now we'd got our ducks in a row. Some years earlier in case of an opportunity such as this, I'd altered the company structure so that we had more flexibility and had given shares to my kids and Chan. Now I made sure that David and Ben also had shares to give them a big bonus when the company was sold.

These were the days of the 'Earn Out' agreement. The purchasing party would offer to pay a multiple of the purchased company's profits. Usually the first payment would relate to the last year of trading, the second to the current year of trading and the final payment to the next year. The multiplier in our case had been agreed at 8.

So, if in the last year we'd made £150,000 we would be paid £1.2 million. Then in the current year, if we made £300,000 we would be paid £2.4 million (less the £1.2 million we had been paid already. Finally, if we made £600,000 the next year, we would be paid £4.8 million. Those were, in fact, pretty much our targets so the easy bit was agreeing the 'Cap' in other words the maximum that Granada would pay – £4.8 million.

The major items for discussion were what exactly they were buying for their money (by then we had a dozen or so trading companies); how the profits were to be computed and what currency (what combination of cash and shares) they would pay with. Naturally, they didn't want me to disappear so we had to agree a service contract length, terms and conditions.

Well, it was all fascinating and we managed to get it all done by that night.

The next day, we all had a lot more security and I had become a director of the new Granada Travel Plc and a senior executive of the mega-rich, mega-powerful, mega-well-connected TV, leisure and media company Granada Group. And I had a big salary and benefits to match.

I thought that was it! Security at last.

Granada were truly lovely people to work with and for. It was a family company that had just grown through the entertainment industry. We were obviously in the entertainment industry too so to all intents and purposes it was a good match.

Sydney Bernstein had started by operating cinemas in 1930, and when television had become the thing in the 1950s he had managed to get the government franchise to create and broadcast programmes in the North of England.

And what programmes – the first big soap: Coronation Street. The first big blockbuster dramas: Jewel in the Crown and Brideshead Revisited. Great news programmes like World in Action. Its production values were superb, everyone respected them.

Plus they were hoteliers and restaurateurs. As a result of another franchise – catering services on motorways – they had established restaurants all over the expanding UK motorway system and nearby hotels – their executives boasted of over 100% occupancy rates. Why? You may ask! These functional hotels were situated at motorway service stations both pretty anonymous. People could rent for the day or night so often both day and night were sold, doubling the possibilities.

As cinemas became less important Granada had converted many of their picture-houses to be Bingo Halls. And bingo had travelled the world. When I joined Granada they were even operating bingo in Native American Reservations.

TV production, motorway services, bingo. Now educational travel (we came in that category!) was to be added to the mix.

Within a year or so Peter had introduced Granada to a very interesting bunch of travel companies and their entrepreneur bosses who were happy to swap a few years of their independence for a few million quid. And, while the earn-out was in place, they didn't even lose their independence – that would have compromised their opportunity to make maximum profits for a maximum payout after all.

And it should have been a win-win deal for everybody. At the time Granada's shares were valued at around sixteen times their profits for the year. When they bought companies for eight times their profits and then added those profits to theirs – hey presto they had doubled their value with no risk. Accountancy & stock market magic!

As it happened the writing was on the wall. The stock market crashed on October 19th, 1987. They called it Black Monday. I remember it well, half of my initial payments amounting to over £4 million pounds were to be paid in cash, the rest in shares valued at their cash equivalent on October 19th! Naturally the shares bounced back providing me with a massive bonus.

For me it was all an education. The complicated financial deal, the responsibility of being a director of a big public company – everything. But as I swapped my precarious existence for a company car, a fat salary, health insurance and a massive payout, I felt that finally there was security.

And it was fun, getting the behind-the-scenes information from these other interesting companies at monthly board meetings was fascinating. We were a dozen-or-so men in all and one woman. We'd all put our 1980's brick-shape mobile phones on the table in one of the boardrooms at Granada's Soho Square HQ and then the fun would begin.

I was amazed. Every single company was doing brilliantly. At every meeting everyone was going from strength to strength. Making more and more money, doing bigger and bigger deals. And then, as each company reached the end of their earn-out period and always got paid their maximum, they stopped turning up at the board meetings. Because, actually, their company cupboards were not packed with money – they were practically bare.

Granada were very nice people but even they had got fed up after they'd spent over a hundred and ten million pounds on travel companies with no return at all. Also, their niceness had been eroded somewhat by a boardroom coup and a reorganisation. They had been one of the first really big investors in satellite tv and it had not paid off quickly enough. The really big bucks were a couple of years away so good quality heads rolled.

As a result of all this trauma, the group was being split up and the whole division was being changed. We had now been hived off into Granada's bingo set up and although there was logic in the move, I had got rather too avaricious for my own good. I jetted back from a short break in Martinique for a meeting with my immediate Granada boss – the founder of B&Q – David Quayle.

My idea? To buy back my company for a pittance and make a second fortune.

In a bit of unconventional business practice David and I cut a deal in 30 minutes between board meetings – in a broom cupboard. The Land Travel Group, the whole lot, properties, design studio, print business was to be mine again.

When I'd sold it to them it was at least half a million pounds in debt – now the balance sheet was half a million positive (so those nice people at Granada's accountants – the eminent Price Waterhouse – said). Plus the bank said they would stump up another half a million working capital.

I left a quarter of a million pounds with Granada and I got a great solvent, well respected company back. So the first part of my plan had been accomplished. We were all ready to rock!

Price Waterhouse had indicated that they wanted to stay as the company's auditors but David, my financial advisor wanted his company to do the job. He knew absolutely everything about the company's financial situation – after all, his company had been doing the accounts since Land Travel's inception and the auditing until Granada's takeover. Moreover he wouldn't charge as much, plus he'd been an amazing support for years . And he'd done most of the negotiations for the original sale and the buyback. Admittedly, I'd paid him a big retainer and given him shares in the company to cash in on the Granada sale. But now I wanted him on my side and giving him the auditing work would give him more freedom.

After the papers had been signed for the deal, I thought that I was in a great position. Phew!

There was one other thing that was very much in my thinking now I was 45. I had a lot of stuff. Either I could get rid of it – downsize (unthinkable!) or I could go on to much bigger and better things.

My difficult marital situation had become very uncomfortable and I tried to make it easier by spending loads of money. Houses, holidays, art, cars, clothes, pretty much everything had been bought without making it any easier. By the time of the company sale in 1987, I'd bought a chateau in France, bought and renovated a house in the country as an escape route and bought a house in the grand Royal Crescent in Bath (which I'd sold to finance the Granada deal – yes it cost me money!).

By 1990, we still had the chateau and my bolt-hole country house, our family house in Bath was on the market, I'd bought a small country estate in Wiltshire so that my wife could get away from Bath gossip and I'd bought and decorated a very big bachelor pad for myself in Bath. I'd borrowed over a million pounds from the bank to finance all this property but they had the security of the property and the shares I had in Granada – all valued at over two million. So, on paper, I was worth over a million net but it could go either way.

As it happened, it all only went one way – the wrong one. The property market went down, the Granada shares went down and the interest on my bank borrowings was on the way up to an unbelievable 17%.

It wasn't long before the bank would demand that the loan was reduced against the reducing security.

But there was an escape – get Land Travel back and make it so successful so that instead of four million it was worth a hundred million and all the problems would pale into insignificance.

So, naturally, that's what I did!

And the future looked good. In 1992 Disney World was to open up in Paris and the World Expo was to open in Seville. I thought we could get tens of thousands of profitable bookings for both. We had negotiated to charter whole ships for Disney so we had massive capacity.

Plus we had a solvent company, a superbly talented young managemant and around 500 great committed staff including management of our moneypot destinations.

What could go wrong? By now I'd forgotten about the letter from Granada warning me that when we left the group we would have to get our own protection for customers' money.

The first body-blow was from Price Waterhouse who were still auditors under the Granada regime, they refused to give us a set of 'clean' accounts for the period that we were part of Granada now we had left. My suspicion was that they would have been happy to do so if we had kept them on instead of replacing them with David's company.

As it was they insisted in saying in the accounts that they queried our 'Going Concern' status.

That, of course worried the bank who weren't prepared to advance the working capital – leaving us half a million pounds short.

Remembering 1984, I decided to hold off publishing the accounts until we had another set that looked better.

We had to soldier on, cutting our spending and maximising marketing. By the end of the year our cash-flow had improved dramatically and the future looked golden again.

1992 started great – we had over 40,000 bookings already – mainly to Disneyland with big profits. Fantastic.

And then the second body-blow happened. On April 9th European Ferries reneged on their deal with us to provide whole ships for our passengers. Disaster. I still have no idea why, although I can imagine that there was some malign conspiracy – so far I can't prove it.

Now I made a non-decision that certainly changed the rest of my life. We'd managed to get through this sort of problem before, we could do it again, I thought. In retrospect I should have put up a bigger fight against European Ferries and not moved from the spot. What we did do was to offer all kinds of options to our 40,000 customers. They wanted money, and we didn't have it – not all of it anyway. All the media from TV to the local press slammed us. Bookings stopped. All of the staff were sensational, nobody was prepared to give up.

The next three months were a nightmare. All our staff were dealing with customers ringing with just problems, so normal service, normal productive business didn't exist.

I couldn't understand what was happening. It felt like we were in a war and, try as I could, I couldn't it find anybody to come to our aid or buy us out. Our business that had been worth over £4 million just 3 years ago seemed worth nothing now.

Our one major creditor/cooperator needed to be told that she was not going to be paid. Sandra had been working with us for years providing travel services and accommodation in Holland. Her bill at the time was nearly a million pounds. She was by far our greatest creditor. I picked her up from Bristol Airport, drove a couple of miles and stopped. I explained the situation – I thought we were likely to stop trading in which case she wouldn't be paid anything she was owed. I knew she owned her company herself and this would be a massive hit for her.

After a perfunctory conversation I drove her to her hotel. At least she knew and would be prepared.

At the end of July I went to, guess who, a local branch of Price Water-house with my mortgage (a floating charge on the company that I had been given in exchange for my big loan). My idea was to put the company into administration myself with the assistance of the accountant.

They were having none of it. They wanted the bankrupcy winding up job and the fees (effectively everything the company owned) I blinked, they won.

First thing the next morning their team arrived. I'd told all the staff what was going to happen so on their last day they turned up for work in their party clothes. The accountants decided that they would save the cost of telling creditors direct by making the biggest media story they could.

Their PR man said – "this is the dream story" there were over 40,000 passengers, many abroad, the PR man said "Stranded" which, of course they weren't. TV, radio, press – all the media loved it and Price Waterhouse made the very most of it. It made the news, there were statements from the government. The PR shit had really hit the fan.

During the day, the police arrived and I was taken away in handcuffs. My home was searched and I was held in the cells all day. I declared myself bankrupt – the Price Waterhouse liquidator had told me if I didn't do it then he would.

So that was it. End of story for Land Travel. In the end we were 12 million pounds in debt. My next step was the creditors' meeting at which I made a fulsome apology before water and various other things were thrown on me. That, of course made the front pages of the newspapers too.

God knows what the liquidator got. Price Waterhouse sold our prize asset – our enormous database which had taken sixteen years to build for a song but 90% of what they sold went directly to them.

I then spent the next four years trying to make a bit of money while creating my legal defence with my lawyer Angus. The result was that I was imprisoned for 4 months on an agreed charge that I had traded fraudulently from 9 April until 30 July – in other words we had no hope of surviving once the ferries had been cancelled and I'd done nothing other than tried to carry on.

Of course, I should have stopped Land Travel trading and sued European Ferries to fulfil their part of the deal. I had blinked twice. For me the only redeeming feature of the whole disaster was the amount of support that I had from my staff and creditors and family, all of whom I had let down.

So, just before my 50th birthday I was banged up in Horfield Prison. Back in Bristol before being transferred to Erlestoke in Wiltshire.

My eldest son, Adam, much to my mother's disgust, had given me a T-shirt emblazoned with a picture of me in Venice's St Mark's Square with pigeons all over me. "Save the Birdman" "Val Tjolle Innocent" said the text. Now he dared me to wear it in court under my shirt. Of course I did.

I celebrated my half-century with a strong coffee, my one remaining cigar, and my dozens of birthday cards and letters, while outside my lawyer held a champagne party for my friends.

While I was in prison two things happened – my wife began divorce proceedings and I was asked if I was willing to give evidence against my fellow directors in return for having no further action against me. I refused so all the proceedings were focused on me and my final disgrace was my being banned as a company director for 15 years – the maximum.

For a couple of years, I tried to repeat the Land Travel formula with other partners but none of it really worked. I'd even taken work with my old buddy Venetian Angelo to help him promote the New York weekends and had been there a few times to help guide his groups.

It was just a few years after the Earth Summit and talk of sustainability and sustainable tourism was in the air. Now, I'd been exposed to green travel by my directors at Land Travel and hadn't been too impressed. Our job was to get the best offers at the cheapest prices to our clientele then try to make a profit out of it. The nearest that I'd got to sustainable tourism was our sustainable competitive advantage that I had been so proud of.

By now the International Ecotourism Society had been formed and I'd heard that they had over 30,000 members. All Americans with home-knitted knickers I thought.

But as the travel industry was growing so fast, I recognised that the opportunities were not being fairly dished out. When I was a kid, everyone had a chance – now the industry was coming to be controlled by a few big companies. Plus I didn't think that clients were really getting optimum benefits from their travel experiences.

Then one day I was in Paris with a group of people – giving them guided tours and I had a half day to myself. Wanting a little reviving peace and quiet, I wandered off to Paris' most hallowed and most powerful spot – the place on the River Seine that had been a religious centre for literally thousands of years – the spot that Notre Dame Cathedral now occupies.

Sitting in peace and quiet was doing me some good, I thought, when a coachload of tourists burst in. In ten minutes they took pictures of everything and then... they were gone, back to the bus with their haul of photos. Nobody had stopped to see, or smell, touch or hear in this incredible place. I had been in the travel industry all my life – had we done this?

Selling superficial unfulfilling experiences where nobody benefits. What a pity, what a waste of time

What a shame.

What an opportunity to reverse the trend profitably. Sustainable Tourism may just be the way forward. Of course it was, it must be – all the signs were pointed in that direction. It would only be a short time before the whole market would DEMAND it!

<cm>CHAPTER 6

The Pearl of Africa and other Sustainable Destinations

By this time as you may imagine I was a little bit dejected. My life as a tour operator, having promised so much, seemed to have come to a shuddering halt. My credibility was pretty much shot (with me, anyway!) my personal relationships were on rocky ground to say the very least. Anyone would have forgiven my thinking that, now 52, I was washed up. Moreover, it seemed to me that it was all pretty much my fault.

As the result of yet another strange scheme hatched up with some ex-Granada pals I was to meet a therapist. I was hoping to sell cruise ship places on voyages of inner discovery, complete with aromatherapy, meditation etc. My friend, ex-Land Travel copywriter and now green marketer, Rob was to write the copy and help with the marketing. We weren't only to sell therapy voyages, included in the offers were Jazz trips and dancing ones. Of course we'd chartered a whole ship for these experiences. Annie was to be the therapist on the inner discovery cruises; when I rang to apologise that the whole thing had fallen through, I realised that I needed a bit of therapy myself. Now I realise that I was very close to some sort of death. Anyway, Annie helped me to recover from the brink – and thought it would be a good idea for me to go to Africa – "it's hot and moist" she said.

Africa = ecotourism, I thought! I needed to investigate. At this time a few years after the Earth Summit it all seemed a pretty good idea. I bought a cheap ticket to The Gambia and off I went.

Immediately I got off the flight I met a lady sitting on a cart that served as a luggage carousel. She was one of the ladies who'd come to Africa years ago, met a local man and married him – pretty romantic at the time, but less romantic a few tears later. Anyway, she hadn't run home but made a life for herself and, by now and had made many local friends too. Joan had been back in England on a visit.

Not all expats, but locals too, were in her circle. She noticed that I was interested in the place, was interesting, and may be able to offer something so she decided to take me under her wing.

What a fascinating experience. Joan took me around in her bashed-up jeep and introduced me to all her friends. I got to meet the beach bums looking for white women to look after them, I talked to the people running the 'Roots' slave experience, I met people doing cruises into the hinterland along the Gambia River. Finally, I was introduced to a beautiful Swedish couple who had built a fabulous igloo-like lodge with bottles for windows. They ran African drumming courses.

This was, of course, the other side of tourism to The Gambia. The rest was hideous, exploitative mass tourism where the visitors got cheap stays in skyscraper hotels and the locals got little benefit. All of the profits got siphoned off by the ruling clique. Sex tourism seemed the easy route out if you were moderately attractive and young and could pick up and keep a needy tourist.

Anyway, I came back with the idea that ecotourism could change the world and immediately set up a partnership with Sandra (who was still supporting me after losing her million) and Rob, called Ecotourism Marketing Associates. Both of my partners had been creditors when Land Travel folded – Rob for a few thousand and Sandra for over a million, but they had both been incredibly supportive since.

Both of them were inclined to view life philosophically. Rob had chucked in his job when the sustainability boat had seemed to be coming and went fully new-age. Sandra has philosophy in her DNA, I'd met her a decade or so ago when she was in her 20's and running the biggest à la carte restaurant in Europe – the floating Chinese palace in Amsterdam – with ease and grace and I knew she loved tourism and was extraordinarily well-connected. So between us we were 'EMA'.

And after a load of trying we were getting totally nowhere. Until I decided that what I really needed was a country that I could organise all the tourism for. Preferably a small country, probably in Africa.

Then an opportunity arrived. There was to be an Africa Travel Market event in Johannesburg and it may be possible for Sandra and me to get there.

She had a friend called Paul Trustfull who wrote and published a magazine which he distributed through airlines – particularly KLM, the Dutch airline. Paul lived on barter and he could often barter copies of the magazine and advertisments for flight tickets. In this case a fairly complex barter deal was done – in exchange for one first class ticket (for Sandra) and two business class tickets (for Paul and me), the airline got some free advertising. Paul was also trying to interview Nelson Mandela (or any other big name he could find) and I was to write a few articles. Sandra made up the difference with cash. There were also two rooms available with the deal, Paul and I could possibly share one – Sandra got the other. Great – we'd be on our way!

Obviously, Paul and I were lower down the food chain than Sandra. First of all we were blokes, secondly, whereas Sandra and Paul both came from Surinam, Paul was a snappily-dressed black man, Sandra was a rather more sophisticated Catholic lady of Indian origin. Me, I was a relatively unknown quality, so the die was set.

Back in Bath, my rich and inventive friend Caroline hove into view, she had decided that, as her 30th birthday was close, she was going to have a party in a different place every night for a whole week and, naturally, I was invited to all of them.

Caroline had a penchant for parties, creative visualisation (she visualised her parking places so one would be free when she needed) and a mentality that expected that everything would be available. It helped that her dad had the same attitude and hence they were all loaded. And a bit (maybe a lot!) unconventional. One regular happening was Caroline's Monday soirée. The idea was that she'd invite about 50 interesting people to her house, a few people would make some food, Caroline would provide some drink and she'd get somebody to hold court. Often a bishop or a monk or a pagan would talk about religion, a well-known philosopher or a historian would talk about their subject, or a new age guru or whatever. The guests were pretty interesting too ranging from musicians to poets, even gangsters.

Anyway, Caroline's events were always interesting – it was difficult not to accept an invitation.

Although I'd been expected to attend all of Caroline's birthday parties, I was not sure that I had the stamina. But she said that I definitely had to go to one in particular. She said that she'd invited a beautiful South African countess – Julie by name, and she was not only beautiful and interesting, Caroline said she would look after me in South Africa and introduce me to her interesting friends.

In the event I went to four of Caroline's parties. At one I met a man who'd been in the same prison as me and a woman whose dad had – lots of unusual reminiscences there! At another a rather nasty fight broke out, and at another I began a friendship with a monk who was a headmaster of a posh boys school – maybe that was why he loved fine wine and good cigars. Finally I met Countess Julie, she was fun, energetic and had a lodge complete with lots of land and an enormous astronomic telescope just outside of Johannesburg.

Julie and her husband both loved wild animals – so they had loads of them including baboons, elephants and even a few pumas (naughty Julie). Sadly she told me that she would love to have hosted me but she was full when I would be in South Africa, but she promised that she would look after me. That meant that Paul and I had to share a room. Never mind.

We would be off to Africa in search of ecotourism business. Ecotourism, this new way of travelling, a new adventure.

By the time we strange three – the skinny old English gent, the rich Asian lady and the pimped up black dude – pitched up in Johannesburg it was already going to a bit to worms. Sandra was feeling unwell, Paul was hyped up and I was tired, what could happen?

Anyway, Countess Julie had invited me to the ranch for the day and how could I refuse, and when Julie came to collect me nobody else wanted to come. It was totally fascinating. Like many Africans, Julie just loved wild animals, so I got introduced to them all, particularly interesting were Julie's pet pumas – not the sort you'd take for a walk unless you wanted to massacre the local cats and dogs! More friendly were her elephants, the young ones I thought a touch overfriendly for my taste as they jokingly squeezed me up to a tree. Time to beat a quick exit I thought. The next evening I had agreed to go with Julie to a big wine tasting, God knows why, as a non-drinker it didn't hold any pleasure for me but Julie persuaded me – I could drink water, she told me.

Well, the next day at the Africa Travel Market was rubbish. I watched a few presentations and visited a few stands but my dream of getting a small African country's tourism to control seemed way out of my grasp. And tonight was the great wine tasting – yawn – better show willing.

By 7pm I was bored witless, there is only so much water I can drink and I'd reached my limit. I made my apologies to Julie and joined the long taxi queue. In those days I used to smoke cigars so, naturally, to while away the time, I pulled out a cigar and lit it up philosophically. No sooner than the contented plume of smoke was rising from my lips than a posh voice penetrated my meditation "I say can I have one of those?" Shaun Mann said.

We finally got a taxi and shared it back to the hotel. En route we discovered certain shared passions – horse racing, cigars and writing amongst others.

And I found out that Shaun was in charge of a substantial budget for tourism development, which he had sourced, in Uganda. Wow.

Anyway, we decided to have dinner together and I wandered up to my room to get the box of Montecristo No. 2 Havana cigars that I had lured Shaun with.

It was a very interesting dinner indeed and concluded with Shaun inviting me to Uganda to pitch for their business.

The rest of the Africa Travel Market was bathed for me with the rosy glow of anticipated success but it was full of characters who would pop up again and again in my life for at least the next 20 years.

Pretty much everybody who thought about it was then convinced of the benefits of tourism sustainability and of Africa. Two blokes in particular held my attention.

The World Travel and Tourism Organisation was, and is, a very powerful club. It was formed of the bosses of the world's biggest 100 travel organisations – hotel groups, tour operators, car hire companies etc. Geoffrey Lipman was its Chief Executive and had just founded

Green Globe which was to lend authenticity to sustainable tourism initiatives. In other words an initiative whereby businesses, destinations, even countries could hand over cash to Green Globe and they would provide a green audit and a green certificate. In effect this third party certification would add value and credibility. Right up my street.

The second bloke was another visionary – Noel de Villiers. He had made plenty of money in the travel industry as Avis Car Rental South Africa franchisee and had now moved on to his big vision – Open Africa, an idea to link all Africa natural parks together into one all-encompassing initiative. His powerful vision was based on Africa's spiritual, environmental and cultural ability to change visitor's perspectives, changing their lived for the better drawing on Carl Jung and others' philosophies. Nelson Mandela, even, had agreed to be its patron. Unfortunately, over a quarter of a century later, it is still getting itself off the ground.

My Africa travel market experience convinced me yet again of the coming power of sustainable tourism and with an invite from Shaun to visit him in Uganda to talk about what we could do together, I thought that Ecotourism Marketing Associates was on its way.

On the basis that I'd write him an article or two, Paul was willing to get me a business class ticket to Uganda which he would barter for advertising space in Executive Class magazine and as soon as I possibly could, I was boarding the Alliance Air flight from London Heathrow Terminal One.

Paul sent me a message to say that I should be excited and you can bet your boots that I was.

I knew very little indeed about Uganda. That it had been a British protectorate that it had been ruled by the notorious Idi Amin and that 'Having Ugandan Discussions' was Private Eye satirical magazine shorthand for having sex had been the extent of my knowledge.

We passed Mt Kilimanjaro as dawn was breaking and soon after we landed in Arusha – the gateway to the Serengeti and Ngorongoro, two of Tanzania's incredible national parks, and, of course Kilimanjaro. A few passengers disembarked, then we were on our way over the enormous Lake Victoria to Entebbe.

My preparatory research had informed me that in 1972 Uganda had been the top tourism destination in Africa, that over 15% of the country's land was devoted to national parks, that the staple diet was plantain with groundnut sauce, and that now the country had a sober liberating president in place of Idi Amin and Milton Obote – two ruthless dictators. So much for boring stuff.

I now knew that this was the place that had a snowy mountain range (in the heart of Africa no less) known as the 'Mountains of the Moon', its Murchison Falls National Park was fed by the surging River Nile, the frighteningly-named Bwindi Impenetrable Forest hosted groups of some of the world's rarest primates – the last three or four hundred Mountain Gorillas. Moreover Kibale Forest – another national park – had groups of habituated chimps whose party trick was to pee on visitors. No point in fighting back they're at least ten times stronger than you! And all that, I was to find, was the teeniest tip of Uganda's wildlife and environmental iceberg. No wonder it had been Africa's top destination in the 1970s.

Shaun was rightly called 'Tarzan' and bore a more than passing likeness to Robert Redford (looks) and Arnold Swarzenegger (presence) met me at the airport in his Defender Land Rover, smoking a cigar.

"Breakfast?" he said. How could I refuse? So we drove to the Windsor Lake Victoria Hotel for what passed for a full English breakfast followed by a full situation briefing from Shaun followed by a bit of a tour. The tour involved Kampala (the capital) and Shaun's office. Then a spot of steak and kidney pie for lunch at one of the expats' haunts, a bit more briefing followed by a visit to another expat haunt then back for the night to Shaun's house to meet the family. Finally the steel shutters were drawn to secure the house against raids or burglars, etc. Chilling.

At the end of my visit, Shaun asked me to quote for the production of a brochure to promote travel to Uganda. This was a very big job and involved actually creating a tourism programme from scratch to fill the brochure. This meant checking hotels, operators and destinations all over the country. The one thing I was not allowed to do was to promote tourism to see Mountain Gorillas – they had enough of this sort of high value élite tourism already. So the brochure was to be part public relations image-creation and part product suggestions, we decided it was to be called the Uganda Trail.

So, I went back to the UK, quoted, got the job and went back to Uganda to get the information I needed to make it happen.

By now I'd learned a lot – about Uganda and about how Shaun's project worked.

And, as usual, being totally fascinated with the job I had done massive amounts of research on Uganda and its potential... which was enormous.

This, as I saw it, was Uganda's story. Once upon a time, just before Uganda was ruled by the infamous dictator Idi Amin, it was a pinnacle of African tourism. Now, tourism was practically non-existent.

But Uganda had no less than 15% of its land in glorious national parks from Kibale, noted for its groups of habituated chimpanzees, to Bwindi Impenetrable Forest with its Mountain Gorillas. It was the source of the Nile. It had more species of birds and butterflies than almost anywhere in the world. It had Africa's most respected university.

On the other hand it was unknown to modern-day tourists except for the fact that it was a darkest Africa country which had been run by an unstable bloodthirsty dictator.

Anyway, my job was to create a new image through a new set of messages and tourism opportunities. All of this was to be embodied in a new brochure.

There was one kind of tourism that worked in Uganda – and still brings in lots of high spending tourists, so many that the number of visitors has to be limited. Gorilla tourism. The world population of Mountain Gorillas is around 400. They are truly gentle giants. They all live in and around the Bwindi Impenetrable Forest in Uganda, the Volcanoes National Park in Rwanda and the Congo (all countries with a challenged image for tourism). A visit to meet Mountain Gorillas is a true life-changing experience.

Everybody that knows about it wants to do it. So, they pay big bucks to do so.

This is great for the agency that issues Gorilla Permits (The Uganda Wildlife Authority) and it brings in an amount of money. But not much help in developing a diversified sustainable tourism offer.

Maybe this is the time to talk about what sustainable tourism actually is. I try to talk about it as little as possible because those two little words combined with my enthusiasm have been known to clear rooms!

This is how I feel about tourism...

Tourism happens when someone goes from their home to a destination and stays one night or more and goes home.

Think of a destination like this... your family owns a lovely stately home estate and you have the responsibility to care for it on behalf of your kids and their kids etc., and you have limited funds. You decide that visitors may pay to visit your home. Your marketing is quite successful, so visitors come. They pay an entrance fee which you use to keep your estate in good order. You build a teashop and employ some people to make teas; your visitors buy them so you make some profit. All your profits go to the upkeep and to pay your staff – the rest, if there is any, goes to you and your family.

So, your house is a tourism destination where you, obviously, have control of the finances and, of course, your property and the people who come you allow in.

The global tourism industry didn't develop like this though.

It was largely developed a few hundred years ago by visionaries like Thomas Cook who wanted to take their friends and other people to see interesting things in interesting places. Travel obviously changing their perspective on life, while Thomas tried (and failed, actually) to make a sustainable income out of it.

Before that the only three forms of tourism were wars, pilgrimages and, at the top end – the Grand Tour. The great thing about this was that everybody knew exactly how to behave. Killing, raping and pillaging defined war tourism, spiritual seeking defined pilgrimage behaviour and 'noblesse oblige' usually defined the Grand Tour.

Of course, the destinations that welcomed Thomas Cook's tourists were glad to have the business – these tourists paid for hotels and meals and guided tours etc. And everyone who wanted benefitted a little. Anyway, there weren't lots of tourists so nobody cared much. Plus the tourists made life a bit more interesting, being exotic specimens worthy of a look by the locals. Everybody was content.

So everybody loved tourists. Until...

In the 1960s a new breed of tour operator appeared. Rather more commercial and less principled than Thomas. These were real businesses that knew that the difference between what your customers paid you and what you paid your suppliers represented your profit and the reward for your work. Hence they tried to pay the least they could whilst charging the least they could. Why not charge the most? Because the easiest way to sell anything is to sell it cheap. Plus, there was this formula which was fashionable at the time of mass production – marginal costing – tiny profits but lots of sales.

Plus, charter flights where operators bought the use of the whole plane not making a profit until they'd sold 95% of the seats. Plus market share – everyone knew that unless you dominated the market you couldn't get the best deals. So travel became mass because the prices became cheap and vice versa. The prices are cheap because the suppliers are paid little. And the industry has got addicted to cheap travel because its customers want the cheapest deal, naturally. They are always right, of course. Why would the customer care how little everybody that served them got paid?

Don't believe me? Currently TUI is the biggest tour operator in the world. It's easy to see that currently TUI makes a profit of €4 per passenger on every holiday thay sell. Good for TUI – they carry 30 million passengers every year. But the small businesses that carry fewer passengers concentrating on service – how could they operate on those sorts of margins?

And now the situation has been dramatically expanded with the advent of the massive online travel agencies (OTAs) such as Airbnb and Booking.com. Whereas tour operators take responsibility for their actions in destinations the online agencies are only responsible to their shareholders.

Let's go back to our stately home destination. By now they've got used to a nice genteel tourism activity and to be fair there's not much else that they can do. But now the new style tour operators bang on their door and say that they are only prepared to pay 25% of what they were paying per person, but not to worry because they would bring ten times as many visitors so there would be more money-making opportunities. Everybody was going to be rich!

And, of course the tour operators and the OTAs have all the trump cards. If the destination refuses or tries to get a saner price, or doesn't spend money to keep fashionable, the tour operator could just move on. And they do. Frequently.

Tourism is simply a buyer's market.

Every destination has the same problems, the bigger the destination is, the more complicated the problems. The problems of a stately home are the same as those of a complex destination only smaller and simpler. The critical issue is that people actually live in both and if tourists come, they will always affect their lives, for better or for worse.

And almost every destination is somebody's home. Most people like to keep their homes clean and tidy and comfortable. Most people treasure their privacy. Most people don't like strangers making muddy footmarks on their carpets or tramping through their rose-beds, clogging up their shops and streets or taking pictures of them.

People are responsible for their families and their homes. Communities are responsible for their people and their destinations. Sustainability is defined in terms of the economy, of culture, of society and of the environment.

Clearly it would be good to have sustainable communities and sustainable homes. Clearly tourism impacts on this sustainability. Clearly it is important that communities understand how best to manage tourism to benefit their economies, their cultures, their environments and their communities' societies. As tourism grows and affects more and more people (it is said that globally one in eight people work in or depend on travel and tourism for their livelihoods) these issues become more and more important.

Here's an interesting fact. When I started in tourism just 50 years ago there were about 25 million international tourists a year. This year there will be over 1.4 billion. And that is the figure for international tourists; if you include those that holiday in their own countries it's a staggering 7 billion-plus. A success, but for whom?

My own simple definition of sustainable tourism is 'the use of good tourism practices to create and sustain places that are good to live in and good to visit'

Easy enough to do when you have manageable numbers of tourists. But 1.4 billion and still increasing by at least 7% a year?

And tourism is so full of opportunities in which everyone can share. I knew, after all I'd seen them!

Back to Uganda and I thought that it was just the tourism job of a lifetime! All of my experience had led me to be able to do this job.

Here, I thought we could really do it! Create offers that would not only give tourists awesome experiences but benefits for locals too. Here we could help build places that were good to live in and good to visit.

First, I did a phenomenal amount of research. I went to Murchison Falls National Park – the second place in the world that moved me to tears. How could it not affect anyone, I thought, as I stood by the water watching crocodiles slip into the water with pods of hippos, dozens of pied kingfishers swooping, and giraffes walking gently while baboons played. There were elephants, too. What an amazing sight – just what the Garden of Eden must have been like.

And that was just the tip of the astonishing Uganda iceberg. Murchison Falls was only one of their amazing parks. I went to Kibale National Park where I was pissed on by annoyed habituated chimps, and I went to Queen Elizabeth National Park where I was chased by an angry mother elephant and surrounded by lions. I went to the Mountains of the Moon in Rwenzori National Park where groundsel was growing to five metres high (the result of Afro-Alpine gigantism or the power of hot high sun) and I encountered billions of lake flies as they rose for the full moon on Lake Victoria.

Basically I went all over, and simply everywhere there was yet another fabulous wildlife discovery and I met crazy, passionate, fascinating people everywhere.

And the land was so fertile that they said you could plug a walking stick in the ground and it would flower.

Plus Uganda had other stuff. For instance, it was slap bang on the Equator which meant when you poured water one side it swirled one way, on the other side, 10 metres away it swirled the other.

To help me I brought my mates to Uganda for a few days. Rob the green marketing guru and Angelo the Venetian who'd been in my life since 1965!

Shaun, my contact and paymaster was initially dubious when I told him our plan. In the end everybody raved about it.

I'd researched and created "The Uganda Trail" which linked all the major national parks in tours and linked all the communities and the tourist lodges.

Now for the promotional material – in those days, a glossy brochure.

Rob's copy and the images were phenomenal – the heading "Ganda – all that's missing is U" led into sensational copy that wooed everyone – the brochure was remarkable. Fabulous images, super words, phenomenal design.

We'd managed to do deals with all of the serious international quality media to run our Uganda tour offers and Angelo was to take the bookings, plus he'd lined up a couple of celebrity journalists to visit and write.

Now Uganda's reputation for security was better and the government had become stable it looked like we were on a winner.

On the strength of it all, which represented 2 years work, I got another fascinating project – to help three ex-Soviet satellite areas (in Slovakia, Czech Republic and Macedonia) to develop sustainable tourism.

I'll never forget getting off the plane in Vienna on the way to Czech Republic when I got a telephone call from Shaun in Uganda. "The shit's hit the fan, mate – tourists have been kidnapped". A group of Rwanda rebels had captured some tourists staying in the upmarket Abercrombie and Kent lodge. It was going to be difficult to promote Uganda for a while.

The the damage had been done. But that's the problem with tourism, it's fragile.

Anyway, I carried on working with Uganda for a couple of years, constantly promoting, creating new tours and programmes, new ideas, but nothing was going to get really better unless something important changed. While tourism operates in local situations that are politically, culturally or socially precarious it can never be truly sustainable.

I bid to get the next 5-year contract to develop a true sustainable tourism environment for Uganda. The proposal I put in partnership with a top development agency in Brussels would have linked together all of the separate elements – local communities in particular. Although our project was the best our charge was too high – it went to an agency that just ticked the boxes and took the cash.

Then I bid for a fascinating development project in Butrint in Albania. An astonishing place – just like ancient Greece. I had been told that if I bid together with an Italian agency (the funding was coming from Italy) I would get the contract. I didn't!

Finally, I tried for a World Bank project which I really wanted to do in Ethiopia which has an astonishing tourism opportunity. Like Uganda 50 years ago its tourism assets were at one time world-renowned. The country's cultural legacy is astonishing. But no was the reply again. At least the months of research I put into the bids was rewarding – I learnt lots about East African and Albanian tourism!

Even though developing more tourism for Uganda seemed like a distant possibility, it certainly didn't finish my relationship with Africa. I was desperate to see the pinnacle of wildlife tourism – the fabulous African game parks in Tanzania – in particular the Serengeti and the

Ngorongoro Crater, and I was really keen on seeing the Indian Ocean and Zanzibar.

So off Pam and I went for a couple of weeks. I'm not very good in Uganda's game parks, I'm far too ditzy. Earlier that year I'd been pissed on by chimps in Uganda's Kibale Park, then chased by elephants in its Queen Elizabeth park. On this trip, I committed a cardinal stupidity of taking a pile of breakfast boxes from one 4WD vehicle to another to the sound of screams. The vehicle I was taking breakfast to had stopped to watch a lion yards away – well I didn't see him, did I?

Anyway, Tanzania would be different – and it was. Much more game than Uganda, but much more organised and much less relaxed. The fact is that Tanzania makes game tourism work. They have sensational natural assets and an extremely efficient tourism industry.

The Serengeti is unbelievable. For anybody interested in the natural world it is simply a dream come true.

It's just like watching wildlife on TV then walking through the screen, sitting in an open Land Rover and swapping your armchair for a hard, dusty, bumpy seat. But you are THERE, you can smell the smells of the almost treeless, over 5,000-square-mile grasslands. You can see for miles and miles and miles of wildebeest, zebra, gazelles, impala, giraffe and occasional big cats and big birds – predators and carrion eaters – the ubiquitous vultures and the loping hyenas. The surprise to me were the delicate wildebeest – that's the problem with TV – you don't see size. And here on the African plain – there is no easy close-up unless you're as stupid as I am.

The Ngorongoro is completely different: whereas the Serengeti is enormous and unbounded as far as the eye can see, the Ngorongoro is an enormous crater. And it is full of wildlife, much of it very close. So, we got to see legendary white rhino and my favourite – dynamic, amazingly accelerating cheetah. And there was one big plus – a pair of copulating lions which we watched for what seemed like hours.

These are memories that you won't ever lose. And it's these guaranteed top-level sights that brings people from all over the world to Tanzania.

Nowadays, if anybody asks me where is my dream destination I say Zanzibar. Because it has everything – lovely beaches, fabulous history and culture, extraordinarily good food, interesting shopping and fascinating wildlife, plus, so far, it has few tourists. It still has, unfortunately, a tourism and human rights problem but their problems are certainly not as big as many other destinations like Maldives, Sri Lanka, Turkey or Egypt.

So, we got the very little plane from Dar es Salaam to Stonetown in Zanzibar, were picked up and driven to the sea. Here we splashed into the water, climbed onto the little boat and, within 15 minutes, were getting off on Chapwani – a private eco-island.

Chapwani is an inexpensive paradise in the warm Indian Ocean. A family-owned haven from which we could explore Zanzibar. There were some fascinating things to explore on Chapwani too – the wildlife on a walk, the little British cemetery, the lovely views but like the massive colony of fruit bats on the island, as dusk fell, we were off to explore Stonetown.

A colourful history has created a colourful town. Once upon a time the island was a centre of activity for the Arab slave trade. At one time it was the ridiculously rich royal residence of the Sultans of Muscat and Oman. Finally colonised by the British and made into the centre of the spice trade, as slavery was banned. Now it relishes its position as an UNESCO world heritage site and the little alleyways and dusty old shops are a real delight to poke around in.

Plus, there are many great beaches and superb relaxed restaurants. Plus, the thoughtful, well organised and funded Aga Khan Development Network is here, preserving the buildings and sustaining the society.

I'd go back there at the drop of a hat. But sensational Zanzibar was the last I'd see of Africa for a year or two!

Just as my full-on relationship with Uganda finished, I was back to Europe to complete the project in Macedonia. Another amazing place.

Nothing warns you when you are about to experience an amazing place that you've never heard about before.

Ohrid is one amazing place that I'd never heard of before. Ask any Serb about Ohrid – they all know it! Ask pretty much anyone else, they have no idea what it is or where it is.

I've been privileged to have experienced three of the world's very special tectonic lakes including the Caspian Sea and Lake Baikal. Lake Ohrid was the first.

Part of their mystery is the simple fact that because of the depth of the water and the luxuriance of the surrounding woodlands – the oxygen level is extremely high with enormous health and energy-giving qualities.

Anyway, apart from the health issues, Ohrid has more than one other thing that makes it very, very special.

In the beginning (in Ohrid's case about 7,000 years ago) there were human settlements around the lake. Obviously they became quite rich as the centuries went on. Golden masks, golden sandals and golden bracelets were unearthed recently to testify to the population's love of bling and their wealth.

Then the legendary Phoenician Cadmus arrived. He'd been banished from Thebes and was looking for somewhere to build an important city. The shores of Lake Ohrid were clearly perfect and so the city of Lychnidos (city of light) was born.

A couple of events later made the city even more important. First the major Roman Road (the Via Egnatia) was built right through Lychnidos on its way from Durres on the Adriatic to Constantinople (then Byzantium) which naturally added to Lychnidos' power, importance and wealth.

Then, a few hundred years later a couple of monks arrived in the area. Kliment and Naum are probably not the best-known monks in the world but around 850AD Kliment created the first Slavic alphabet – Glagolitic script, the precursor to Cyrillic.

Ohrid then became the world centre of Slavic literacy, spirituality and culture. This spread across the world, especially in the Slavic east. Ohrid's Literary University at its height had over 3,000 students. The power of Ohrid in those times cannot be overestimated as Slavic literacy is the force that binds all Slavic people from the Greek border all the way up to Russia.

Today, Ohrid is a true delight with a year-long festival programme in beautiful, unbelievably powerful surroundings.

And a fascinating and beautiful array of things to see and do. The town of Ohrid itself is dominated by its massive medieval castle, a stunningly elegant amphitheatre and, of course, the splendid lake. There are cobbled streets liberally dotted with little shops selling hand-made local specialities – from glorious ikons to delicate filigree silver work and a unique speciality – Ohrid pearls harvested from the lake. Naturally there are lots of bars and teahouses. There is unspoiled countryside, and stunning Byzantine churches, basilicas and lakeside monasteries – even ancient cave churches.

Plus, another lake – Prespa is partly in Macedonia but also in Greece and Albania. It drains into the deeper Lake Ohrid via underground streams. All of that area is part of a wonderful biosphere reserve.

There is food and wine everywhere in Macedonia. The area around Ohrid was a real market garden.

So, what was I meant to do there? Develop tourism, of course! I was part of a two-person team with a lovely lady development consultant – Jenny Holland. My job was the marketing of the area through the creation of a tourist heritage trail. We were paid by the European Union who had got 50% of the money from the local government.

Of course, a place like Ohrid had had tourists for ever, it had been a thriving destination for hundreds of years – but now, almost none. Before the Second World War there were regional tourists, but after the war Macedonia had become part of Yugoslavia where tourism had been centrally controlled. This was not a bad idea in fact as most workers had free holidays. There were a few agencies that controlled tourism – the biggest were Putnik and Globtour. International sales were handled by Yugotours who I remembered from my days in London. So everybody got nice holidays and the way it was structured Ohrid did pretty well both internationally and regionally.

Then came 1989 the Soviet Union was disbanded and Yugoslavia broken up into its separate parts.

There was no future for regional centrally managed tourism except for high visibility mass tourism destinations. So, the Yugoslav (now Croatia, Slovenia, Montenegro) destinations came to the fore and the others were denuded of tourism. I thought that this was a temporary aberration.

Anyway, Ohrid was left out in the cold and it was my job to bring it back into the warm, and my partner Jenny's job was to make sure that we did it sustainably.

There was a community tourism group already in existence which had been set up by the local partners. The group consisted of a local teacher, a hotelier, the director of the famous Ikon Gallery, a local tourist guide and a local politician. The idea was that I would teach them tourism marketing and they would teach me about the area's tourism assets. At the end of a few weeks we were to come up with a plan.

And we did. The project was then judged by the local EU auditor who came from Bulgaria to check us out and obviously we passed muster so I got paid.

The Slovakia, Czech Republic and Macedonia projects all followed the same format. And with the same result – a proposal for the future. I followed the groups for a while but eventually they lost their way. The fact is that tourism is driven by the marketplaces where tourists live rather than the destinations that they'll visit.

It's a real pity because the result is that 99% of tourists even now go to 0.1% of destinations. The tourists miss out on sensational places such as Ohrid and places like Ohrid miss out on great tourism opportunities.

At the time I was still doing some work with Uganda, mainly helping the parks to create guidebooks to their astonishing treasure chests of the natural world, but my projects there, although not my relationship, were coming to an end. I hadn't got the ongoing contract so there would be other masters.

Then one morning at 3am I drowsily answered the telephone. It was Alexis, my youngest son, who had been living with my ex-wife. "Mum's dead" he said. Frozen to the core, I got up, quickly dressed and drove to her house. The little street was flooded by the flashing lights of police cars. I found it all difficult to believe – we'd been talking just a few days ago, apparently, she had had an anaphylactic reaction to a new combination of drugs prescribed by her doctor and died instantly.

To say that I was shocked and gutted would be an understatement.

Whatever our current relationship was, for many years we had had a loving and productive one. I was completely unprepared for the waves of grief and guilt and shame that engulfed me. Although now they have abated somewhat, they haunt me to this day.

After the funeral, I was back to work with the knowledge that I was a sole parent to my sons, now 19, 27 and 29. Certainly I had not been the best father so far, what could I do in place of a mother, whatever their differences, that they adored. Maybe just let them see me, with all my faults.

Luckily, they have all grown into sensitive courageous husbands and fathers. And I am totally in love with their wives and my grandchildren.

Now I also had other stuff to do too. Mainly trying to convert the travel industry to sustainability in the process of getting more tourism consultancy work.

To do it, I started writing lots of articles about the benefits of green tourism and pushing them around the new internet with the hope that potential clients would like my words and give me interesting work.

Luckily a few did and with a nucleus of clients and some marketing consultancy work from Sandra in Amsterdam (my ex supplier to Land Travel and ex partner in EMA), I started a weekly newsletter with lots of hints about sustainable tourism, stories plus a bit of evangelical zeal.

And I did bits of sustainable tourism consultancy. On top of which I wrote a self-help book for B&Bs – it was called 100 ways to B&B Success.

My vision for sustainable tourism wasn't becoming reality anywhere near quickly enough. And the B&Bs weren't buying enough of my books quickly enough. So, I started a series of masterclasses around the country. The idea was that one nice B&B would host me and the masterclass in exchange for a free place and I would promote the event with the local tourist board to other B&Bs.

Finally, I sold the books through a company that sold all the stuff that B&Bs needed, soap etc. And I stopped doing the B&B masterclasses. But it was fascinating at the time even though I was left with thousands of books and a big bill for their printing.

By now my inability to squeeze money, rather than just good words, out of my activities, had nearly bankrupted me again and, as a result I was practically homeless. I simply couldn't pay my rent and would have to find somewhere to live – and quickly.

By now I was writing an annual Sustainable Tourism Report which was packed full of information. I sold it to my small group of clients and it was supported by some well-known names – such as Virgin Holidays and Thomas Cook. It made a tiny bit of money but at least I was doing something I believed in. I was also running a yearly Sustainable Tourism Masterclass.

CHAPTER 7

Applecake Days

The absence of money led me to wonder just what I could do to get some to tide me over until the next job came in – whenever that may be.

Pam made soap and sold it in the local market, I noticed that food stalls made money, she had an apple tree and by now on a wish and a prayer I'd moved in with her. Eureka I'd make apple cake using her apples and her kitchen and sell it in the market.

I've always loved applecake. Not stuff that masquerades as apple-cake, but real applecake like they make it in the low countries. Laden with spices, laced with plump sultanas and raisins and topped with juicy glazed succulent apples.

So that Friday evening, in Pam's spotless kitchen, I handmade 10 big applecakes – not a kitchen machine in sight. Finished at 1am I was ready to take them to market and sell them to cake enthusiasts at a sizeable profit.

The next day I was there at 8ish with cake for sale. Cut up into 12 slices per cake I had 144 slices to sell at £1 each (much too much thought the market traders). Anyway, as a result of my predatory activity wandering around the market dishing out samples, I sold or gave away the lot. This was largely due to the delicious potency of the cake and my hijacking anybody who looked like they may buy one with a free sample. I reckon I made about a hundred quid – not bad.

And that was how Oncle Valere's Belgian Applecake – "made to an authentic family recipe" – was born.

My son Adam dubbed it "Cinnamon-coated currency" because I could use it to barter for anything else on offer at the market. Cheese, meat, applejuice, mushrooms, flowers, pies, eggs – whatever! Life was good, at least we weren't going to starve!

So, for a couple of years, until the end of 2007, I baked cake every day whilst still writing and promoting my Sustainable Tourism Report and organising and promoting my Sustainable Tourism masterclasses. The clients loved both of them – particularly the masterclasses which were held twice a year in different but interesting locations. They were held in posh sustainable hotels like the Zetter (Mark Sainsbury's pad) and the Aldwych (very posh, very sustainable where Henry Dimbleby spoke), even at the Royal Geographical Society. We always went some-where nice for lunch and the masterclasses were great fun. Of course they depended on the buzz that was generated by the participants – like a party – and plenty of buzz there was but not plenty of money.

The masterclasses like the Sustainable Tourism Reports were a means to an end – the idea was that they would eventually make some money and lead to consultancy contracts. But in the meantime I was baking and selling cake to keep body and soul together.

Pam decided that it was a bad idea for me to live with her so I was homeless again. Time to move the bakery. I had a friend with a small estate (big house, little cottage and some grounds). He offered me the cottage to live in for a while and its kitchen to bake in.

So I used the cottage and kitchen for a while, got a few part-time staff and baked even more cake until we were up to oven capacity.

It's strange how life seems to often run in concentric circles. Remember the printing company I'd bought in 1979? Trymprint it was called. It became part of my little empire at Land Travel. Now it was a bakery making and selling thousands of organic pies and I'd been offered a lease on one room with ovens.

So, I moved in and started work. The idea was to make money out of good cake. Now I was producing not only applecake but baked cheesecake, Sachertorte and Plumcake. Over a hundred cakes a week had to be sold. On Saturdays I left at 5am to sell cake in Chelsea, on Wednesdays I left at 6 to sell cake in Bristol, on Thursdays in Soho, Fridays in Spitalfiends. Plus cakes had to be created and baked.

One day in 2005 I had got an email. It was from the owner of a global travel trade website called TravelMole. It asked if I wanted a chat about working with them.

When I talked to Charlie Kao, the boss in question, he said he loved my way of writing and did I want to edit his Vision on Sustainable Tourism newswire. No money but he'd help promote my products and services in exchange for my work.

Sounded like a good idea to me. All I needed to do is to learn how to post stories online – and how to write online stories.

And even TravelMole had its roots in my past. In its infancy as a little website it was born in Bristol's Small Street next door to the Assize Courts Hotel where I'd had my last drink.

Run by a very young Richard Hammond, he'd sold out to Charlie on the basis that he'd get paid some money. Richard set up the Vision on Sustainable Tourism newswire.

So what did TravelMole do?

TravelMole was, and is, a news medium for the global travel and tourism industry. They boast 400,000 subscribers all over the world and they send out a number of newswires on different facets of the industry. The formula is that stories get placed in the relevant section – travel agents, shipping, green travel etc., where they are visible to all and then individual editors choose the most appropriate stories to put into newswires. The newswires could be daily, weekly or ad hoc.

I was appointed one of the editors, so I wrote the stories that went into the green section and chose the ones that went into the Vision on Sustainable Tourism newswire. The recipients of the newswire were subscribers – about 30,000 of them who had ticked that particular newswire box.

So, I went to events, did interviews (often video) and wrote stories. I didn't get paid but the quid pro quo was that I got to promote my Sustainable Tourism Reports and masterclasses through my own stories. This worked to an extent but never sufficiently to make me a real living even though people paid up to £1,000 for a report and for sponsorship. It was a fairly tough life, but it could be fun.

At the beginning I sent the newswire once a month but Charlie had pushed me into making it weekly. The fact is that researching and writing up to 10 stories a week, getting pictures, etc., takes time, so I was back into too much work, too little money!

I had a good deal with Charlie though about advertising sales. He was to pay me a reasonable commission on advertising space I sold. And there was a time that it looked like I could make a serious income from this; certainly I believed so.

Plus, we were both convinced that, as climate change awareness kicked in, the carbon market would take off in a massive way and tourism would be an enormous part of it.

The carbon market? OK this is how it works: airplanes emit greenhouse gases while they fly. Obviously the longer the flight the more the emissions plus emissions at high altitude are multiplied – they are more toxic than those on the ground. In my view these airline emissions have to be capped because as flights increase so do emissions – the higher the emissions, the faster the climate change. There is a system called 'Cap and Trade' whereby airlines are given a limited amount of emissions (tons of greenhouse gases) that they can make in a given year and if they exceed it they have to buy a similar amount from someone that has not gone over their cap. The most effective of these markets was the EUETS – the European Union Emissions Trading System, it was properly organised and policed. The other opportunity was that airlines and others could buy Carbon Credits. These are quite simple and rely on the fact that certain activities create emissions (those that rely on fossil fuels) and certain activities that reduce emissions (tree growing, renewable energy etc). Plus Carbon Credits gain more value if they are created in a developing country and if they are rigorously audited.

Very quickly after the Earth Summit in 1992 companies and initiatives were created to make this process easier. They packaged up all these Carbon Credits and sold what they called 'Carbon Offsets' so if you wanted to make your corporate or personal activity emission-free, you just bought the relevant amount of 'Carbon Offsets' and hey presto you were effectively 'Carbon Neutral'.

There were a number of reasons put forward that this was not a good idea – buying Carbon Credits didn't reduce emissions. You had to do that for yourself. The green brigade didn't like rich people getting off their share of the problem. I think that they wanted perfection rather than just 'better'.

Personally, I thought that there was no hope whatsoever that people would reduce their emissions if they weren't forced. So I had great hopes for Carbon Offsets because it seemed everybody could gain.

So now I was producing the Sustainable Tourism Report, running Sustainable Tourism Masterclasses and was Publisher of Vision on Sustainable Tourism and TravelMole's Sustainable Tourism Editor. And I truly believe that sustainable tourism is the most important opportunity/challenge that the tourism industry has ever faced.

Plus, as we've seen, since I've been involved in the industry it has grown from moving around 25 million international tourists a year to moving over a billion of them. If you add tourists that stay in their own country you multiply both those figures by a factor of six. It's big!

And in 2007 it was all kicking off finally, I thought. Largely due to the efforts of Geoffrey Lipman who was now Assistant Secretary General of the United Nations World Tourism Organisation (UNWTO) – the Davos Forum on Climate Change and Tourism was set up. Everyone who was anybody was there. It was a seminal occasion. Now there appeared a straight, strong line from the 1992 Earth Summit to the tourism industry.

All of the key scientist participants and people from UNWTO and the UN Environment Programme came to Oxford to present their document outlining the problems and the solution. I was there.

Another tourism conference was convened for Gothenburg by Lipman and UNWTO – the Symposium on Tourism and the Green Economy was held in September 2009. The idea was that this would draw on the Davos Forum and lead onto the upcoming key world conference on climate change in Copenhagen that December. The pivotal COP15 UN Conference on Climate Change.

It was believed that COP15 would come up with a binding agreement on maximum emissions that all the countries in the world would adhere to. It would have been the next sensible step on the road to climate sanity.

In the event COP15 lost the plot. It was to take another 6 years (the Paris Accord at COP21) to get anywhere near the potential that the Copenhagen Conference had. The energy behind the process had been lost.

Why? Maybe the global financial meltdown of 2008 had the most influence on the conference's failure. But certainly the drive behind sustainable tourism had faltered.

Of course, the key difficulty that thwarts tourism sustainability is air travel – this represents some 80% of tourism-related emissions.

And the insoluble problem is that airplane construction and air travel are largely protected industries. When the European Union tried to force international airlines to engage in the EU cap and trade system (EUETS) if they landed in Europe – the world's planemakers and big governments played hardball forcing the EU to stand down and kicking the problem into the long grass. The long grass being the International Civil Aviation Organisation – the organisation that ensures that no airline pays tax on fuel or spare parts. The ICAO was meant to resolve the problem by 2016. At the time of writing, it has still not happened.

The problem? If tourism, and air travel carries on increasing at its current pace, by 2030 it alone will represent 30% of total global emissions and we will have no hope of hitting emission reduction targets.

So COP15 threw a big fat wet blanket all over the prospects of tourism sustainability.

The next big sets of opportunities would not be until 2015, 2016 and 2017.

The first big deal was in 2015 when the United Nations held its first big development meeting since the Millennium Development Goals were set in, obviously, 1999!

I've always been a big fan of the MDGs. I believe that they recognised that a world with less poverty, less stupidity, more rights for women and children and more freedom is a world to be worked for. In that aim I am pleased to be supported by President George W Bush who set up the Millennium Challenge Corporation as his presidential legacy with an initial endowment of $9billion.

Anyway, tourism has always been recognised as a big opportunity for development for poor countries with sun. But sustainable tourism development was something new (well, since 1992, anyway). Since then pretty much every rich country's overseas development budget (they all have them!) USA (USAID), China, Germany (GTZ), France (AFD), Netherlands (SNV), UK (DfID), and apart from the World Bank, there are a bunch of regional development banks. So a lot of my projects (including Uganda and eastern Europe) were funded by these development agencies.

The great thing about the 2015 UN development summit was that it set new development goals for the next 15 years. And specifically included sustainable tourism as an integral part of these goals.

All this led to the UN declaring 2017 the "Year of Sustainable Tourism for Development"

Anyway, by the end of 2008 all this was a dream or a nightmare, or a bit of both and the fact was that I was thinking of chucking it all in.

I'd been slogging away writing stuff for years while still making applecake. And the financial results were nearly nil. I reckoned that I was working over a hundred hours a week for less than £1 an hour. I'd had enough.

Then I got an email from Charlie Kao – he'd been invited to Kazakhstan to cover the General Assembly of UNWTO and he couldn't go – would I like to do it instead. No pay but all expenses covered.

CHAPTER 8

The Silk Road...

Astana is literally unbelievable. It is a dictator's surreal dream and a sustainable nightmare. Built on the vast steppe specifically to be the new capital of Kazakhstan it is too hot in the summer and too cold in the winter so its residents have to make use of artificial environments all year round.

Anyway the 'father' of the country Nursultan Nazarbayev got the most expensive, most famous, most iconic architects from all over the world and gave them free rein to create their most commercial nightmares each shouting on the others. Of course, he had the money from Kazakhstan's vast oil wealth and power (he was 'elected' in the Soviet regime and has held on to it ever since – some 28 years so far). Actually, most of the young people I met liked him – after all he paid all their expenses personally if they went to foreign universities provided they came back to Kazakhstan for 5 years.

So, the UN World Tourism Organization held its 2009 Annual Assembly in Astana with over a hundred ministers of tourism in this surreal city. Surrounded by vastly expensive, architectural 'master-pieces' by the likes of Kisho Kurokawa, Norman Foster and Zaha Hadid, the Disney meets Bart Simpson meets loadsamoney style of architecture made an appropriately ridiculous meeting point.

The event itself was fascinating – and I got to meet and interview dozens of ministers of tourism from all over the world. I met ministers from big countries like Brazil and Spain, France and India and little countries like Sri Lanka and Georgia – totally amazing!

And, of course there were seminars and events – most of which included vast amounts of Kazakh food. At these, I got to know many of the country's ruling cadre – like a little dysfunctional family. The food was quite interesting too, consisting mainly of horse done as many ways as possible but mainly boiled; and the aptly named ubiquitous Plov. The Kazakhs truly love their horses and their traditional horse-riding games are fabulous.

So naturally one afternoon I was taken to see Kokpar (Grey Wolf) where two teams with about 5 riders in each grappled over a decapitated goat, which they tried to deposit in their opponents' goal. The more romantic Kyz kuu literally means "catch the girl". Two horse-riders (a man and a woman) participate in this game. The female rider sits on her horse at a certain distance behind a horseman. She starts riding at full speed and, as soon as she reaches him, the male rider moves. Both race towards the finishing line. If the man wins, he has the right to kiss the girl. Otherwise, she may beat him with a whip. More fun than eating the horses!

And the Kazakh women were absolutely knock-down gorgeous. Tall, athletic, beautifully dressed in traditional clothes and they are brave powerful riders. Frightening to boot, I'm sure – particularly if they are wielding a whip at you!

Not quite as frightening as my last night's meeting though, with the president himself. As he gripped my hand, I realised my total lack of moral fibre.

Next day we were all flying south and backwards in time – to the old capital of Kazakhstan and even now its biggest city, Almaty.

For the next few days our little group of international journalists were to be in the hands of my friend Alla, ex-Intourist (Russian State Travel Organisation) and reputedly a KGB officer.

Alla and I get on fine, now she's accepted the fact that I don't join in the many, many vodka toasts obligatory in any Russian formal or informal dinner. So now we've been many places together. Her Russian and other languages plus her presence have come in handy on many occasions throughout the strange and worrying network of ex-Soviet states.

And she introduced my nice stalker as Dagmar Shreiber ("who likes you") who came to be a firm friend.

Both these lovely ladies came from the same background. Alla is a Moscow-born, Moscow-educated translator/guide who worked for the state taking foreigners around Russia and its satellites until the walls came down and she got seconded by the governnment to work for the UN World Tourism Organisation in Madrid.

And Dagmar is an East German Moscow- and Leningrad-educated green tourism entrepreneur who brings people from Germany to Kazakhstan and other ex-Soviet countries and writes and photographs and creates guidebooks and works with the Kazakh ecotourism organisation. Plus, she is a fearless ecowarrier in the East, which sometimes makes me fearful for her safety. Plus, she had a fabulous apartment in Berlin.

So, after Astana, I spent a few days happily exploring Almaty, visiting its amazing markets and astonishing shamans and the less interesting museums. I discovered that here, on the foothills of the TienShan mountain range on the border of China – both the original apple and the original tulip were discovered.

And then I got ill. Not terribly ill, possibly suffering from a surfeit of horse (Alla kindly told me that it was because I wouldn't drink vodka). Anyway, I was ill enough not to go on a helicopter trip with a crazy Russian drunken pilot into the mountains and far away. Bye bye Kazakhstan.

But a few years later, I was back in the area. Why? Because of an American casino-owner. Mark Advent had teamed up with Swissport and another few investors to create a big scheme.

Near Almaty, he proposed to create the land of Oz. Oz would have its own airport, more than 48 individual casino-hotels, a big-time racecourse, and everything that the high-rolling modern-day tourist requires. He even proposed to create cities like Venice and New York within the boundaries of the land of Oz. His estimate of visitors – 15 million a year. Now for a country like Kazakhstan with less than a million tourists (if that) the prospect of all this business and all this currency set eyes alight. Particularly the minister of tourism and the president.

As Mr Advent explained to me – Kazakhstan is placed between China and Russia, both big-time gambling populations. They would go for it in a big way.

It was no problem to Mr Advent that there were not enough trained hospitality personnel in the area. He would set up a tourism university to train them.

So, all bases covered, plus he had the backing of Mr Nursultan Nazarbayev and the minister of tourism. What could fail? Never heard of it since.

And the next time Kazakhstan came up? When I came to the support of Dagmar the ecowarrior.

Another mega-project, this time potentially much more damaging than Mr Advent's. This was to create a massive ski destination.

All the money-grabbing politicos and oligarchs were up to their necks in it and Dagmar was wild.

She had been involved in organising a mass protest against the mega ski resort in this rare snow leopard territory

The central part of the National Park – Kok-Zhailyau gorge – was slated to become a place for a new huge ski resort and real estate development.

Plans for the construction encompassed a huge swathe of land up to the border of Kazakhstan and Kyrgyzstan, which is the prime habitat of the extremely rare snow leopard plus the Turkestan lynx and other precious species

She said that the ski resort was only a disguise for the actual plan, which is to build private luxury houses, hotels and a golf-course in the very heart of the National Park. The Almaty Mayor's Office and private business interests were lobbying the legislature to make amendments to laws and regulations so that they could not be accused of breaking the law.

Almaty was then rated as number 4 in the list of the most polluted cities in the world the city got most of its fresh air and water from the "disputed" part of the National Park.

The battle went on for years during which Dagmar was threatened by the authorities and others and went to court to protest. Luckily she was never thrown in jail, but her card was certainly marked.

So that's Kazakhstan and my first engagement with the Silk Road Project.

But more important events were on the horizon. As 2010 dawned so did the prospect of my eldest son, Adam's 40th birthday. As it happened in January, he thought that it would be a good idea to have his party in the sun. We had friends in South Africa, and England were playing cricket there, so as far as Adam was concerned there was no reason to look further. He booked a house in Knysna (near Cape Town) and the whole family was to fly there for a few weeks to celebrate his 40th.

I had a relationship with Cape Town Tourism and a friend was running a sustainable tourism project in Namibia, so I decided to sandwich the celebrations between writing a couple of stories and seeing if there was any chance of more consultancy business in Cape Town.

Cape Town Tourism were stars in my tourism firmament. They really understood how tourism works and how the city could benefit from it. They had arranged for me to stay for a few days in a very green hotel with its own recycling set up and then meet some young black tourism entrepreneurs.

It was all great, and South Africa was enthusiastically looking forward to hosting the World Cup, plus lots of great building was going on – so everybody was looking forward to a sensational year. I was looking forward to a great day of cricket in the January sun before my dinner meeting with the bosses of Cape Town Tourism.

The cricket was great, the sun was hot. When I visited the toilet before my important meeting, I realised my mistake – my face was bright red! I struggled with my embarrassment during dinner. And I'll always remember the then director of the organisation – Mariette du Toit Helmbold – one of the best tourism professionals I've ever met. Her quote – "We don't want one-night-stand tourists in Cape Town – we're looking for tourists who want a long-term relationship."

The fact is that Cape Town has pretty much got everything that could support a truly sustainable tourism industry. And they know it! Plus they understand how it works. They should – the whole concept of sustainable tourism was created as a part of the 2002 Johannesburg Earth Summit – in Cape Town. The Cape Town Declaration on Responsible Tourism is like sustainable tourism's Bible. It embodies all the things you need to do to create forms of tourism that benefit both tourists and local communities.

In the modern tourism world, South Africa has got everything. It even, for a while, had a ministry of tourism who actually knew their jobs – from the minister Martinus van Schalkwyk down.

South Africa creates great wine in glorious vineyards, it has extraordinarily good food grown in beautiful fertile lands, it has possibly the world's best seafood swimming in sensational seas. It has some of the best-run and best-stocked game parks anywhere. It has superb beaches, wonderful hotels and restaurants. It has friendly, attractive, hospitable people. It has a lovely climate, a delightful environment and scenery. It connects all of these diverse assets in one tourism offer. But above all, it has a population that really get sustainability and sustainable tourism at a deep level. They truly connect sustainable with culture, economics, society and their environment. It is the only country that I know where people naturally call each other when there is a great sunset.

So South Africa is tourism paradise, it still has reasonable numbers of tourists, it is not yet overcrowded. The only thing that can get in the way of its sustainable success is its government.

After Adam's birthday another country was in my sights – Namibia.

Well in fact Namibia has been in my sights for many years – it's got form as a global leader in ecotourism, willing and open to develop sustainable tourism to its nth degree.

It had been a hard day. The 4WD has smashed into an ex-river course and broken a tyre so it had to be changed in the baking sun/ torrential rain. We're late, so no time to stop even for a drink before we have to engage the Defender's 4-wheel drive and scramble up a muddy, almost vertical incline to the tented camp. A welcome soft drink, cold towel, and welcome from the manager – my kind driver departs, leaving me to a briefing from the assistant manager/ lodge pilot – nice South Indian guy from Kerala.

The briefing involves: "We"ve got a few black scorpions and occasionally see puff adders" – "So no armed guard to see me to my room and frighten the lions like last night, at your other camp then!" – "No but you're our only guest tonight so we don"t want to lose you" – "Only me?" – "Only you!" "How many staff?" "Thirty-four". Wow.

Time to wash and change, admire the view from the veranda (stunning vast, deep, long basalt rock-strewn valley made green by the recent rain) and explore the room/tent (style and utility combined – toiletries, tea, big shower, comfy bed, large veranda – no scorpions or snakes).

Dinner for one; small table right in the middle of the restaurant with a view. Set for two? Local custom? No, the manager, Lena, sits down beside me. "They want to know what you want to eat" she says – "Do I have to choose" – "No, we"ll have everything on the menu, I want to try it ALL!"

I realized that Lena was a larger than life character. This is confirmed when she shows me her feet "Size 10, you know, because I didn't wear shoes until I was 12 years old – none of us did – plastic bags sometimes, but not shoes – and we didn't have money either"

So, what's the story? Lena's grandparents had been moved from South Africa in the 1960s to make way for a military camp. She'd spent her early life as a goatherd, bored out of her wits, she was constantly getting into trouble. And when her community was one of the first to apply to organize a conservancy, with a tourist lodge – Lena had applied for a job as manager. "I could do it" she said. But her brother had got the job, because he had precedence, and she'd gone to another lodge to work, very hard, because now she had something to prove.

When her brother had fouled up ("due to them having given him money," she said – "it was new to us, we didn"t have money before.") Lena had got the job and here she was.

"But you're a real professional, Lena!" I said – "Yeah, they train us, they even sent me to the Kansas City Ramada to work – all those cream cakes I'd never seen before – I was a skinny little thing when I went there, look at me now! I did everything, marketing, front of house, chef, washer-up, reservations, reception, chambermaid, waiting, concierge – everything. You can't manage staff until you can do their jobs yourself, can you?"

"Wilderness Safaris and the Conservancies change people's lives, you know"

I'm in Namibia and this was a typical conversation, not just at the award-winning Damaraland Camp on the country's first conservancy – Torra. The country is riding high on the success of the unique conservancy programme which allows local communities to take charge of their local wildlife and manage them to their advantage. The programme delivers financial benefits, a sense of ownership and pride to the communities; a burgeoning wildlife population to the country, the tourists and the environment; and major commercial opportunities to SMEs like Wilderness Safaris. Plus, of course, it's a successful formula for the knotty mix of tourism and conservation that is an exportable, transferable commodity.

I wasn't surprised next early morning to be shown round the conservancy by one of the brightest, youngest and most accomplished wildlife guides I've ever met. Raymond explained that he was training an assistant, Anthony – and they both managed to give me a morning to remember. We tracked desert elephants and found them again and again – added to a vast variety of other wildlife that the pair knowledgeably identified in the remarkable terrain.

Later, in Windhoek, I talked to Rob Moffat of Wilderness, a passionate advocate of both Namibia and the conservancy system. "It really works, you know," he said, "we plough back everything we can and we get total commitment. At the end of the day it boils down to ownership and involvement"

So far Namibia is a real success story. The conservancy system is working so well that, spurred on by the Ministry of Environment and Tourism the rich US Millennium Challenge Corporation is in the process of investing over $300m in the country including a hefty $60m in tourism – in particular the sensational Etosha National Park.

And for some very good reasons…

Namibia was the first African country to incorporate protection of the environment into its constitution. The Government of Namibia has reinforced this by giving its communities the opportunity and rights to manage their wildlife through communal conservancies. In existence for over 20 years, the Community-Based Natural Resources Management (CBNRM) Programme is a successful multi-faceted approach to rural development and conservation.

Covering a massive 16% of the country over 130,000 square kilometers of prime wildlife habitat, the conservancy movement has grown dramatically over the past decade with 59 communities (with over 230,000 members) already registered and a further 30 were in the pipeline when I was there.

Economic benefits to communities have increased tangibly since the start of the CBNRM programme, from less than N$600,000 in 1998 to N$41.9 million (US$5.7 million) in 2008. Most of this growth has come from tourism. As tourism to the normal destinations in Namibia has grown, there has been a parallel growth in the level of interest demonstrated by tour operators, lodge investors and independent tourists in the remote wildlands of Namibia, much of which are now covered by communal conservancies.

Many of these conservancies contain spectacular scenery, rich cultures and burgeoning wildlife populations including elephant, rhino and lion, all of which make them highly attractive to the tourism sector.

Within the Communal Conservancy Tourism Sector, there are now 29 formal joint-venture lodges and campsites (like the relationship between Torra and Wilderness Safaris) that work in collaboration with the host communities to achieve both conservation and development objectives at the local level. And, when I was there, therewere another 15 on the way. Then joint ventures conservancies represented 856 beds, 789 full-time jobs and over 250 seasonal positions. More than N$145 million (US$19 million) has been invested in tourism in communal conservancies in this way by the private sector since 1998.

In this way, tourism contributes direct cash payments to conservancies, salaries for employees, staff training, and related benefits such as payments of cash and in-kind contributions (equipment, donated services, etc.) to village development committees, local schools, etc. These are new or additional activities which give many households access to cash and other benefits that they never had before, and that would not have been possible prior to this innovative conservancy legislation in 1996. This has directly translated into conservation benefits with poaching being almost totally eliminated, communities setting aside land for exclusive use of wildlife and resulting in expanding populations of all wildlife even including animals such as elephant, lion and black rhino.

And there are many less tangible social benefits like greater confidence and empowerment, on-the-job training, travel opportunities, improved governance, accountability and transparency. Namibia's got some of the most sensational scenery and wildife in the world, and it's being turned to real community advantage by a potent cocktail of enabling legislation, private sector involvement, and massive, educated, donor funding and technical assistance.

The proof of the pudding? A dramatically enhanced wildlife count, strong and stewarded cultural values, a prosperous and growing tourism economy, satisfied visitors, a profitable private sector but most importantly enthusiastic, educated and committed people like Lena, Raymond and Anthony – the necessary seed corn for a truly sustainable tourism industry.

Back to the UK and I was straight off on the Silk Road again. By now I had found out much more about the project. As I understood it the idea had come from UNESCO (the UN organisation that looks after culture and heritage sites) and UNDP (the UN organisation that looks after human and economic development). Their brainwave was to reinvent the historic silk road as a massive modern-day tourist route – or a series of routes all the way from the far east to the far west.

This had opportunities from everybody's point of view. There were massive development opportunities and an extraordinary cultural and environmental heritage from the Great Wall of China through Samarkand and dozens of amazing cities all the way through undiscovered places to Greece, Italy and the west.

No wonder all the involved (and less involved) countries joined when the UN World Tourism Organization took the reins. When I got involved there were 27 member countries – including almost all the 'Stans' of central Asia.

So, during the winter after my Kazakhstan experience, I helped promote and moderate Silk Road events in Europe and as a result I was asked to come and report on a country right in the heart of the action.

With half a dozen other international journalists and communicators, I was off to Tajikistan.

Now Tajikistan has a bit of a spotty reputation. While it was a Soviet state, it was known to 'own' large blocks of business in Moscow and provided millions of unskilled labourours in mother Russia. Even then it was the most remittance-dependent country in the world with almost half of its income coming from remittances from Tajiks working abroad. It was also said to own much of the east-west drug trade. Geographically there was trouble too. The country is very mountainous, very easy to get lost in and is positioned between Afghanistan, China, Uzbekistan and Kyrgystan. Uncharted territory then, great for bandits, smugglers, brigands and all sorts of ne'er-do-wells.

The plan was that we would fly to the capital, Dushanbe, stay for the night, have a tour round, meet local VIPs and then we were to be hosted by the AKDN (The Aga Khan Development Network) who would fly us through the Pamir Mountain Range to Khorog, beside the rickety bridge to Afghanistan. We were to get a briefing there, stay a couple of nights and then fly back to Dushanbe and thence home.

The first day or two were fascinating. We stayed in the president's dacha (all chandeliers, gold plate and mirrors) we had a nice walk around town met the new, young minister of tourism and got him to take us to a night club (very revealing). Plus I got to buy kilos of fabulous dried fruits and nuts both preserved in honey and loose.

Unfortunately the day we were to fly to Khorog, the weather intervened. There were storms in the mountains. There was nothing for it but to drive. Obviously there are no motorways in Tajikistan so instead of a comfortable one-hour helicopter flight in the Aga Khan's helicopter we were faced with a minimum two-day drive in bad weather on unmade bumpy roads. Fascinating!

I piled into one 4WD vehicle with a couple of other journalists. A nice young lady from Sweden and a cool Canadian gent. Our driver spoke absolutely no English. And off we bumped through the mountains up and up and up for miles, hours and hours and hours until we arrived at a makeshift spa – a hot plunge pool set in snow some 4,000 metres high.

Only two of the blokes were willing to have a go. Naturally stupid me and another crazy Brit. It was easy enough to get my kit off and get into the tiny mountaintop pool, but getting out and getting dressed was another issue. Firstly, we'd forgotten we needed towels when we jumped in and secondly had not taken into consideration either the bad weather (a snowstorm) or the height and the lack of oxygen. Anyway, eventually we got out and away – looking forward to a good meal, a blazing fire and a warm bed.

As dusk fell, we bumped up to our hostelry for the night.

We were a group of soft middle-aged journalists not a bunch of young fit backpackers. There was food of course and naturally vodka but bedrooms? Ladies only (well one lady had a bedroom) the rest of us had to sleep on the floor. At least it was warm. And the toilets and bathrooms? Well there was a big piece of land outside with a water tap. Great. At least Yuri our Russian journalist was happy as he plodded outside with his spade over his shoulder "Just like home," he said!

The next day we arrived at Khorog and a real Indian hotel. Big Indian family, big hotel, Indian restaurant, cleaning service, shop – the lot. I used the cleaning service for my linen suit. They washed it, It came back clean but tiny!

Khorug is a totally fascinating place. Its position has been key to its importance ever since the Russia v Britain 'Great Game' took place all around it. Right beside the Panj river, right on the bridge to the Wakhan Corridor – it is a major crossroads even now.

Apart from everything else (including a bit of armed dissent occasionally!) Khorog hosts the weekly Afghan market (traders just pop over the bridge) and the extraordinary 'Roof of the World' music and culture festival.

Naturally, the really, really, young enthusiastic Yale-educated bright AKDN American kids bussed us over to meet Afghan travel agents who were equally determined, intelligent and interesting. Then we explored a tiny bit of the Wakhan and met some adventure tourists (British, naturally). There were thousands of them all over Afghanistan including a group of Italian lady skiers (aptly named "The Lipstick Blondes"). It's a strange world. But by then the Taliban had blown up and destroyed Afghanistan's hitherto amazing tourism draw, the massive Buddhas of Bamiyan.

The next day, on our bumpy way back to Dushanbe, I was in a flyblown Central Asian mountainside café, looking at the beehives on the incline opposite and listening to the furious roar of the ice-fed river swirling and gushing outside.

Neatly lined up on the café's glass shelves were thin plastic second-hand 2-litre water bottles full of an amber liquid and on sale for 50 Somoni ($11) a go. What's in the bottles? Honey apparently. Each bent and buckled bottle holds 2kg of honey from those bees opposite. Pure authentic honey 100% sustainably sourced, packaged and delivered.

That's the thing about Tajikistan: In this poorest of the ex-Soviet republics, sustainability was not a mantra of the middle classes – it's an imperative.

The journey to our stop in the café had involved a full-day drive along a dangerous track perched high on the Tajik side of the sensational Panj river gorge (the border between the Tajik part of Badakhshan and the Afghan bit). All day we'd bumped along uncomfortably in our 4WD, negotiating the occasional landslide and frequent water fords collecting bruises, but also grabbing memories of fabulous soaring sights, and gut-wrenching views of the people on both sides living truly gruelling spartan lives.

After such tough days, you feel you truly deserve a comfortable, not to say luxurious, night. This is very rarely to be had in Tajikistan. That is not to say that good accommodation doesn't exist, it simply depends on your interpretation of the term 'good'.

That night we had a bed each at least, a bunk bed but it was a bed. And we needed it!

The sad fact, or, perhaps the great opportunity, is that tourism infrastructure in the Pamirs and Badakhshan, in truth, doesn't yet exist.

The AKDN had earmarked tourism as a cross-border development opportunity and is was working to create methods for Tajik and Afghan SMEs in the area to take advantage of it but there is a very long way to go indeed.

A very big prize is on offer. The AKDN's chosen venue, the Wakhan Corridor, originally created by the British as a buffer between its Indian (now Pakistan) interests and China, is a stunningly beautiful wilderness. On the one side of the river, Afghanistan and on the other, Tajikistan – divided in 1925, kept separate and patrolled vigorously, latterly by the KGB, until 2006. The AKDN sees the potential in this area for tourism, economic development and, perhaps, harmony and a bit of peace!

Anyway, after a good Russian breakfast (without the vodka for me) we were on our bumpy way spurred on by the fact of a bad weather forecast in the mountains.

The further up we went, the colder and snowier it got – and we had a long way to go. Given the weather we'd been told that it was every 4WD vehicle for itself and in any case, it was dangerous to go in convoy.

Our vehicle's company comprised our non-speaking Tajik driver, a cool Canadian journalist who'd been everywhere, a smart young Swedish lady and me. Obviously a Tajik, a Swede, a Canadian and a Brit in a car on a mountain are the ingredients for a joke. But we didn't think it was a joke when our driver threw us out at the summit of the mountain and chucked out our luggage. The Swede screamed, I wondered what to do and the Canadian relieved himself as the vehicle disappeared at midnight around the corner of the snowy mountain.

What next, I thought? Another vehicle, obviously – phew. Yet another 4WD eventually arrived, driven by yet another taciturn driver. Off we went over the snow around the bends in the early hours of the dark morning!

Where are we? We have no idea. Are we hostages? Who knows? And on and on we go, sliding around hairpin bends until finally at around 3am we stop in amongst loads of other cars and people. There are tents, there are lorries there is smoke and the hubble and bubble of crowds. Beards, scarves, smells – it could be a scene from Arabian Nights.

Our driver (swarthy, unshaven) gets out, it looks like bargaining is going on. Is he selling us? Is this a big heroin market? After all Tajikistan is right in the middle of the heroin trade route.

As if to confirm our suspicions the driver returns with something concealed wrapped in newspaper. He offers it to us.

It's rhubarb. With relief I take a stick, to show my knowledge of the vegetable, forgetting how it's grown I stick it in my mouth and take a bite with relish! Yuk it's shit. I mean real shit, it's grown in it! Off we go back to Dushanbe for what's left of the night at the president's dacha and then home.

Until I got the next call from Alla, my Russian Silk Road friend at the UNWTO. "Darleeng would you like to come to Shiraz – it is wonderful!" "We are having a Silk Road Mayors' meeting and you can help". Before you could say Magic Carpet I was on my way.

My arrival in Iran was not very auspicious. Getting off the plane I got on the wrong bus. Well it was late at night and I hadn't thought of myself as a VIP so I got onto the ordinary bus, wondered where the rest of the group had got to and made my own way through immigration. Not good. I got a four-hour grilling, had my fingerprints taken with wet ink and was told off heartily because of being British. Finally, I was let go and got a strange taxi to my hotel – luckily I knew its name. All the way from the airport through the city full of tents in parks and stark buildings – poverty and housing crisis I thought.

Eventually I got to the hotel, an ex-Sheraton. Four-star yuk, but the room was OK except the internet was full of forbidden pages. Even my emails wouldn't open. One in particular was financial news – 'Naked Shorts' was the headline which obviously confused the Iranian censors!

Next day dawned gorgeous and I awoke in a new dimension. To start the day my breakfast was an incredibly beautiful one – delicious fresh fruit juices from pomegranate to persimmon; sublime pastries; sensational yoghurts, exceptional eggs – heaven on a plate. Sitting beside me at the feast was the young Minister of Tourism from Tajikistan. "These women are soooo beautiful" he said. And he was right, the headscarves all the ladies were wearing simply added a demure grace to a sort of sophistication that has been removed from today's in-your-face fashion.

My walk after breakfast took me to the tent cities in Shiraz's parks where I realized that rather than alternative housing this was extra special sunshade for local people who liked to picnic in the park in the evening. And who wouldn't, given the local food and wine and the need to party! Everybody wanted to talk to me "Why do you say such nasty things about us?" They asked.

The mayor's forum was interesting but rather formal – nothing ever started until the local Mullah had arrived, been embraced by a few people and taken his seat.

It was made much more interesting by my participation! Our UNWTO top speaker had failed to arrive so I had agreed to give a talk on tourism marketing.

Thinking that flattery would get me everywhere, I waxed lyrical about everything I knew about Shiraz and how wonderful it was. My presentation went down very well, naturally. The rest of the day proved to me that my flattery was, rather, understatement.

The first result was a request from the regional deputy that I give a little marketing class to local tourism bosses. Within an hour I had a dozen big blokes ranged in front of me waiting for pearls of western wisdom. Somewhat fearful that they may either eat me or rough me up, I started with a question – "How many of you read and recite poetry every day?" Every hand went up! How could a poetry-loving group be nasty to me? Or anyone?

Tonight was my night of poetry. After another sensational meal, I was in the rose garden tomb of Hafez, Shiraz's 14th-century lyrical romantic poet. The scene was rose-scented grace and I was lucky to be with a bunch of friends well-disposed to revel in the unique atmosphere. To bed with sweet-scented dreams.

And the next day was divine. The musical perfume of poetry was everywhere. All of my professional friends from all over the world dressed in keeping and enjoyed it. Russian, Japanese, Iranian, Chinese, German – they all looked a little more sophisticated and glamorous for their headscarves. And a bunch of colourful blokes – mainly Central Asian mayors with wild Silk Road ideas – took the podium. It proved to me once again that a big idea gets blokes going!

And the thing I found fascinating was the wild ideas below the surface of each of the demure ladies I met, particularly those from Iran. If one day they are freed from imposed constraints the world had better look out.

Yes of course we saw the astonishing world heritage site of Persepolis but Shiraz, with its superb food, scented gardens, poetry and serene wild ladies was a true insight.

From the sublime to the sublime, my next gig was to be in Budapest. The European Union presidency rotates every six months to another EU state. For six months this year it was Hungary's turn and their president had decided to have a EU symposium on sustainable tourism as his special event to celebrate his presidency. Dozens of people were invited to present in the subject – including me. It was amazing – everybody I knew was part of the symposium. And lots of people I didn't.

The presidency paid for our flights, our stays in top Budapest hotels – and some great dinners. I got to see belly dancing, eat goulash, take a dip in the famous Gellert art deco thermal spa – hang about with my mates and meet the team from UNEP – which was a big deal.

Why so big? Because the UN Environment Programme is at the heart of everything I do. It was UNEP under Maurice Strong – Geoffrey Lipman's sage – that organised and ran the Earth Summit in Rio 1992. And it has been central to the progress of sustainable tourism ever since. And it organised a later Earth Summit (Rio+20 – in other words 1992 +20).

Back to the Silk Road! A few months later, I was to run the World Tourism Conference in Borneo for UNWTO and then I'd fly to Uzbekistan to give some Silk Road presentations in Samarkand, have a look at Bukhara and Khiva and a lot of other Ghengis Khan and Tamerlane stuff and then fly home, writing all the way.

Great stuff – fascinating places. Borneo was a delight. The conference – all about sharing tourism success stories – was held in a posh hotel in Kota Kinabalu. But I had the idea that Borneo was an uncivilized wilderness and I was disappointed in that.

And then off to Samarkand, Tamerlane's home town. I was excited to go to the heart of Central Asia. I was not disappointed.

Night one in Tashkent. Wow? Not really, boring is a better description. Unfortunately, much of the city was destroyed by an earthquake and now it's mainly functional communist-style architecture and style.

But Samarkand was amazing. Truly, truly amazing. There are two big tourist hits in Samarkand. The Registan, where we were lucky to be holding our Silk Road conference, is truly beautiful. The only way I can describe it is as a glorious city square started in the 15th century and still pristine today. The white buildings are magnificent, better than the Taj Mahal because they seem to be still in use and relevant. OK they have been tarted up recently since the soviet era but they are rightfully at the top of UNESCO's world heritage list.

The other big hit in Samarkand is Tamerlane's mausoleum. Gur i Amir is one of the models for later mausoleums including the Taj Mahal. When Tamerlane's descendents swept south taking their wealth and power to create Moghul India they took with them their rich artistic icons which became the lush, sensual emblems of north India.

Back at the conference, the idea was to create a Silk Road action plan. Of course, in principle it's a totally brilliant idea. The Silk Road runs right through a massive swathe of world history with an art, architecture and cultural treasure to match. Connecting the far east to the far west, it is as much a route of the future as a route of the past, it is chock-full of myriads of exceptional tourism opportunities. And that is the problem – there is simply too much.

In the beginning the project was quite simple. It was impossible to travel the Silk Road because there were too many countries who all needed individual visas.

So an original idea was to create one tourist visa that allowed the bearer to go through all the Silk Road countries. It's not happened yet. Another idea was to brand the Silk Road to enable joint marketing campaigns where lots of countries put in money and expertise and got benefits. Yet another idea was a Silk Road airline, yet another a Silk Road hotel group, yet another a Silk Road City badge. There are loads of ideas and there are loads of entrepreneurs, marketing people and city fathers toting them about. Even Mark Advent, the Las Vegas bloke with the idea of the city of Oz based it on the Silk Road and set it amongst its marketing plans.

But there were more – all-seeing opportunities in the heady mix of two UN organisations (UNWTO and UNESCO plus maybe UNEP), ministerial politics, big ideas, NGOs, and the scent of power, global respectability and money.

But with a bunch of 33 country-members as disparate as China and San Marino and with hundreds of mayors of Silk Road cities as disparate as Macclesfield and Kabul (where another mayors forum was to be held) it is difficult to formulate a cohesive marketing strategy.

Of course, sustainable tourism and fair trade and tourism for development and cultural assets are talked about at length but how to get anything happening in practice is elusive.

However, talking is good as is the employment of consultants to create yet another series of colour brochures. And, maybe something good will eventually coalesce.

Then we had a great dinner in Bukhara where our senior journalist after a few drinks suggested that we'd behave ourselves if we weren't thrown into their pit. The reference to the Victorian emissary of Queen Victoria who was kept in the notorious bug pit having a daily shower of rats and scorpions and tortured for four years before he had his head chopped off – didn't go down too well with our local hosts.

Next stop Japan – another Silk Road country. This was just one year after the tsunami and I'd been invited to Sendai which bore the brunt of the disaster to see how they had got on with reconstruction. I was to combine this with a visit to Tokyo where the Tourism for Tomorrow awards were to be unveiled.

Tourism is important in Tohoku, the northeastern enclave of Honshu Island. Originally one of the poorest parts of Japan, the area's fabulous apple harvest and iron ore have provided great cash crops while latterly its breathtaking display of cherry blossom, its rugged mountain countryside and its thermal baths and astonishingly good food and hospitality have proved powerful local tourist draws.

A deep love for the natural world and an appreciation of good food are characteristics of Japanese life and nowhere more so than in Tohoku, where each season represents an opportunity for a massive party (with, of course huge feasts!). And the biggest party of all starts the year with a swing – cherry blossom time brings literally millions of aficionados to the best and most bounteous glorious white displays. Vast audiences watch the "Cherry Blossom Front" on national TV moving north through Japan until it reaches its most natural showcase – Tohoku.

The Sakura (Cherry Blossom) Festivals are curtain-openers for further festivals, later in the year there are great warm summer festivals, which in turn give way to wild autumn harvest festivals and, finally a startling winter wonderland exposes Tohoku in a glittering garb of icy jewels celebrated by snow lantern festivals.

So, on the morning of March 11 2009 people all over Tuhoku were looking forward to welcoming the cherry blossom and planning to host the annual spring pilgrimage of millions of visitors at the start of the festive year when doors would open to tourists and the cash tills would ring to bring economic benefits to Tohoku businesses and local communities.

In Hirosaki the castle park with 2600 cherry trees was cleaning and painting ready to welcome its annual over 2 million visitors while the display of magnificent floats was being tidied up.

At the charming Akita Nairiku local railway carriages were being polished, stops cleaned, whistles buffed.

At Lake Tazawa the lake's gilded maiden statue checked, shops prepared for business and the Komagatake Kanko Hot Spa Hotel was going through its hospitality training.

The Samurai village of Kakunodate was preparing its unique houses, museums and craft centres ready for business.

The enormous agricultural enterprise at Koiwai Farm was preparing its grounds, cafés, restaurants and ice cream parlour for hungry guests and the fabulous World Heritage Zen Monastery of Chusonji Temple was making sure that all paths were clean and bells shiny.

By the sea at the bay of Matsushima boats were being prepared for pleasure cruises around the picturesque islands, the local Samurai house readied for tea festivals and the fabulous Entsuin Buddhist temple readied for visitors.

At the castle city regional HQ of Sendai, the final touches were being put to the year's tourism action-plan.

By the afternoon all plans were swept away – one of the strongest earthquakes on record (level 9) hit the Tohoku Region, triggering up to 40-metre-high tsunami waves that caused massive destruction and loss of human lives in areas along the Pacific coast. TV news around the world showed heart-breaking scenes of homes, cars and humans tossed around as if they were puppets on massive, powerful walls of water.

I was watching the television at the time. It was appalling.

After the disaster the locals set to clearing up the chaos in their own inimitable understated way. The 15,854 dead were buried, the 26,992 injured were treated, the 3,155 missing were searched for, the million damaged and destroyed buildings begun to be rebuilt.

International tourism had taken a real beating in 2011 – Sendai city staff said that even though it was not official, the statistics showed that in 2010, there were 90,000 nights in which foreign visitors stayed in Sendai, but 2011 saw only 9,000 nights.

By the time I got there a year later, tourism was set to begin again in Tohoku, the quality of food, accommodation and welcome undiminished.

The cherry blossom was again in full bloom and tourists were ready to be welcomed to this tear-jerkingly beautiful area with such an unbelievable wealth of natural and cultural heritage, good things to do and see and mouth-wateringly good food and drink.

Above all that year's crop of tourists were to receive a heartfelt welcome from a people to whom hospitality is a way of life.

I travelled all over Japan, received gentle, perfect hospitality everywhere from public baths to grand restaurants and hotels. Even in earlier disaster cities Nagasaki and Hiroshima, the quality of welcome was undiminished. In Japan, I realised that hospitality is a true art form, always rendered immaculately.

Actually, Japan astonished me in many ways. Primarily I was constantly amazed by the thoughtfulness, respect and even tenderness that the Japanese gave to everything around them – their homes, their clothes, their food and drink, their bodies, their environment – simply everything. I didn't see one single bit of litter, I didn't see a tree or a plant or a flower that wasn't properly tenderly looked after, I didn't see a dawn or a sunset that wasn't adored. And as I was there at cherry blossom time, I couldn't miss the crowds and the festivals set up to revere this beautiful nationwide natural phenomenon.

The fact is that the Japanese are simply natural ecologists. I was in awe.

Back in Tokyo, I had put my time into interviewing contenders for the tourism awards – I'd done video interviews, specific stories outlining why one destination would win.

My money was on Destination Roros and I'd got quite friendly with their team so I was over the moon when they actually won!

The reason I backed Roros so heavily? Because it is a whole town in the north of Norway totally committed to hospitality. And it's a very new thing because a little while ago Roros was a copper town, totally 100% committed to the production of copper. Now its focus is tourism and it is 100% committed to delivering a sustainable tourism experience to its visitors. From exceptionally good accommodation and extraordinarily good food use is made of local materials and produce. Local people are trained as guides and providers of local experiences from husky mushing to rambles in the lovely countryside. Tourism is totally rooted in a sense of a very particular place. You could say from brown field site to green tourism success. Plus I'd used the destination as a case study in one of my sustainable tourism reports.

It was time to leave Norway in Japan but not without a thought for the World Travel and Tourism Council – the WTTC, who had organised the massive tourism summit.

You could say that while the UN World Tourism Organisation delivers the politics of tourism the WTTC delivers the business end of the industry.

The WTTC started as a kind of big round table – of the 100 most powerful people in the industry – the CEOs of the biggest 100 travel and tourism companies. As it happened the first Executive Director of the organisation was a certain Geoffrey Lipman – remember my trip to Johannesburg in 1995? While he was the boss of WTTC, Geoffrey had found time to start Green Globe, which should have been earthshaking – well, we all believed in the dynamism and power of sustainability in those days!

Green Globe was simply everywhere, providing sustainability certifications for travel companies, hotels, resorts – even whole countries, for a fee of course – economic sustainability is part of the plan. But, unfortunately that part of the plan didn't work out. Green Globe got fragmented although it's still alive. Geoffrey moved on – to UNWTO as it happens and eventually, we became friends.

There is nobody who has done more to promote commercially sustainable sustainable tourism than Geoffrey. And maybe he is the reason that the Tourism for Tomorrow awards have landed up under the umbrella of WTTC. But unfortunately, a global organization effectively representing the developed world's big companies' interests are possibly not the best people to share the proceeds with destinations who are less well-heeled and less powerful.

Unfortunately, in the last 50 years or so tourism has been used less to develop the countries who host the visitors and more to develop the balance sheets of the companies who profit from the activity without investment in infrastructure. The dramatic growth of Wall Street's Booking.com and Airbnb are testimony to this unbalance.

Another Silk Road destination called – this time a conference 'Flavours of the Silk Road' in Azerbaijan – how could I refuse?

Off to Baku – "you'll love it" said Alla.

Maybe I'd forgotten that the Eurovision Song Contest was held here. If so, I knew zero about Azerbaijan.

This kingdom – I can't think of a better word for a kind of family dictatorship – is full of more facts that I didn't know, like Baku (its capital) is set on a tectonic lake, the Caspian Sea, the biggest enclosed expanse of water in the world; the country is full of oil, in fact enough to fuel the whole of the first world war with some to spare, It has some of the longest-lived people in the world, the food and wine are both exceptionally good and the tea is phenomenal.

Azerbaijan has pretty much everything a country could want including a massive harvest of fruit and veg and wine, bags of culinary understanding and cultural heritage, a lovely sea in which the world's most valuable fish – sturgeons with caviar swim PLUS the world's first major oil economy that stretches back to the 19th century.

And its history is fascinating, Zoroastrians travelled to Azerbaijan somewhere in the first millennium BC and created their fire temples all over the area. Even after Soviet depredations – you can still see some temples with flames fuelled by gas now, rather than natural gas straight from below.

And Azerbaijan was so taken with the religion that the major Zoroastrian Persian festival – Nowruz – is still celebrated as the Azeri National Day. Azerbaijan actually means "Protector of Fire"

Plus, the country sits astride the Silk Road with travellers bringing ideas and cultures to this intriguing land, Azerbaijan is also famous for its exquisite hand-woven carpets. Here, too, carpets are a lifestyle, lifelong issue – the Azeris say you are born on a carpet, you receive your guests on a carpet and you are buried in one too.

Although there is evidence of oil being used as far back as the 3rd century – it really came into its own in the latter stages of the industrial revolution.

By the beginning of the 20th century, Azerbaijan produced more than half of the world's oil.

The massive amounts of easily accessible oil and the ready markets of countries gearing up for industrial capacity and the Great War – made dozens of Baku billionaire oil barons and a really wealthy, architecturally stunning capital city of Baku.

Interestingly, three of the first prospectors to get rich were Alfred, Ludvig and Robert Nobel who used the wealth created to begin their munitions business – the funding source of the global prize.

And even now Baku looks like a billionnaire's dream. Flashy illuminated high-rise buildings, harbour full of gin-palace yachts, expensive night clubs flowing with champagne and escorts, top restaurants and hotels, glamourous shopping malls and probably the richest-looking car parks in the world.

Coming hot on the heels of the Eurovision Song Contest, the Flavours of the Silk Road was a classy event. Top chefs from France and Spain, Turkey and Italy came to show off their skills and demonstrate the opportunities for Silk Road gastronomy. And, of course there were conferences and presentations and gala dinners. Naturally a report on gastronomy and tourism was created and there was a closing declaration for world posterity.

After the food event, we ventured off into the countryside for a little less sophisticated entertainment. We went to see the old folk. to a village full of centenarians, we stopped in a village hostelry and were confronted with a massive heaving table. It was laden with dozens of dishes including perfectly cooked local lamb created in a number of ways barbequed, roast, with dried fruits. And with pomegranate sauce; Caspian salmon; a massive platter of the Azerbaijani version of the Silk Road staple – saffron-scented Plov; delicious chicken kebabs and beef shashliks; a variety of different prime vegetables and peppers and spicy condiments including saffron and sumac.

Naturally local fruits and nuts and dates and figs, local wines and cherry and raspberry juices completed the spread.

After this feast, there was an opportunity for a well-deserved rest at a riverbank teahouse in a glade of pomegranate trees. For refreshment we enjoyed local black tea with a range of local jams and sweet delicacies.

Then we went to the village famous for its centenarians. The happiness of the old people and their hospitality was touching. More good food – home made butter and bread, yoghurt and cheese. Clearly the secret of longevity is not being abstemious!

Back in Baku – the rich capital of the country beside the Caspian Sea wealth is palpable. The old walled city is beautifully kept – not a bit of litter anywhere, but outside in Baku's 19th, 20th and 21st century boulevards the throbbing heart of a wealthy modern metropolis beats to the tune of hordes of top of the range SUVs.

The skyline and the corniche is astounding, modern architecture at its blatant best – buildings with night-time light shows, staggering skyscrapers and towers – all the way to the seaport and the spectacular 12,000-seat Crystal Hall created in just eight months for the Eurovision Song Contest.

As far as tourism is concerned, the country has set its sights on being just like Dubai and already there are over 3,500 five star rooms with all the top hotel brands in Baku and building has started on the local version of the Palm – the $100billion Caspian Khazar islands development was set to provide residences for a million people, even a Formula 1 racetrack and the highest tower in the world until the oil price crashed and the project stalled.

But Azerbaijan has one trump card – its gloriously fertile land. Here you can experience 9 of the world's 11 climates – producing a fabulous harvest of food and wine and oil. And it's already set to produce much more, its oil production is still increasing and its economy is again on a recovery track.

But does Azerbajan really need tourism?

A clue to the answer is perhaps Baku's International Jazz Festival. It's a little-known fact that Azeris are absolutely 'sent' by jazz – they have been big aficionados since the 1920s with, even, their own style (a blend of Jazz and Azeri music). Even when jazz went underground in the Soviet era, Azeris supported it.

But for great jazz, you need a great party, and for a great party you need great guests – could this be the real reason for Azerbaijan's tourism drive?

Azerbajan was a real revelation but then I was off to a destination that completely blew my mind – where the Silk Road merged with the Tea Road.

Together with a bunch of Chinese, we were to attend a conference where I was to present a marketing case for a joint promotion, right in the cold heart of Siberia just by Lake Baikal.

Ever heard of Kyakhta? Buryatia ? No? Me neither!

Buryatia is a country just a bit bigger than Germany with a population of less than a million – in itself that indicates quite a lot of space and masses of wonderful peace and quiet and mountains – 60% of the country is mountainous.

Not content with these extreme statistics – the country also has some 60% of the shore of Lake Baikal. Formed at least 25 million years ago, it is the world''s deepest, clearest and oldest lake – yet another tectonic lake – like the Caspian Sea and Lake Ohrid.

But maybe you guessed where the Republic of Buryatia is. Right slap bang in the middle of Siberia between Russia and China.

Whatever my preconceptions I saw that the country is lovely. Its friendly people are unbelievably warm and hospitable and very keen to share with us their country's unique heritage and peerless beauty. After years of repression, a quartet of religions – Tibetan Buddhism, Russian Orthodox Christianity, Shamanism plus a group of "Old Believers" – are brushing up their places of worship. Their tolerance and integration with each other was never in doubt – hence, maybe such nice hospitable people!

As Russia's centre of Buddhism, the country has always been a major pilgrimage destination – the temples are now beautiful and very well-kept. This steady flow of pilgrims for learning and reverence has been dramatically increased recently: the local Buddhist Dashi Dorzho's body, buried since 1927, was exhumed in 2002. His body still shows no signs of decay. The body, which scientists say may even be in hibernation, is now on show to pilgrims, who arrive in reverential groups.

The Old Believers existed before the modern Russian Orthodox church and were effectively hounded out of Russia in the 17th century – to Siberia naturally. In Russia they were tortured and had to pay double taxation (plus an extra beard tax).

Now it looks like they are making a comeback in exile. An Old Believer Village had set up an extremely successful community tourism initiative and welcomes guests each day – displaying an authentic picture of Russia in the 17th century. Before they were expelled.

And the Buryats are not only Siberia's largest ethnic population but many still practise their own 'Old Religion' Siberian Shamanism. Of course, many converted to Buddhism but a large minority still practise their traditional female-generated beliefs, full of music, art and culture and respect for their Earth.

But, of course the most important cultural and natural asset Buryatia has is Lake Baikal.

Rightly revered throughout the country, the lake is quite astonishing. The water is cold, clear and clean – there are not many lakes in the world where you would draw water and drink with impunity!

Unbelievably, the lake has at least 25% of the world"s fresh water. It is the deepest lake in the world (1.7km) and hosts some 1,700 varieties of plant and animals – 70% of whom can be found nowhere else in the world – including the Baikal seal, a variety of salmon called Omul and the Baikal sturgeon – all swimming in the crystal-clear water.

No wonder a great deal of delicious fish is consumed in barbeques around the lake!

There are a few tourist villages around the lake full of weekend dachas for residents of Ulan Ude, Buryatia's capital; but apart from that there was little tourism development in this pristine area – thus far.

The most exciting tourism opportunity that has recently emerged is the fascinating, rich and historic city of Kyakhta. Given that Russia is known as one of the greatest tea-drinking connoisseur countries in the world (where would a Russian story be without at least one samovar?) it is another astonishing Buryatia fact that almost all tea consumed in Russia was transported through and traded in Kyakhta – which, given the massive profits that tea offered, must have been the extraordinarily wealthy gold-rush city of the 17th century.

Maybe it will be again. Both Russia and China had taken an interest in the area and are providing funds to renovate the city and develop the "Great Tea Road". Our conference hosted speakers from China,

Mongolia and Russia plus people like me to develop a Tea Trail.

Given the fact that the Trans-Siberian express already traverses Lake Baikal; that the Chinese have now committed to a Silk Road including high-speed trains all the way to Germany; that the global top tourism market of Beijing is less than 1,000 miles away and Tokyo less than 2,000; that Buryatia offers a quality of pristine environment rarely nowadays found; that the eyes and ears of world tourism are now showing a real interest...

You can be sure that the Great Tea Road will soon be hosting flocks of tourists drinking tea, visiting historical Kyakhta, taking saunas and splashing in Baikal discovering that it's just their cup of reviving, invigorating aromatic tourism experience tea!

Anyway, I was amazed, and the tea is delicious.

Much more delicious than the teabag tea we drank as we travelled Upper Class Virgin Rail from London to Macclesfield. The final leg on this particular Silk Road experience.

We were going to the UK terminus of the Silk Road. Just outside Manchester, Macclesfield is a commuter haven now. But two hundred years ago Macclesfield meant silk. Even now the city hosts a silk museum and their football team is called "The Silk Men". The reason we are here is as part of a UN delegation to ask the local authorities to join the Silk Road Initiative and complete a route all the way from China to the north of England. Job done and my Silk Road experience over for a while.

CHAPTER 9

My Italian Adventure
Romagna Mia and more strange songs

It all had seemed harmless enough to start with. We two old geezers, Angelo and I, had known each other well for more than half a century by now. We'd both been in the travel business for all of that time. I'd blagged a trip for us to Emilia Romagna on the basis that we'd write an article on the destination's green credentials.

As it happened, we were eminently well qualified for the task. We both knew the travel industry like the backs of our hands; I'd been writing about tourism sustainability for more than 20 years and Angelo was still a travel industry politician. Although he was a bit biased towards the Veneto (he was a Venetian, after all!) we both loved and knew Italy from top to bottom and side to side, having worked there and travelled around together and apart for nearly half a century.

And Emilia Romagna wasn't just picked out from a hat. With its well-earned reputation for incredible local food and drink, its community-based offbeat left-wing politics and its reverence for regional culture and history – I felt it was set to be a real star in the green tourism world.

Anyway, Angelo had been banging on at me about the delights of green bike-city Ferrara, and I had been desperate to see the extraordinary mosaics in Ravenna for at least forty years. We'd both been to Bologna – the region's capital – many times and we knew just what an impossibility finding a bad meal was in this red city. So, if the rest of the region was up to the same mark, we would be in for a real feast.

Angelo was detailed to negotiate details with his friends at the Italian tourist board and before you could say Parmesan, Parma Ham or Balsamic Vinegar we were off to the home of all these and much more.

In Bologna we stayed in a 'Right-on' B&B – actually a big apartment in an enormous palace, with 4 letting rooms run by a youthful crowd of home-knitted organic-eating students.

As soon as we pressed the apartment's bell and entered the massive doors into the old stone courtyard, we got the picture. We checked into a quirky green apartment in a Bologna palace – now a student co-operative and got ready to eat Bolognese lentils.

Here, student kitsch met massive medieval walls and a sustainable ethos – what the guiding co-operative called "respect for nature, values of organic, energy conservation and sustainability". We got the picture.

Not an ancient stone had been left unturned to demonstrate the organic, low-impact products in this funky establishment right in the heart of Bologna's medieval student quarter.

For the rest of the evening Angelo and I wandered what seemed like all the atmospheric medieval city's 38km of porticos and dozens of squares pursuing our Bolognese hobby searching for a bad meal – no luck, happily.

We walked and ate with the benefit of Angelo's Michelin Italy and a little deft questioning of locals. The highlight of the visit for Angelo was eating Culatello di Zibello – possibly the rarest ham in Italy. "What's the difference with normal culatello" says Angelo "Five kilometres" replied the waiter. For me, it was the Mostarda – pickled sweet fruit – hot and sweet and delicious all at the same time.

Next on the itinerary was Ferrara. Here we stayed in a chintzy B&B in the old Ghetto, we cycled around to eat and we went to Venetian-style Commachio to see the eel-fishing industry and eel-canning factory. The poster of Sophia Loren, hands above her head exposing her little tufts of underarm hair attested to the date (circa 1954), of the film it promoted – La Donna del Fiume – and reminded me of the passion of my youth. Canned eel, though? Not to my, or Angelo's taste.

But something quite strange happened to our perceptions in Ferrara. Lucrezia Borgia. Our local guide took us to where she was resting still looked after by nuns. And revered. They were all talking about her as though she were still alive "Poor maligned, misunderstood Lady Lucia", they said. She'd certainly had a tough life – married off many times, little opportunity for her real love and a life of kindness and charity – quite different from the 'Femme Fatale' she has been depicted as – but still alive? Maybe it's the Italian penchant for the present tense, I thought.

Anyway things got a lot better when we arrived in Ravenna. A local tour guide, Cinzia, met us at the station and walked us to our B&B. Well, palace in the city wall, to be more precise. Both of us had massive suites, mine included a dressing room, a library an enormous bathroom plus a vast, enormous four-poster bed of which more later.

So with Angelo and I happily settled in our palace lodging suites, Cinzia proceeded to show us around.

Ravenna is a very strange place both very dead and nearly alive at the same time. Thinking about it now gives me the shivers. But you've got to see it. In the world of undiscovered amazing places it's a must.

So we tottered out of the palace with Cinzia and down the road to the mausoleum by way of a very dark, very old basilica.

Let me explain; Ravenna's times of glory and global power were twofold – the first at the height of the Roman Empire's power and the second just as Rome was losing its grip. So, for about 500 years,

Ravenna was THE place to be. A pivotal eastern backdoor to the warring western world where East met West met North met South. Or in other words Byzantium came face to face with Rome confronting the Goths fighting the Vandals. And in the 5th century AD Ravenna became really, really hot.

Cinzia took us by our hands and led us there... right into Ravenna 465 AD. In the Basilica of San Vitale we met Theodora the dancing girl mascot of the charioteers who became empress in a love match with Emperor Justinian. Inside what seemed like an enormous Byzantine domed dark blue jewel box we met the empress Galla Placidia in this, her mausoleum. Here this shockingly powerful woman created her own final resting place festooned with deeply coloured mosaics glistening to us now as though they were made and polished yesterday or, indeed today.

The sheer opulence of it all made us blink. And then, as Cinzia carefully brought us out to the present day we blinked again. Time travel is hungry work. "Lunch" said Angelo "Will you join us, Cinzia?"

So we all had a nice lunch together after our time-travelling and Cinzia told us that it was her birthday tomorrow "Great," says Angelo "You can put on a miniskirt to show off your beautiful legs – I know they're beautiful – and you can join us for dinner too." God knows what he was doing but at the moment he seemed to be on a roll.

Cinzia was nice enough, tall and slim and very attractive in a Russian ikon or Modigliani kind of way with a touch of the Mona Lisas but she seemed to be rather sweet, and a little tame to tell the truth. Anyway, now we'd got behind the task of getting Cinzia out for dinner there was no going back. The die was cast and the first step of my challenging future made.

Our afternoon was spent innocently enough tasting sublime olive oil up in a Venetian conquered village on the brow of a hill with soaring castles and a microclimate, you've guessed it, absolutely perfect for growing the top variety of olives. And wine, as it happens, and honey, and lots of other good things.

Why? Because the hill is actually made of gypsum. Anywhere else they may have knocked it down and sold it as aggregate – but not in Romagna. If you can grow good stuff on it, grow it.

So Brisighella was fabulous and so was the olive oil – plus we'd learnt a new skill. Olive oil tasting was obviously an art in itself – and, according to Cinzia we were naturals!

We were in good spirits on the way back to Ravenna, undaunted by Cinzia's decision to join us only for dessert and a coffee that evening.

But she did turn up in a mini-skirt, at least, and posed for photographs with us at the hotel door. And wrote her email address on a restaurant napkin for me – another step as it was to turn out.

The next day we were to leave for Angelo's beloved Venice and the magic of Ravenna could have stopped there, except for the fact that I'd already asked Cinzia to join us. "No problem" he said "Could be a bit of fun" obviously relishing the thought of having double the audience.

And that was it except for one thing, maybe it was the time-travelling, maybe it was the Ravenna air, but somehow my life had opened up to exciting but dangerous possibilities and I could see uncharted territory. I was, of course, blythely unaware of this, happily having an enjoyable trip but deep inside me my internal imp was doing pressups.

How did the rest happen? I really haven't a clue. Suffice it to say that none of my fail-safe devices worked and I was to be drawn so far out of my comfort zone that my life was to be in danger far quicker than I could imagine.

Anyway, Cinzia didn't come with us to Venice and didn't come to see us in Venice either, but it wasn't for the lack of my trying. Egged on by Angelo, I tried every trick in the book in my text messages and emails, but she wasn't going to budge from Ravenna.

Angelo and I, as ever, had a great time in Venice. The Venetians had pulled out their stops for us and we were staying in an unknown ex-military island in the lagoon – fascinating and just a couple of stops from Piazza San Marco on the waterbus. We went to see his mates and his favourite places, we ate great food, we popped down to the Lido, we walked and we boated around. All the time chatting and looking, and in my case, emailing and texting to Cinzia in Ravenna.

Gradually, imperceptably, a virtual bridge was being built between me and Ravenna – into the land where time took on a new identity and was to shake me to my roots.

Some new ideas from a new and rather strange person were creeping into my life and altering my perceptions.

Every day for the next two months, Cinzia and I talked by text and email and then skype.

And I set to finding out more about Ravenna, where she lived, now the contested capital of Romagna, once capital of the Roman Empire, a very strange place indeed, but totally, utterly, dangerously fascinating.

So, day after day, I learnt about Ravenna and I learnt about Romagna and I learnt about Cinzia too.

Cinzia now became my guide. Somehow her words and her sweet enthusiasm bridged the gap between 21st-century Britain and 5th-century Ravenna taking me back a couple of millennia to Classe, the Ravenna suburb where she lived.

And soon enough I was there, physically in Ravenna. And that year I kept coming back to enjoy a bit of deft guided time-travelling with Cinzia. She would pick me up at the airport in her little ecocar and take me places. We'd see extraordinary things and eat extraordinary meals, stay in extraordinary places and then she'd dump me at the airport to go home. I would write an article for each visit and I was finding it more and more addictive.

Clearly, Romagna was a potent mix of everything I loved. Romagna? What the hell is Romagna?

A classic Roman strategy in conquered territories was to build roads through them and cities in them, so when they advanced north east of Rome first they built a classic new city with all mod cons on the Adriatic coast called Ariminum (today's Rimini). Naturally they built a nice new road from Rome to connect. It was called the Via Flaminia. What to do next?

In a kind of tacking move, they built a road from Ariminum towards more conquered territory in the north west. They called the road the Via Emilia and it followed the line of the Apennines towards the other sea coast – the Med'.

They now controlled a territory bounded by the mountains in the south and north (the alps) and seas in the west and the east, in the middle there was an astonishingly fertile plain watered by the powerful Po river.

Roman generals at the time had one big problem – providing pensions for their retiring soldiers, particularly if there wasn't too much booty to go around. In these cases, generals often just captured some land and gave it away in nice retirement packages to soldiers as a working pension.

This method had a double benefit – not only were ex-soldiers looked after, but also the presence of soldiers added a bit of security. Naturally it was not a good idea to settle retired soldiers too close to overcrowded Rome.

So as soon as returning troops got through the Alps it seemed a good idea to find pension plots quick. What about that fertile land on the plain? Perfect! Before you could say Marcus Aurelius it was full of Roman soldiers living on pension plots. In other words, it became the land of the Romans or ´Romagna'!

Romagna had a few pretty strong selling points. It was close to the Adriatic (lots of seafood and lots of trade with the east). It was sandwiched between the Alps and the Apennines (lots of safety). It was astonishingly fertile (lots of great food). It had great transport options (two major Roman roads and the sea).

So for the centuries after the Romans arrived and it got called Romagna, it became a rich, elegant and important place.

First, arriving over the Alps from Gallic conquests, Julius Caesar used his first major stopping place, the then-walled island city of Ravenna, to gather his troops and make his journey over the Rubicon to take Rome and become emperor.

Although Caesar's campaign ended in his famous assassination, one thing was not lost on his adopted son and later emperor. Augustus recognised the invincibility of Ravenna and created one of the empire's biggest ports and massive fleets in the city which then became a major international city-port.

By the time Ravenna became imperial capital of Rome it was surrounded by riches. The Via Emilia was like a glorious necklace dotted with sumptuous art cities from Ariminum to Bologna; the fertile plains were producing fabulous harvests and the hills and mountains were alive with vineyards. The scene was set to create one of the world's great cities of art, resplendent with mosaic-stuffed basilicas. An astoundingly colourful mix of Italy and Byzantium.

In later centuries Romagna's riches brought warlords to the green hills and the fat cities. The Borgias, the Malatestas, the Estes, the Montefeltros brought violence, commissioned art and castles and people like Leonardo da Vinci and Dante to work in the area.

And even later Romagna became a pilgrimage place for artists, writers, connoisseurs and cognoscenti. Shelley and Byron, Freud and Jung, Versace and Armani, JRR Tolkien and Oscar Wilde amongst thousands of famous others trekked to Romagna to experience its colourful, world legacy treasure chest. And then they stopped coming, the second world war had allowed them to forget and for Romagna to drop off the Grand Tour itineraries.

By the time I arrived the treasure of Romagna had been forgotten for at least half a century. Now I was on a voyage of discovery, starting with Ravenna itself. Cinzia was determined to help me experience simply everything.

And we started with a meal, naturally. In a beach restaurant right on the Adriatic we ate a massive feast of fish. Simple dishes, spaghetti with juicy clams followed by a heap of mixed perfectly grilled fish.

Wonderful fresh fare with dozens of diners enthusiastically piling into their dishes, eating with knowledge and gusto. With the warm sea breeze, the scent of great food wafting from the kitchen and Cinzia, proud of her region's food, tucking in with relish, I felt at home.

History is strange and extremely partial. Like many kids at school I was taught quite a lot of history involving Britain. I was lucky also to learn some Latin and I knew a bit about Rome and about ancient Greece. After school and during my work I was lucky enough to learn a bit more about our past. Travelling around the Silk Road had informed me a bit about one massive gap in my understanding: the Roman empire post 300 AD was to be another quite amazing untold story. Cinzia had decided to hold my hand, guide me on this exciting journey of discovery and show me everything she had. She was to become my teacher, my guide, my interpreter, and my muse as she gradually unveiled Romagna and herself to me.

Again and again I returned to see and hear and taste its tempting tale – to savour this massive experience to its fullest. And every time I returned, door after door opened and veil after veil was lifted as I discovered Romagna's unbelievable story.

OK I knew a bit about Romagna already... but now I was taken to the depths of the 5th century AD and Galla Placidia. Obviously Cinzia was besotted with her. But actually, who was this unknown lady? Cinzia explained...

Galla Placidia was born in Greece – Thessaloniki actually, the daughter of the soon-to-be Theodosius the Great emperor of Rome – so power from her father's side. But her mother's line may actually have been a little more tough. Her gran was the gloriously beautiful Justina who seduced and married emperor Valentinian and gave birth to the equally beautiful Galla who as a teenager, in turn, seduced Theodosius.

Beautiful, tough and powerful, when Galla Placidia was given the title of 'Most Noble Child' and her own household and income, she looked set for a life of power and glory. But it was not quite as simple as that. First her mum died, then her dad was killed and shortly after the whole of her fiancé's family was slaughtered for trying to grab power. Galla Placidia was living in Milan then and she naturally decided to flee.

She chose Rome as her safe spot, but unfortunately it was under seige by Barbarians when she arrived and she was captured by Ataulf, king of the Goths who wanted to hold her hostage for ransom. Naturally a big price would be demanded for such a high-grade prisoner.

Who knows how she did it, but Ataulf fell head over heels in love with Galla Placidia and decided to forego the ransom and take the girl. Their marriage was consummated in Forli and they had a massive wedding ceremony in Narbonne (the then capital of the Gothic lands) surrounded by many fortunes of captured booty. Galla Placidia became Queen Consort of the Goths.

So, loved-up and happy for once, there is yet another turn in her tale. Taking a bath in Barcelona, Ataulf was slaughtered by a rival who proceeded to kill the king's ex-wife and his six children. Galla Placidia was again used as a ransom but not before she had been marched in front of her husband's murderer.

Her half-brother Honorius had a cunning plan. Now he was in charge of the empire, he would ransom Galla, his half-sister, whom he had designs on, marry her off to his friend, the soldier Constantius, and while he was away in battle, Honorius would have her all to himself. So in 417 Constantius married Galla Placidia then off he went to fight

It didn't quite work out like that. Honorius moved everyone to Ravenna from Milan and to get the ménage a trois working properly he made Constantius joint emperor – so when Galla Placidia married she became Empress Consort in the Western Roman Empire then she had his two children Justa and Valentinian then of course Constantius died!

By now Constantius had become the real power behind Honorius' throne and Galla Placidia's protector. Knowing that she was in danger without his protection and fearful of the anger of the Ravenna population at her perceived incest with her brother, Galla Placidia fled to Constantinople with her children.

Mind you by now Constantinople was about as safe as Rome had been when Galla Placidia had fled there. The Eastern (and most important) capital of the Roman Empire was pretty much under seige by Atilla the Hun. There was sufficient danger for a wall to be built to secure Constantine's beautiful new city.

Then her half-brother Honorius died.

In Constantinople with her half-nephew Emperor Theodosius, Galla Placidia decided to make a bid for power for her son Valentinian.

In the meantime local civil servant Johannes had seized power in Ravenna and was negotiating to become emperor.

After getting Theodosius' support for Valentinian plus an army and a fleet of ships, Galla Placidia left the Bosphorus to take 'impregnable' Ravenna. She went by land with a small army and her captain Ardaburius went by sea.

Ardaburius and two of his galleys were captured by forces loyal to Johannes and were held prisoners in Ravenna. The prisoner was allowed the freedom of walking the court and streets of Ravenna during his captivity. He took advantage of this privilege to get the city gates open to let in his troops. Johannes was taken and his right hand cut off; he was then mounted on a donkey and paraded through the streets, and finally beheaded in the city's main hippodrome.

All Galla Placidia had to do was to make peace with the Goths waiting for spoils and she was in! Now she was Empress Consort on behalf of her 3-year-old son. Real power at last!

Thus began Ravenna's age of Roman glory. Now not just a port, it was Imperial capital of Rome – and its empress – twice married, twice widowed, twice ransomed, humiliated and bartered now glorious Galla Placidia.

In 425 she started a building campaign that is evident even now, nearly 1600 years later. She built beautiful basilicas, commissioned glistening mosaics, started to create glorious Ravenna. Beautiful, rich, powerful, opulent, impregnable, global, stuffed full of Byzantine treasure, Rome's window on the east was also full of intrigue, decadence and seedy goings-on.

Galla Placidia, though, was empress at a time when the whole world was in chaos. The city of Rome had fallen, the known world was full of millions of refugees due to famines.

Whole peoples were roaming the world to find fat territories to ravage and plunder. In China there were massive famines, hunger and death; in Europe malaria had reached the hitherto cold northern countries. Atilla the Hun and his vicious tribes having been bribed to go by Theodosius, were on their way to Italy. Rome's western empire had fallen apart, the Vandals had reached North Africa, and closer to Ravenna the lands were full of Ostrogoths, Visigoths, Barbarians, and many other tribes who relished the opportunity to ravish the great city.

It's lucky for her that Galla Placidia was a woman of steel forged in conquest and defeat.

But for another two hundred years Ravenna's power did not wane. Galla Placidia was followed by more colourful rulers, in particular the Gothic hero Theodoric who shepherded half a million of his people over the Alps to populate the area. This powerful man built more palaces and basilicas, this time in the Northern Arian style. And then, gradually Ravenna slid back into obscurity.

Cinzia guided me around the city. Every time I returned there was something to see. She took me to the fabulous basilicas, some dark and haunted like the church of San Vitale decorated with astonishing mosaics depicting the dynamic emperor Justinian, writer of western law, and his seductive dancing-girl wife Teodora. She took me to the museums and art galleries, ex-monastries and churches, and she took me to the extraordinary basilica of Sant'Appolinare in Classe. This massive edifice with its glittering mosaics seemed like it lived in a land of light, delicately reflecting all the glory of its 1600 years.

Then, when the visits and the delightful tours seemed to be over, I came back to Ravenna so Cinzia could show me what happened after Ravenna's power lapsed. She took me to see the tomb of Dante Alighieri and showed me her favourite basilica just by it – the 7th-century basilica of San Francesco. This classic basilica had something very special – goldfish swimming in the crypt.

The sea had receded from Ravenna – denuding the city of its canals and natural moat. Then it was no longer an island and robbed of the massive natural protection of the sea, it was invincible no longer and slowly it has begun to sink.

This is nowhere more evident than in the mosaic-floored crypt of San Francesco. Now it is full of water and is the home to a family of goldfish.

Back to the tomb of Dante, Cinzia proudly told me the story of the greatest Italian writer ever – she was besotted with one of his tales, the ill-fated romance of Francesca and Paolo which took place close to Ravenna. Poor dears, they both ended up in Hell!

Dante had been exiled by Florence in 1302 and had wandered the country making trouble before being taken in by the Polenta family near Ravenna where he died of malaria in 1321. He was buried by the Francescan monks.

Naturally as Dante was a Florentine, and one of the world's great poets, the Florentines wanted Dante's remains in their city. Knowing that they would stop at nothing, the Franciscan monks hid Dante's coffin. For the last nearly 800 years, the Florentines have tried to get back what's left of their star poet but with no success. Dante Alighieri was pardoned by Florence in 2008!

Carrying on the literary theme, Cinzia led me to Ravenna's 'Street of Poets'. The via Mazzini is a lovely long cobbled pedestrian street which winds through the pretty 18th century part of Ravenna. At the time most of the street's palaces, houses and shops were created, Ravenna was a magnet for rich and educated Grand Tour visitors from all over the world. They came to imbue themselves with the magic, history and art of this then-iconic, city.

Following in Dante's footsteps came Oscar Wilde and Sigmund Freud, Alfred Lord Byron and TS Eliot, Henry James and Herman Hesse and all up this lovely street there were small placards with their comments about Ravenna.

As it happened, Cinzia was very fond of Lord Byron who came to Ravenna and seduced Teresa Countess Guiccioli, the wife of a rich Ravenna merchant. Appropriately Byron was writing the first five cantos of Don Juan at the time.

Following on the Byron theme, Cinzia decided to take me to Bagnacavallo the little country town where Byron had his love-nest. Rather more than pretty, Bagnacavallo has a spectacular miniature 17th-century perfect oval piazza, a street of love, and the ancient convent where Byron unceremoniously dumped his two-year-old daughter Allegra. She died there at the age of five. Sad I thought; romantic thought Cinzia.

Now we'd moved our centre of interest outside of Ravenna, Cinzia decided to take me for two meals in two very different and very special places.

The Adriatic coast municipality of Cervia had been an ancient salt city with enormous salt-pan lakes, owned by the Popes. In the 18th century they built an elegant new model town and port to house their vastly wealthy salt businesses and the people running it.

We walked around the colourful port and into the 'New' model town with its piazzas and porticos, its salt market and salt museum, its delightful 18th century theatre and its art-stuffed cathedral. By now, naturally we were hungry and it was just a short walk to a sublime beach-side restaurant.

And I was introduced to Strozzapreti. Made of just flour and water (no eggs) these short lengths of pasta twisted as though a priests thin neck were between your fingers – "Strangled Priest" pasta is something very special and totally fabulous with a sauce of fresh fish created by someone who truly knows. Even more fabulous if you're eating it in a classic restaurant on the beach and your bare feet are twisting with enjoyment in the warm sand – as Cinzia's were. A long lunch, even more delicious fresh fish and we took a walk along the beach towards the glitzy part.

In the 19th century seaside tourism developed as a health-giving activity and Cervia's beaches and its vast pine woods came into use to welcome visitors.

Obviously the pinewoods, the lovely beach and the historic town (and the sublime food and wine all around) were attractive to visitors. By the time Cervia had a railway station, visitors were arriving from as far away as rich, fashionable Milan and a few Milanese took interest in the lovely area.

Then, at the beginning of the 20th century an agreement was reached between Cervia and the Maffei Family from Milan who bought a large piece of Cervia's land by the sea. On this land, they built villas, parks and gardens to transform the area into a superb Art Deco holiday resort. It would be called Milano Marittima (Milan by the Sea).

The man chosen to lead the development was Milanese painter Giuseppe Palanti who had been influenced by Ebenezer Howard (the force behind the Garden City movement – thought to represent the perfect blend of city and nature).

In 1913 the Garden City Society built the first three cottages and the following year four more, including Giuseppe Palanti's villa. All these cottages were in the heart of the pinewoods and in Liberty style (Italian Art Nouveau). In a few years Milano Marittima became a smart new middle-class beach resort within Cervia's municipality.

The beneficial effects of Cervia's health spa have been known for centuries and the centre has been visited by many people over the years. "Selva e Mare" – 'forests and sea' was the first theme used to publicize the spa at the start of the century and today is still considered the winning formula of the city.

Cinzia loved it. "Selva e Mare" plus fashion, elegance and food certainly did it for her!

And she loved something else about Cervia – flamingos – thousands of them. Like most of Romagna's coast, the area around Cervia was waterland – just a few hundred years ago it was mainly seawater and now it is mainly land. Hence the vast salt-lakes, and hence the flamingos and all kinds of other water birds, but mainly flamingos, beautiful graceful flamingos. As the area around Cervia is a massive natural park, it is kept natural and protected. The environment is pretty much untouched – great pine forests, vast amounts of water, great empty beaches, paradise for flamingos.

I came back to Romagna for the last performance of the Ravenna Festival and we arrived in the sultry July evening heat at the massive San Giacomo palace, the seat of the power players in Ravenna – the Rasponi family.

"Can I tell you something" said Cinzia Pasi conpiratorially, as she waylaid Cinzia and I at the gate "They are making a factory here" "It is going to ruin our beautiful area – have a leaflet" "Do you want to see the mayor, it's his project – he's standing there".

To be honest, in the balmy evening with a hundred or so people sitting on the grass and enjoying fabulous world music – it didn't seem appropriate to stand and demonstrate or talk to the mayor.

So, we queued up at the trestle table and waited while three delightful local people laboriously wrote out tickets for a couple of ice creams – we paid our 2 euros and went to the bar to be served. Who cared about the global financial crisis, the possibility that a factory would be built. We'd got our ice creams, the musicians were drumming and singing and playing weird stringed instruments and the bureaucratically-bought ice cream tasted good. The crowd was happy and everything in Italy was in its place.

The concert ended late and after happily getting lost in the grounds of the old Rasponi palace, church and art gallery complex (there was always a great art gallery!) we made our way back to another Rasponi establishment – the Palazzo Baldini.

With its air of peace, understanding and plenty, you couldn't find a more sublime place to sleep.

To be honest, you wouldn't have marked out our hosts as medieval barons. At the Palazzo Baldini, Filipo (a veterinary surgeon) is a young impeccable, well-travelled 'Front of House' and his mother (a Baldini by birth) and his father aided by two inspired chefs look after the hospitality in depth.

It was quickly clear that just everything has been chosen with the best possible taste. From the superb white-sheeted beds, through the thoughtfully-restored and now glazed air vents in the drying-room to the miraculous ravioli, the taste, visual and culinary, is simply perfect.

And these Baldinis don't stand on formality. For breakfast mother brings out a tray of melt-in-the-mouth just-baked cookies and father asks if we'd like some fresh fruit.

He reappears two minutes later with peaches, apricots and nectarines still warm from the sun and just plucked from the trees. With a little perfect espresso, it's the breakfast from heaven.

And while dad grabs more fruit for us to take away, mum gives the tour of the garden – sample ripe figs, see the goats and chicken and rabbits gambolling and forget about the fact they're going to be lunch!

It's time for coffee. Hastily grabbing our bags and gratefully accepting a box of at least 10kg of fresh fruit ("for the journey!") we leave to have morning coffee in Bagnacavallo, the tiny astonishing marvel of Italian medieval architecture, slumbering in the morning sun. Lord Byron must have loved it.

Now it really is time for lunch, up in a hilltop historic vineyard city, why not? Bertinoro has history. When the Empress Galla Placidia arrived, touring her area, they offered her wine. In fact they offered her a cup of the sublime Albana wine of which they are justly very proud and was the first wine in Italy to have a DOCG accreditation.

Savouring the terra cotta beaker of delicious wine, she said (in Latin obviously) "This wine is so good it should be drunk in gold" Hence the city's name – Bert in Oro (drunk in gold in Romagnolo dialect).

Since then, for over fifteen centuries the locals have been perfecting their wine-making craft and the city became rich and powerful. The archbishop's castle dominates all the lands around and was once the fiefdom of Frederick Barbarossa. Now the locals just specialise in wine – and food, of course.

Perched on the side of its grand square, with astonishing views, Bertinoro's best restaurant has an enormous wine museum and unbelievably good food. Because it's at least fifteen kilometres away from the sea, it specialises in meat rather than fish. Like many Romagna restaurants it serves wonderful tagliatelli made fresh each morning and it's served with very special 'Ragu' sauce. This sauce is the pride of every chef and normally includes chopped local pork and beef and many delicious secret ingredients. Sublime! It's normally followed by an enormous plate of selected grilled meats including sausage, liver, chops, ribs, "Castrato" lamb, steaks and patties. Enough!

Finally Cinzia thought that my food education was in need of refreshment so she took me to the Via Emilia city of Forlimpopoli to learn from Pellegrino Artusi. Ever heard of Pellegrino Artusi? I hadn't!

If not, like me you have some wonderful eating, drinking and living to do in the warm company of the father of Italian home cooking.

In 1891, at the tender age of 70, Pellegrino Artusi, a rich travelling Florence-based merchant got his final refusal from yet another publisher.

This energetic gentleman's life's work was to travel the length and breadth of Italy prior to unification and collect authentic local home recipes from all over soon-to-be Italy. And, of course, each recipe had both a story and a taste!

Obviously Artusi had a passion for food and his ambition was to share his carefully annotated recipes with... everybody.

Anyway, Artusi, not deterred by the publishers' refusals, went ahead, self-published his first volume of 475 recipes called "Science in the Kitchen and the Art of Eating Well", and, of course it quickly sold out. 122 years later it is still one of Italy's best-selling books and has never been out of print.

Artusi had travelled throughout the Italian peninsula. He became familiar with many of the regions and their culinary traditions, and he began collecting recipes that later became the foundation of his book. Family wealth enabled him to retire at the age of 45 and he devoted himself to his passions, culture and cuisine.

Born in Romagna in the town of Forlimpopoli, this successful fabric merchant and bon viveur had moved to Florence as a young man. Luckily for us, because when Italy was unified in 1861 only 2.5% of the country's population could speak Italian. So the book, written in Italian was a unifying force in itself – speading opportunities and understanding together with fabulous food.

And it's no wonder that the book has been so successful, Artusi himself was leery of books about cooking. In his preface he says, "Beware of books that deal with this art: most of them are inaccurate or incomprehensible, especially the Italian ones. The French are a little better. But from either, the very most you will glean are a few notions, useful only if you already know the art."

He considered his book a teaching manual, "To practise using this manual, one simply needs to know how to hold a wooden spoon," he wrote. "The best teacher is experience. Yet even lacking this, with a guide such as mine, and devotion to your labours, you should be able, I hope, to put something decent together."

But, most importantly, and typically, – in his 14th edition he says this "Finally, I should not like my interest in gastronomy to give me the reputation of a gourmand or glutton. I object to any such dishonourable imputation, for I am neither. I love the good and the beautiful wherever I find them, and hate to see anyone squander, as they say, God's bounty. Amen"

He saw 15 editions published before his death in 1911 at the age of 90. Originally containing 475 recipes, the last edition of the book contained 790 recipes.

Casa Artusi where Cinzia took me for dinner was established in 2007. It is a tribute to the man who singlehandedly put Italian home cooking on the culinary map. Housed in a renovated monastery and church in his birthplace of Forlimpopoli, Casa Artusi has a restaurant, a culinary school, library, meeting space, art exhibits and museum. It is a place to read, learn, practice, taste and appreciate the treasure that is Italian home cooking.

In the restaurant – l'Osteria – Cinzia and I ate magnificently. They serve traditional, regional dishes and prepare some of Artusi's recipes, depending on the season – all at incredibly low prices. The wine cellar has over 200 different kinds of wine from the region. And then, of course, she gave me the tour including the sensational 16th-century chapel – the whole establishment is set in an ancient convent complete with serene cloisters.

Finally she took me to the heart of the foundation – the cookery school. Here they offer home cooks day classes with some of the area's best chefs. These lucky people get to work with 'Mariettes', experienced and trained local home cooks named after Artusi's helper of whom he said, ". . .Mariette is both a good cook, and a decent, honest person. . .".

I vowed to be back for a special occasion Forlimpopoli holds an annual gastronomic event dedicated to Artusi, The Festa Artusiana. For over a week every night between 7pm and midnight, Casa Artusi and the historical center of the town came alive with music and events as a "city of taste." Streets, alleys, courtyards and squares, named after types of food – fruit, veg, gelato, sweets, throng with happy crowds.

The next time I returned to Romagna that year, Cinzia had a task for me. She had spent months researching two important places in the area and I was to be her guinea pig. She would guide me around and I was to comment on her English language, how easy it was for me to understand her and how interesting it all was – I was to tell her the truth – no holds barred. Obviously it wasn't going to be all work and no play – we would have some fun too.

We started in Faenza with a poetry reading. Romagnolo poetry is great stuff – even if you can't understand the dialect – you get the expressions and the tone of voice. The idea was that the poetry would be translated into English too, and Cinzia had decided that would be great for me – and it was! The Welsh lady who translated really put her heart and soul into the task and the crowd was lovely – they all wanted to talk to us in their version of English.

And then, after a superb dinner, we wandered around Faenza's cobbled streets and vast, rich piazzas. And Cinzia told me the story of this lovely city.

By the 16th century Faenza was one of the richest cities in Europe, creating a product that simply every royal court in the world wanted. You could call Faenza 'Ceramic City' and it lent its name to the richest of porcelain – Majolica or Faience ware, some of the most sumptuously decorated and most colourful that ever existed. And ceramics are, even now, everywhere in this city – artisan factories, talented designers, great displays, beautiful ceramics are even plastered on houses. And Faenza is clever, ever up with the times: the ceramic museum houses stunning ceramic pieces by current artists as well as those illustrating the fashions in art and style over the last five hundred years.

Now every year there is a massive exhibition of ceramics that takes over the city 'Argila' or clay!

And, with rich architecture and lively, lovely tiny piazzas and a thriving Café Culture the city is a delight.

Then we took on somewhere a bit different – San Marino. A little more challenging because Cinzia had decided to take me all around this mountaintop republic by foot! Up and down, down and up we went – with Cinzia guiding and talking and pointing and making sure that I was listening and looking in the right direction everywhere.

I've always known that San Marino was special – certainly from my days bringing a thousand happy travellers a week to nearby Rimini. Special? Very special and extremely profitable. Mountaintop republic, short coachride, stunning views, castles, passport stamp from another country, duty-free branded shopping – a classic excursion opportunity. A thousand passengers a week who would all pay a tenner to go up the mountain meant ten grand a week in excursion revenue plus commissions on shop sales – yummee!

Anyway, this was different and even more rewarding – Cinzia doing her speciality was taking me back twenty centuries or so to the time of Saint Marinus the mountaintop hermit saint. I even crawled into his cave-lair sleeping place and saw his silver death mask. Of course he had a story and Cinzia knew it. He was a stonemason from Dalmatia who worked with his mate Leo – they both found mountains, performed miracles and created sects – Leo created San Leo on one Romagna mountain and Marinus created San Marino on the other. Marinus was rather more independently-minded and hence San Marino asks nothing of anyone – its motto 'Liberty'

It's beautiful, atmospheric and quirky – serene San Leo was promised for another time. By the time dinner – the usual sensational food – was over I was exhausted and then on my way back to the UK.

My adventures in Romagna, I thought were over, just seven months seemed like a lifetime after they had begun. But by now I was hooked.

"I wanna go to the Veneto" moaned Angelo! "We've got an invite to the Po Valley. Rovigo – the fabulous waterlands where they've got this amazing rice. I wanted to sell cruises down the river there. They'll feed us wonderful food – you won't believe it. "And we'll go on a boat" Angelo enthused. "And if we're lucky they'll put us up at a place like that Tenuta Castel Venezze – remember?"

So, we went on another adventure. I filled my car up with a month's worth of stuff. The plan was to go to Italy via the South of France resort of Arles (where Van Gogh painted all those great pictures) then we'd stop at one of Angelo's mates' hotels on the Med then swing around Ravenna and have lunch with Cinzia. Whizz across to the Veneto and then come back to Ravenna for a few days or weeks, whatever.

The trip was a doddle, we wizzed down to Arles, which was amazing. There was a lot of Van Gogh stuff everywhere and some very good restaurants, plus we stayed in a glorious hotel cheap – I've still got the posh key to prove it. Dinner was superb – both Angelo and I have a penchant for classic old fashioned fishy French cuisine so we feasted on soupe de poisson and bouillabaise to our heart's content.

The next day we were in Italy and on our way back to Ravenna for supper with Cinzia. Or not – she declined our invitation. It was as though we were back on home territory that night staying in the Casa Masoli 16th century city palace B&B.

Massive rooms with enormous four-poster beds, good antique furniture, dressing rooms, posh bathrooms and big libraries. What more could we want? Well we weren't going to get that but we did breakfast well on ham and cheese and eggs, good bread and butter, fresh local fruit and home made pastries and cakes and great coffee and superb blood orange juice.

Chat, walk, coffee and time for lunch with Cinzia. There's a Venetian restaurant in Ravenna and, homesick maybe, Angelo wanted to go there – at least we could sit outside as we ate our Venetian specialities like liver and onions and cold veal.

Cinzia said that if I wanted to stay longer there was a massive Mussolini-era Colonnia by the sea in Marina di Ravenna. These colonnias were all along the coast, built by Mussolini in the classic brutalist art deco style to give kids and workers free seaside holidays, they have now either disappeared or, like this one been made into blocks of apartments.

As we left Ravenna on our way along the coast to the Veneto we popped into this colonnia and I haggled for a flat for a month. We dumped a load of my stuff out of the car giving Angelo a bit of room to move and we were off to see the Po valley.

Obviously, the Po valley is full of water. We'd been invited there by a company which wanted to hire out boats for people to enjoy waterborne holidays. Like many people in the industry they were giving us an experience in the hope that we would promote them. Seemed a good idea, at least it wasn't mass tourism and local people were involved.

"We've been here before" said Angelo when we arrived at our accommodation for the night. "Yes – the Castel Venezze – fab" I replied.

I remembered the village down the road, San Martino where everyone downed tools and stopped work at six in the evening to dance in the town square – delightful.

Our accommodation was superb. Since we'd stayed before, they had cashed in on cookery classes led by the manager's mum, the Contessa.

All over the world TV cookery programmes had started to get big audiences. Masterchef, for instance was getting millions of viewers from Australia to Italy. Other cookery programmes are becoming a staple on the TV menu. There are often so many viewers who wish to try the recipes that supermarkets stock up in advance with specialist ingredients.

Just when Angelo and I arrived the cookery craze was beginning to offer opportunities for posh struggling old hotels.

No more so than around Italy's fertile Po Delta where hotels and agriturismo establishments were learning new ways to reap the harvest of wonderful produce and of high-spending quality tourism by creating cookery classes.

Veneto, extending from the Dolomites to the Adriatic Sea, is one of the richest provinces in Italy – full of culture and history and jam-packed with absolutely sensational food and wine.

There is an astonishing range of vegetables. Veneto has no less than seven with DOP protection and richness of waters (the sea, the lagoons, the lakes, the rivers) also gives local people an ample supply of fish stocks. As far as meats are concerned, there is also an amazing variety. The lagoons around also produce superb rice.

And the wines are no less wonderful – Just think of Soave, Valpolicella, Amarone, Bardolino, Garganega , Prosecco, Pinot Grigio, amongst dozens more, particularly great whites, fabulous reds.

Hence there is a huge range of recipes and preparations in the kitchen. Great specialities, world-renowned foods.

Castel Venezze's family were determined to collect their bit of the opportunity and become leaders in high quality cooking holidays. In a superb setting, hands-on cooking lessons were now being run by the Countess Maria Giustiniani in the kitchens at the castle. As the estate was set in thousands of acres of woodland, green fields and kitchen gardens they really had something special to offer. The idea was that here, under the steady eye of Contessa Maria, a special menu would be created every day culled from their own local earth.

It was a simple next step for guests to experience the bounty of this rich soil with their own hands quarters and cook it themselves. Hence the Tenuta Castel Venezze cookery classes.

The countess is more than happy to help guests cook and with the aid of a qualified sommelier, assists them to put together a simply amazing lunch.

A typical day's cooking could include a whole sumptuous meal with wine. After gathering required herbs and vegetables on the estate, participants would repair to the estate's kitchens where, under the instruction of Contessa Maria, they prepare a seasonal lunch, usually consisting of a risotto, a typical meat or fish dish (depending on the best ingredients) and a dessert. The created, hopefully superb, lunch will be eaten with local wines. During the day participants also learn about the Veneto's fabulous history of cuisine.

After lunch there would be time for a walk on the estate before beginning the fine eating process again in the evening with an aperitif and an excellent dinner created again with the best of local produce.

Good enough for Angelo and me then. And after a nice sleep in yet another four-poster, we had our big local breakfast in the awesome dining hall. Today we were off on the river.

There can't be many more tranquil experiences than slowly negotiating a beautiful Italian river towards lunch.

As it happened lunch was to be something very special indeed. Something neither of us had tasted before, something sublime. Obviously we were in rice field country so it had to be risotto, but what more local and totally deliciously appropriate than eel risotto. Maybe it's something about the oil in the eel but the dish is a truimph. Angelo couldn't stop talking about it all the way back to the colonnia in Marina di Ravenna.

The next day we went off for lunch in the little port of Marina di Ravenna. A fish lunch, naturally. Astonishing. The port has a street full of fishmongers that are also restaurants. So we got starters of pickled fish – little octopus, anchovies, Branzino, clams, shrimp, squid and cuttlefish and prawns – the lot. Then spaghetti alla bottarga (with mullet eggs) delicious. Naturally Adriatic fritto misto followed and grilled fish too. And then he was gone – Angelo was on his way home leaving me in my Mussolini apartment.

I had decided exactly what I was going to do. I would research Romagna myself and I would write a magazine about the place. I thought people would love it.

Of course, I'd published magazines in the past. I'd even owned and run a weekly newspaper, so I knew how it worked. A massive saving was that I didn't have to print it. I could do it all online.

But first I had a job to do on the other side of the Adriatic.

By now I had an assistant – Jasmine – a highly-educated tourism academic who wanted to work with me. She edited my Sustainable Tourism Reports and produced a report analysis for me on cynical attitudes to tourism sustainability called the 'Greenwash Report' Together we created something called the Integrated Tourism Development

Initiative and a beautiful part of Slovenia was to be my first project.

Slovenj Gradec and Misilnja were two communities in the Styrian part of Slovakia, practically on the border of Austria and just by the European City of Culture – Maribor. They were beautiful, historic and fascinating and they had no tourism.

We had convinced them that we could help. The idea was that tourism is not just about visitors coming and looking at things. Tourism can involve the whole business community at one level or the other – and can benefit them. That's why the initiative uses the word 'integration'. If tourism could be used by the butcher, the baker, the farmer etc., they should be involved in creating and developing the tourism project. Plus they could bring more ideas and more commitment.

So, we got a two-day workshop organised which Jasmine and I were to jointly moderate and enthuse, but first we had to learn by travelling around and seeing the opportunities on the spot.

Something new for me. We got to a 'Tourist Farm' and they asked us to take our shoes off. Not when we got to the farmhouse, but when we got to the land. Soil and grass between our toes, we entered the farmhouse for a little 'refreshment' actually a fabulous treat of local (well, from the farm actually) fresh, organic, sublime delicious food. Apparently there were dozens like this charging ridiculously little money for a comforting wholesome break.

From the healthily organic to the light fantastic. Off we went to a pretty little airport. Here we were to have a taste of 'sport flying', well actually I was! Up, up and away I went with Damian Cehner (not the 666 one) and got to fly his dinky little plane. His company Aviofun owned the airport and did fun things like selling parachute jumps; luckily I wasn't on the jump!

Finally, I visited the magic triangle. Very special! The Magical Triangle of the Mislinja Valley embodied three spiritual points that are related to the mythology of the old Slavs. The top point is at the place where the church of St. Pankraty stands, from where one can see the two other points, the church of St George and the church of St Mary. Within this triangle there is a special mythological story, which includes archeology and mythology. It was a beautiful but a strange place where it is said that all growing things receive extra energy. The idea was to research and create a tourism programme around the area which would help heal visitors' minds, bodies and spirits.

I was fascinated – I'd only ever heard of St Pankraty before in terms of St Pancras station in London!

In the following days we created four local groups at an intensive tourism workshop to visualize these projects and put them into action.

The idea was that local residents would benefit from more tourists coming to sky dive at the Slovenj Gradj sport airport and to enjoy great local hospitality and the natural world on special farm and forest stays. The visitors would also be able to experience health-giving relaxation in Mislinja valley's magic triangle and to try specially branded holidays and locally produced goods.

I really loved the place, the people the food and the potent spirituality and thought it was just a matter of time before it would be a really successful little destination.

Back in Romagna, for the next few months I'd go out and around every day getting stories and pictures and then I'd come back to the collonnia and write them up.

The first edition came out! Wow. Certainly, the cover was a knockout – a picture of a smiling Romagnola girl eating an enormous piadina, that perfectly circular, particularly Romagnolo flatbread which locals lust after – particularly when it's filled with fresh local cheese, prosciutto crudo and rocket!

By now, of course, I'd learnt a lot about the Romagna food and wine, and why piadina (now designated a special DOC product) was so important.

At its heart, piadina is simple, unpretentious unleavened flatbread, but every restaurant in Romagna serves it and competes with all the others as to its quality. It is a simple mix of flour and water, a little salt and strutto (lard) or olive oil. After being flattened it is baked on an earthenware telia, usually made in one specific place – historic hilltop Montetiffi. It is always served hot. Given its simplicity there should be little difference between one piadina and another yet there is. Simply everybody has their way to make the very best from humble homes to grand restaurants and your piadina will always be delicious. It is Romagnolo soul food, like passatelli in brodo. OK, I'll tell you about passatelli after I've told you about the magazine!

It was 48 pages full of stuff about fascinating places that I'd visited and researched. Of course, I went back to Brisighella – the gypsum hill that grew the extraordinarily delicious olives. Naturally I revisited Bertinoro the hilltop wine village where they discovered and cherished the sublime golden Albana wine.

But there were some things that I just hadn't known about after these many visits, that featured in the magazine. Take Mona Lisa and Mussolini for instance.

There was a time in Romagna that borders were fairly fluid between neighbouring regions like Marche and Tuscany. Artists attracted by superb scenery and rich commissions used to work for local warlords like the Malatestas from Romagna, the Montefeltros from Marche and the Borgias from Florence. The artists liked to use the most atmospheric and classically beautiful scenery, in this respect many preferred

Romagna backgrounds. One particular artist is now known to have done so – Piero della Francesca and it is likely that Leonardo da Vinci did too. Now it is possible not only to see pictures by these great artists but see the backdrops that they used too – the sensational and quite magical countryside of Romagna.

And just down the road, on the Via Emilia, is the city of Forli, also very artistic but in a very different way. Mussolini (probably the most important warlord that Romagna ever produced) was born in a village close to Forli – Predappio. The village, by the way, is even now a big-time pilgrimage site. Yes, there are many people who still revere Mussolini. Anyway, the biggest shrine to the regime and that era is Forli itself.

The city is chock-full of what I call brutalist art deco. Well naturally Mussolini was the local lad made good and he made sure that everybody knew it. The Forli masterwork is its railway station and the wide triumphal way that leads from it. Down the route there are massive buildings for railway workers to live in, a university, a flying school with amazing mosaics and other iconic architecture. And that's not all, Forli's public buildings are also massive emblems to 'Il Duce'. I was lucky to be involved with a controversial programme to use these and other totalitarian regime buildings throughout Europe as a gruesome art project.

But the architecture that always chills me in Forli is the ancient town square – the Piazza Saffi. The square's most visible totem is the eagle, it is everywhere, on buildings and on street furniture. The eagles that freeze my stomach are at the top of each lamppost which were also adorned by the bodies of hanged partisans during the war. After the war, of course, from the lampposts hung collaborators.

And another thing that I hadn't known about was Christmas in San Marino. Now apart from bringing me loads of excursion money in the 1980s, San Marino is something very special. Like Cinzia said, it's historic, atmospheric, duty free, another country and it's up its own mountain – Mount Titano, plus of course its economy depends on tourists.

Something I profited from royally for at least 10 years was Christmas (Christmas markets and festive holidays to be precise) so I know a big Christmas-time opportunity when I see one and San Marino is a big Christmas opportunity.

In San Marino, they call it the 'Christmas of Marvels' and I highlighted it in the magazine. Christmas markets, Christmas events, nativity scenes, Christmas lights, Christmas music and Christmas shops wound themselves all around San Marino's ever-upward cobbled streets already dotted with boutique shopping opportunities. And it was all in very good taste and not too expensive as most tax had been taken off. Nearly at the top of the mountain Santa Claus had set up his headquarters served by hundreds of elves. Altogether a great story and one that I thought would run and run.

Naturally the magazine had great write-ups on hotels and vineyards – and restaurants and food. Basically it was a fun set of stories about somewhere very special and quite mysterious and extremely packed with history and food and wine.

Which all reminds me of the supreme Romagna soul-food, a simple but sublime concoction made of left-overs.

That's what they tell you! Obviously, you've got some stale bread in your kitchen, some hard, left-over parmesan, a lemon or two that are past their best and a few herbs and spices plus an egg or two? With this you can make Passatelli.

Just make breadcrumbs out of the stale bread and grate the parmesan finely, mix these two ingredients together with the lemon zest, add some nutmeg and other spices and bind the whole lot together with the eggs. In Romagna you're probably talking about a couple of dozen eggs – just to give you an idea about proportions!

Simple, right? And cheap – that's the Passatelli mix, but you're going to have to make a stock to put it in. They say you should get a big pot. Why a big pot? Well you're going to have to put a big capon chicken into it plus big lumps – a few kilos of beef or pork. You are going to boil all this with herbs for at least a day. A day? Well, you want to make the richest perfect broth don't you?

The rest is simple. Take the boiled meat out of the broth – put it on one side for your second course for which you'll make a cold Bearnaise-type sauce.

Now you're ready to make sensational simple heartwarming Passatelli.

Bring the rich broth to the boil and use a potato ricer to squeeze strands of the Passatelli into it. Serve from a big steaming tureen. It is paradise in a bowl.

The magazine got rave reviews from all the locals that read it. Even though it didn't get mass circulation like I had thought, I loved the place and the magazine so much, I carried on producing them. After all, the fascinating in-depth stories and glorious pictures must be a powerful way of marketing tourism and giving it massive value-added, mustn't they?

Anyway, I was enjoying being a writer, editor and publisher of a magazine that local people loved! And I loved travelling around, finding out stuff, meeting fans and eating great food.

So I carried blithely on and produced another couple of editions. It was hard work, it was costly. I couldn't get anyone to support it financially and I was running out of cash and credit. I had hoped that the magazines and the website would at least generate enquiries, but they didn't.

I thought that the Best of Romagna number 2 was better than number 1. It was chock-full of even more fascinating stories and great pictures.

The first time I had arrived in Ravenna, which started this whole process was 21 March 2012. This was the day that Tonino Guerra died.

It's surprising that more people haven't heard about this amazing man. Tonino Guerra was the writing partner of fellow Romagnolo Federico Fellini on his Oscar-winning film 'Amarcord'. This was just one of his achievements – amongst over forty other great classic films including 'Blow Up' and 'Ginger and Fred'. Guerra was also a prolific poet in the Romagnolo language and a phenomenally good artist and mosaicist. He brought the Dalai Lama to his retirement home, the hilltop castle town of Pennabilli where he tirelessly worked to create museums and festivals. But above all this man, imprisoned by the Nazis for his partisan work, was a true Romagnolo with a passion for food and wine enjoyment and argument.

I got introduced to Tonino Guerra's life and work at a restaurant that he had founded in the town of his birth – Santarcangelo di Romagna. On a research trip for an article in the second magazine this is where I think I discovered the real heart and soul of Romagna.

The restaurant is called La Sangiovesa after the rich red wine that is redolent of the area. It is an insight into the way the Romagnolo spirit works.

Guerra's partner in the restaurant was a publisher – Maggioli, his family had a big palace in the centre of Santarcangelo, complete with a maze of catacombs that were used to store wine. And this is where the restaurant was to be. The idea was to celebrate the best of Romagnolo food and wine and hospitality and naturally it had to be done better than well.

The restaurant was to be the showplace, but the 'tenuta' was to be the workplace. Maggioli also owned a big farm – Tenuta Saiano at the bottom of Monte Bello. Here the food for the restaurant was grown or raised. Here were the capons for the broth, the donkeys for the stew, the posh pigs for the grills and of course the beef. Naturally great cheeses were to be made and naturally there was a vineyard for beautiful Sangiovese wines. Everything would be perfect.

And in the showplace restaurant, of course they started with the design. Rural but serious! Tonino even went to Austria to study heating stoves and came back with an idea he put into practice – stunning mosaic stoves everywhere.

The advantage of being a Romagnolo is that you know exactly how good food is made, so in the Sangiovesa there are four important stations. As you enter the restaurant (actually "Osteria") you see the great boards of cold meats, cheese and jam starters, then the piadina station where ladies make the delicious flatbread. The next station you see is the pasta station where more staff create pasta from scratch with flour and eggs, rolling pins and knives. The next station is for desserts, gelatos and dessert wines where great cakes and puddings are created. And finally, on your way out you'll encounter the cash station and shop where you can buy anything you would like to take home with you!

Then you eat! Any meal starts with great platters of perfect cold hams from every part of the pig, superb cheeses and delightful confections of figs and apricots. Naturally freshly-made pasta follows, then there is a main course of meat and vegetables. Trencherman's food! Followed by perfect desserts – cheesecakes, applecakes, trifles and more. Then perfect coffee! And great wines throughout.

That sort of committment to good meticulous cooking and quality and management of food requires passion – and that's what Romagnolos like Tonino Guerra have a lot of.

So, in the magazine there was a big story about Tonino Guerra and his creations plus a bunch of other tough Romagnolo men and women. The list included the robber barons who owned Santarcangelo among other places – the Malatesta family, Mussolini the Romagnolo who grabbed power and ruled with a rod of iron and lots more.

Then my September came and everything started to close down in Marina di Ravenna. It was the end of the season. I wondered what I should do.

I was having my car cleaned by the beach and the man who was doing it asked what my profession was. "I write" I said "So do I" replied Alessandro. Turns out that he was an off-duty drummer and songwriter for a Romagnolo hard rock outfit and he invited me to a performance in Cesena's medieval castle. How could I refuse?

The band wasn't scheduled to play until midnight so I was looking for a little sustenance. " Where do you come from?" "Can I help you?" said my very new friend Chiara, who found me food and introduced me to her friend Daniela. I had been picked up in the very nicest way. The next day they took me to see 'their' Romagna.

We started off in Cesena, then off to see the source of the River Tiber, Rome's great river which naturally Mussolini had claimed for his own Romagna and moved the border. You can do that sort if thing if you're a dictator! Then we went off into the mountains for lunch in Sarsina – a fabulous pilgrimage site where the priest exorcised my demons by placing a metal collar around my throat. Then it was off to see Daniela's mountain home before dinner.

Up another mountain – Montecodruzzo – we had a staggeringly good dinner provided by the local farmer in his restaurant with sensational panoramic views stretching all the way to Tuscany.

"Where will I go now Marina di Ravenna is closing down" I said "Longiano" said they.

Within a few days Chiara and Daniela had taken me to Longiano for lunch and to meet the locals and within a few more I'd got a stunning aparrment there.

Daniela had a little local advantage as she had worked in the local castle art collection, which is another Romagnolo story in itself.

Local poet Tito Balestra was yet another typical Romagnolo man, passionate, argumentative, chauvinistic, above all lovable, apparently. He had a lot of friends, did Tito, in the years before and after the second world war. Friends like top artists and art dealers and they all gave him gifts – arty gifts. Hence the local castle art collection with great Italian painters represented plus work from artists like Degas and Goya. Wow.

Then one morning I'm working in my apartment and I get a horrible pain in my stomach. I rang the local doctor, Luciano Guidi he came to see me and gave me a jab – "How much do I owe you?" Said I "Nothing" says he. By that night an ambulance has collected me to take me to Cesena Hospital. "I'm sorry" says the lovely doctor "You have pancreatitis".

For the three weeks I was in hospital, every day I had a visit from Chiara or Daniela or both. Each time they came to see me they wore different attractive costumes – very jolly. And their families came too, Daniella's mum worked in the hospital. And my family came, and Pam and, naturally Angelo.

And then I was on my way home to Longiano for a week or so showing Pam Romagna and then I was on my way home to the UK.

Back in Bath for Christmas, I was pretty sure that my Romagna adventure was over. Nobody in the hospital had found out what had caused my pancreatitis so that was fairly high on my agenda. Plus, I had sustainable tourism reports to write.

So, a few months of ordinary work and then a couple of interesting events were lined up. I'd been invited to speak in five places – three of which I was in two minds about – Grozny, Ürümqi and Rostov Veliky the other two I was in only one mind about – Grenada and Hasselt.

Why worry about having doubts? Two minds sometimes work. Well, I didn't like Grozny because of the mayor, I'd met him in Iran, with his henchmen and I never saw him smile once. Apart from that Grozny looked like a horrible place – a new Soviet city. And, by the sound of what I'd heard – full of violence – it was after all the capital of Chechnya full of marauding terrorists apparently. However, I had a rule never to refuse to go somewhere that I hadn't been before. So I checked with the insurance company – given my undiagnosed pancreatitis they wanted a kings fortune. Nobody was going to pay.

Ürümqi was a different story. Someone I didn't know rang me and said that not only would they pay for my flights and accommodation, but they would give me real money too. And the conference was interesting when they emailed me about it. Apart from all that I was fascinated with the story of the Uyghur people – the massive muslim population living in China. And Ürümqi was fascinating too, a major Chinese hub on the ancient Silk Road.

A little current problem was the rioting that was happening as a result of the Uyghur people not getting a good deal.

Anyway, I could get over the insurance by paying the required king's ransom. And then I had another bout of pancreatitis which put the cap on that little adventure.

Rostov Veliky was less easy to refuse being an ancient city close to Moscow and with a fabulous food history, but the combination of my pancreas problems and the cost of insurance knocked that one on the head.

But there were two that I really couldn't refuse. Grenada, I didn't care about the cost of the insurance I paid it willingly. Just the conference that I was to cover was worth it. It was packed with old friends, scientists that worked in climate change, long time tourism luminaries and people that wanted to meet me or I wanted to meet. And I am so pleased I took the risk – it was amazing.

It was a top-level conference with very accomplished people who all talked knowledgeable sense from the country's president to the minister of tourism all the way to the people who staffed the tourism offices.

And I loved the island and its many unique aspects – including chocolate manufacture. I even got to watch a cricket match! Accommodation in a superb eco-lodge was sensational.

But of course I hadn't forgotten about Italy or Romagna!

I'd never met Cristina Ambrosini before but we had talked by email as a result of Charlie Kao's chat with her at some trade show somewhere.

She was the publisher and editor of the Italian travel trade newspaper aptly named Agenzia di Viaggi (Travel Agent). It transpired that Cristina had a great idea, so we had arranged to meet when I finally got to Romagna that year.

I got the dinky little train for the spectacular scenic ride through the Apennines from Faenza right in the heart of Romagna to Florence right in the heart of Tuscany where Cristina was waiting for me.

Naturally we started with lunch. Cristina was keen on introducing me to some Florentine specialities so we started with her favourite – Crostini di Fegatini. Execrable! Maybe the only thing I have ever eaten in Italy that was totally disgusting. Not that I don't like chicken livers but these were horrible! Mind you the pasta and the fiorentina beef-steak certainly made up for it.

Then to our meeting. We were talking to Antonella Chiti from the Florence municipality and Chiara Bocchio of the UNESCO office of the City of Florence to arrange a 'Talk Show' for the event which was to be held in Padua in September.

The Responsible and Sustainable Tourism Prize was sponsored by Agenzia di Viaggi and other big Italian names in tourism to be awarded at World Heritage Tourism Exhibition, which is to be held in Padua around the awarding there were to be other events such as the talk show.

Just the life-enhancing experience I needed to be embedded in my recent memory when, back in Bristol, I sat in front of my consultant and she told me I had cancer in my pancreas. The cancer had been causing my pancreatitis. Meg Fitch-Jones held my hands as she told me and looked in my eyes with such kindness that I knew she had my best interests in mind. She suggested the Whipple procedure – a major 6-8 hour operation to remove the cancer. "If it works, you'll die of something else" She said.

Although I was shaken by the news and the fact that it was a massive operation which would remove some of my pancreas, some of my stomach, all of my duodenum and a length of intestine – there was no choice other than to go ahead.

The operation was organised for mid-September, just five months before my 70th birthday. So, I decided to have my birthday party in one particular amazingly good restaurant in Romagna. All my family were invited and they all said that they would come.

The anaesthetist raised her eyebrows when she heard my plan – "8 months is average recovery time for an 8–hour operation but you have to have something to look forward to – right?"

I spent the next few weeks getting fit and then I was off to Belgium and Italy.

First stop just had to be Ostend on the Belgian coast where my tourism journey had started. Here I needed lunch – not just lunch – my perfect favourite lunch – ripe, sweet beef tomatoes stuffed with real fresh mayonnaise and hand-shelled baby brown North Sea shrimps followed by a fat Sole Meunière (fried in butter) with real Belgian frites, finally a Dame Blanche – rich vanilla ice cream with a Belgian chocolate sauce with flaked almonds. Of course, I found this magical meal. And I followed it with a walk along my familiar promenade.

Afternoon – Diksmuide, where some of my family had come from and the fabulous cobbled square with the Butter Hall – which was still running the annual beer and chocolate festival I'd started 20 years previously.

Now Diksmuide had also become a tourist destination. Just 100 years ago the first world war had flattened the city but now, it looks just like it did before the war arrived. They're a tough bunch, the Flemings. And they're used to war. Resilient – that's the word.

Nearby Ypres had also cashed in on the war centenary tourism – the great thing about which was that it would be a four-year tourism boom – the length of the war. Plus it would be quality high-spending tourism – older people with a bit of money.

And then I was off to Romagna the pretty way – through Austria and the Alps. Another bunch of memories here – like our astonishingly profitable operation in Zell am See and fabulous Salzburg and Innsbruck, both great excursion destinations.

And back in Romagna it was time to eat, drink (well in my case fizzy water) because tomorrow you may die! Plus, I needed to buy some things. I needed a truly great dinner before the op – so I needed great Romagnolo sausage for the 'Ragu'.

I'd promised to do various things (like having great meals) and say goodbye to my friends, and then I was off back home via Strasbourg for the night and a massive plate of Choucroute. Strasbourg is extraordinary, in my view it is the best food city north of Milan. There is simply everything good in French cuisine – great cheeses, amazingly good desserts and cakes (including macarons, eclairs and biscuits), and wonderful salads. For me one of the problems about French and Italian food is bread – OK you've got brioches etc., but where are the superb currant breads? In Germany and Belgium.

In Strasbourg, my culinary problems are answered – there is absolutely superb bread. And another Franco-German triumph – Choucroute. As you arrive in Strasbourg, you'll see great fields of cabbage especially for Sauerkraut. But of course it's not just the Sauerkraut in Choucroute, it's the vast variety of meat too – different sausages, pieces of pork – I've seen 9 pieces of meat and more. With the proper bread and the correct boiled potatoes – it's a meal that will last you a day... or until you spot another great delicious dessert! Too heavy? You can also have a Choucroute with bits of fish too!

Strasbourg has other culinary specialities – like flammekueche (flame cake) basically a pizza but with toppings like cherry or cheese and bacon. Just a half an hour's walk will give you an appetite and food ideas for a week. Particularly in the baker's where my personal passion is Cramique – a confection of brioche, currants and sugar lumps!

If you want a good way of preparing for an operation – Strasbourg is a very effective one, plus it has the great River Rhine for a nice boat ride and the soaring cathedral where you can say your prayers.

Back in the UK, the night before the op, I prepared dinner for my three sons. A massive platter of tagliatelle with great parmesan and a ragu made of pork and beef, lots of different Romagnolo sausages, good olive oil, garlic, tomatoes carrots and celery. I'd made a great applecake with clotted cream for pudding. Bed early because I wasn't allowed to eat for 8 hours before the op which was set for 8am the next morning.

10 hours after the operation had started, I was awake, feeling horrid and minus a lot of my offal. Thanks to the brilliant and very fit surgeon (apparently, he hadn't had a pee for the whole 9-hour op) I was up and about within a couple of days and out of hospital in 10 days. That's not to say I didn't have my near-death experience. The High Dependency Unit where I was taken to after the operation was my nightmare. No natural light completely disoriented me and soon I was having a migraine, unable to feel my legs, unable to see or hear and unable to pass anything in my body due to the lack of plumbing. "Well here it is" I thought as I descended into numbness and nausea. But I wasn't allowed out of the world yet.

It took longer than I thought to get better enough to drive longish distances but by February I was ready to drive to Italy and back to Longiano for my birthday party.

So, off Pam and I set out in the trusty old VW Golf. First stop a fabulous lunch in a forest manor Michelin restaurant near Calais, ready to rock, great food finally. We spent the night in Auxerre – one of my first visits when I was a kid and, although a historic and pretty city never in danger of being overloaded wth tourists. The next night after driving through the Alps, we were in Italy, just outside of Ravenna and the village of San Pancrazio.

Of course I should have realised! I was here the year before last, and in Saint Pancrazy in Slovenia – everything comes in threes – the third was my own pancreas getting wonky!

But here in San Pancrazio was the very rococo hotel Villa Roncuzzi run by a friend, an ex-art dealer and it was stuffed full of pictures, statues and mosaics. Plus all of my family, each a work of art in themselves and well up for a weekend party!

Patrizia, the owner, had asked if we wanted a dinner on the eve of my birthday. As my family were arriving from all over and many of them on late flights, I'd said "just a plate of pasta – maybe."

In the event just a plate of perfect tagliatelle with ragu was produced. After a plate of mixed hors d'oeuvres and before a plate of fillet steak and another bowl of Zuppa Inglese. All of this was accompanied by copious amounts of wine. How nice I thought. But far, far too much to feed a bunch who weren't hungry.

The idea was that the next day we would have lunch in Longiano all together and I'd been looking forward to it for at least a year. For a big lunch – we'd settled on starting at midday and finishing at 6pm – we would all need a good rest – so early to bed.

My birthday dawned bright and cold and after a stamina-giving full-on breakfast we were off to Longiano. So about forty of us sat down for lunch at the superb Dei Cantoni restaurant – all my family plus Angelo and his long-suffering wife Marian and Sandra who'd come from Amsterdam with her daughter. Plus there was a goodly bunch of my Italian friends. I'd discussed the menu with my friends Danilo and Teresa who owned the restaurant and we had decided to do only local specialities plus vegetarian for my sister, her daughter and my eldest grandchild. Anyway, I knew it was going to be good.

And just like the magnificent long banquets I remembered from my childhood in Belgium our lunch would be a relaxed affair including walks around, playing outside, informal fun and very long.

And we started with a walk. Longiano's councillor in charge of the arts and culture Cristina Minotti and the tourism manager Emiliano Ceredi met us and gave us a nice tour – up to the picturesque medieval castle, down to the beautiful picturesque theatre, into the quirky museum of cast iron, before we repaired for lunch.

We started with great platters of antipasto. Some with tender artichokes deep fried in the lightest of light batters, local pork sausage with a mustard sauce and grilled porcini mushrooms with rocket and parmesan; others with great speciality local prosciutto, salami and Squacquerone (the freshest of fresh local cream cheese) served with local sea salt and caramelised figs and, of course fresh, warm Piadina flatbread. Naturally there were also crostini – some with toppings of vegetables and cheese, others topped with roasted Tomino cheese and yet others with delicious sweet/bitter fresh herb salads.

Then came the pasta – all freshly made that morning. Just two! But a magnificent pair – the first – Cappellacci stuffed with Ricotta and Raveggiolo cheeses and topped with fresh local porcini mushrooms and baby tomatoes. The second was baby potato gnocchi with a cream sauce of local strong pit-fermented cheese and bacon.

And now for the main courses! Rabbit cooked in casserole with lemon and olive; grilled beef with sun dried tomatoes and truffles; rare breed local pork with roast potatoes and caramelised balsamic.

And, of course, there was room for the millefeuille birthday cake stuffed with cream and strawberries and laden with icing sugar – and candles.

All was washed down with great local wines, soft drinks for the kids and water for everybody (including me!).

The kids were happy, there was a playground outside and plenty of pop within. At six-ish we raised ourselves to our feet, made more speeches and toasts and then we were on our way back to Villa Roncuzzi.

Where dinner and yet another celebration was awaiting!

My pleas for just a little plate of pasta had fallen on deaf ears and we arrived for a massive banquet just a couple of hours after we had already eaten one.

I'm very proud of my family. Seeing what was about to happen, they just sat down and ate. Another four courses with wine to go with them.

And then the whole event took on a surreal aspect. Alfredo, Patrizia's friend, had arrived from Rimini with what he suggested was very special wine. So, he stood up and talked about it to the whole table for what seemed like hours – in Italian, because he spoke not a word of English. He was only stopped by Maestro Carnevali – an older gent dressed up to the nines with his suitcase full of Ocarinas plus a couple of saxophones. He was to do his act which involved playing a tune on each of his many instruments. And, although Maestro Carnevali was quite happy to go into the history of ocarinas, I'm not.

We trotted off to bed defeated by the food and the hospitality.

One of the guests at my birthday lunch had been Dominique Morroli who happened to be the PR officer at San Marino. Lively, lovely Dominique had come to my lunch with important news – tomorrow was to be a kids' carnival in San Marino – for St Valentine's Day.

San Marino was to be the first stop and the main event on the day after my birthday lunch.

We made our way to the little republic's main square up the top of its mountain where Dominique was waiting for us with the regulation goodies. Masks, hats, swords and balloons (after all it was a carnival) were distributed to all! Everybody had a great time swordfighting, chucking things around and generally wrecking the decorations that San Marino had put up everywhere for the occasion. Lots of photos were taken and all that activity got the better of us so it was time for a splendid lunch.

A stroll up and down the mountain before we went off to Cesena for gelato and a wander around the town's picture-perfect square and a visit to the castle (the scene of my meeting with Dani and Chiara before I got ill). Naturally now Dani was with us all so she gave us a tour before our big dinner in the amazing Malatesta castle.

What a wonderful few days for a birthday – and the sun shone – there was even a bit of picturesque snow!

They all went home happy – even after having to pay for the unwanted but spectacular extra birthday party. And Pam and I stayed for a few more days.

And I stayed for even more days before I drove off to somewhere I'd been going to each year for nearly four decades – ITB Berlin – the biggest travel trade show in the world.

First stop Prague. Strangely I had never been there before. Here, I stayed in a lovely art nouveau hotel, cheap. The streets were nice to walk, brilliant bits of architecture at every corner. And great food too. But cram-ram packed with tourists and tourist guides soliciting business. You could have any kind of tour you wanted free – food tour, fun tour, history tour – even a mathematics tour. However, I found the really offensive tours the ones by Segway. How can you protect and cherish fragile, beautiful places with hordes of young people zipping around on segways and getting 5 minutes to look. Done, zip off to the next spot. Don't worry, I'll rant more about the near blasphemy of overtourism later.

So, thanks Prague, next stop somewhere I've wanted to go to for years – Dresden, the stunningly beautiful city that my country firebombed into oblivion.

Parked up next to a football bus outside a posh hotel in the centre. Walked into the main square right into an anti-fascist demonstration. Doesn't take long, does it? I had a long chat with one if the demonstrators. It's a tough call for Germany.

As you know, Germany is very close to my heart, after all it was this country's beauty and diversity that lured me into tourism to start with. And I've visited many times and watched with admiration as this smashed and defeated state has gradually, meticulously, put itself together again. I never visit without thinking how difficult it must be to engage with the hideous actions that were taken, admit them and make amends. Added to which, they had to deal with the destruction of their homes, the raping of over two million women and children, and the largest movement of people in human history – the 15-20 million post-war homeless German refugees.

Against that background, when East Germany folded, the country had been re-united at great cost with the unreconstructed East Germans now part of the family and fanning the flames of a right-wing neo-nazi movenent. That was the spectre as I arrived in Dresden.

Now, again, Dresden is beautiful. It seemed to me like a frail old lady with a fabulous bone structure. And Dresden is big in tourism with about 5 million visitors a year. Once again Dresden is a cultural magnet; one of its famous buildings, the Semper Opera is home to both a great opera and a ballet company. The city's biggest event, a massive Christmas Market, that mixture of religion, history, eating, drinking and shopping!

Finally I arrived in Berlin for the ITB – the world's biggest travel show, plus the IHIF – the International Hotel Investment Forum.

The ITB is probably my key to the year's events. It was big and important when I first went there in the 1970s in particular because it faced East as well as West and because it was where you knew what Europe thought. Plus it's always been a bit left-of-centre whereas its main competitor the London-based World Travel Market is much more overtly commercial.

Anyway, WTM is in November and ITB is in March so anyone can, and should do both. Now, ITB was big and important 40 years ago when Berlin had a big wall around it and international tourism was a tiny fraction of what it is now. You can imagine just how big it was in 2015 – enormous! And multilingual – possibly just like a million square feet of towers of Babel. At the end of the week of ITB my feet are like raw meat and my brain is blown.

But I am grateful. Although it has got progressively more difficult to distill all the diverse ideas that come from ITB, it really is edgy and thought-provoking.

Plus it's got heart. My friend Rika Jean Francois is the CSR commissioner of ITB and I guess to her CSR simply means "Do the right thing" so she is constantly adding subjects and making people talk about – refugees, LGBTQ, human rights, child trafficking/tourism, climate change, women's rights and empowerment, accessibility, all in a tourism context. It really proves the point that tourism can actually be relevant.

But, above all, ITB is held in Berlin and that means three important things to me.

The first is that more than any other city I know, Berlin changes dramatically every year. Well, I suppose it has to. Just 70 years ago, after five years of war and one massive invasion from four sides, it was completely wrecked. It had to be built again. As a yearly visitor, I've been privileged to watch that rebuilding take place, I've been able to see one of the world's great historical capital cities take shape as it grows from its ruins.

And by ruins, I don't just mean the buildings. What happens to a community when their women and children are raped and abused, when they have to scavenge for food, when their city is razed to the ground and split in four, when they must lose their self-respect just to survive, when their countrymen have become part of the greatest refugee movement in the history of the world?

I started coming to Berlin just 30 years since this utter desolation happened and when still the city was split into two. There was one side beyond Checkpoint Charlie which was grey and impoverished, where you could still buy plastic neckties for useless money – Ostmarks. The west side, on the other hand, was peopled by fascinating international people, often renegades, who found Berlin and its unjudgmental attitude to their liking. I remember walking down Kurfürstendamm at night looking at the glitzy shops, the neon lights and that bright blue light from the gaunt Kaiser Wilhelm church and thinking – this is a demonstrarion of the opulence available in the west.

But things were changing in the Soviet Union even then, and through Land Travel we were a part of it. We were taking people for coach holidays in Poland and Hungary – as it happens many of the coaches brought back cheap caviar and cheap Cuban cigars for me!

And when the wall came down – Bonanza. We brought thousands of people out for weekends in this new colourful destination and we brought back tons of the hideous wall to give away.

The thing I could never understand though was how the local people were dealing with their swap. After all then they all had guaranteed jobs, childcare, holidays, university education, pensions and healthcare and this year they'd swapped all if it for ´freedom'

And the change stepped up a gear. Berlin became a property-developer's delight. You could see them filling up the top hotels and cracking deals to gentrify the city.

Every year when I visit Berlin for ITB, I stay in an up-and-coming quarter that had been rescued from the rubble and is being given the treatment to deliver massive profits. It was and still is totally inspirational.

And every year I learn more about Berlin's trauma and against that background the story is even more inspirational. But the fact that takes the Berlin story into yet another dimension of inspirational is that the Berliners didn't just dust themselves down, get up and start again. They truly engaged with their own country's part in their downfall. Nowadays you can't get very far without seeing evidence of Berlin's and Germany's dark past, displayed and annotated for all to see.

Particularly heartrending are the brass bricks called 'Stolperstein' (stumbling stones) on the pavement in front of individual houses telling the story of the Jewish people (and others proscribed by the Nazis) that lived there and what awful fate befell them.

And then it was back to the UK for a month or two and back to Romagna!

I had a plan and as a result of my visit with Cristina, I had a new friend in Florence. Antonella Chiti was a historian specialising in Dante and the Italian language – she was currently in charge of events in Florence. With a mass of curls and a fun demeanour and was certainly up for a laugh! I thought we would make a great team to check out Romagna's castles – and have a few nice meals together.

We couldn't check them all – there were said to be over 300 of them – but we could at least check out the best, so she came over to stay with me in Longiano as a base for our adventure.

Obviously, the castles are on hills and the hills are around the river valleys. All we needed to do was to take the valleys one by one and work from the sea to the hills on each. The two main castellated valleys were the Conca and the Marrechia river valleys – and as Antonella and I drove around checking them out, these historic valleys revealed a glorious haul of fabulous and very different castles.

We started with the Conca valley and the biggie! A long time ago Cinzia had promised to take me to Gradara "Incredible, romantic" she had said, and now I knew why. First its position was perfect, looking out over the Adriatic on the one side and the hinterland on the other; no one could pass without the Malatesta family knowing. Plus it was really big – encompassing a substantial village. And it had a great deal of atmospheric history. It makes the most of the fact that it is the most likely place that Paolo and Francesca kissed (remember Dante's Inferno?). And the 'exact room' is identified. But above all the touristy stuff it is beautiful and a delightful home for a thousand or so lucky residents – with nice restaurants and tea shops, bars and loads of events. None of the Conca castles were as magnificent as Gradara but they were all truly charming.

You'd think that a castle was a castle wouldn't you, after all in the middle ages there weren't so many architects or designers. The warlords made their own decisions and forced locals to labour. A thousand or so years of standing up in one place changed each castle, though, to its unique environment, so now each castle is very different. As we travelled down the Conca valley we experienced a fascinating range of castle surprises. San Giovanni in Marignano is now one of Italy's most beautiful villages. In San Clemente, the village has forced itself into the castle, each year in Montecolombo visitors stream over the drawbridge to a magnificent strozzapreti pasta festival; in fascinating Gemmano the castle hosts a wild boar festival; soaring Montefiore Conca looks like a modern skyscraper until you get there and see the old stones, gardens and the delightful castle-village. Saludecio, which often feels gaunt and deserted, comes to life each year with its own medieval festival. Mondaino has a semi-circular piazza where each year there is a real 'Palio' complete with soldiers in ceremonial costumes and medieval bands. Finally Montegridolfo is a true classic of Malatesta design with a moat, a drawbridge and a watchtower. As all the castles are on hills they were naturally surrounded with historic vineyards producing wonderful wines.

And the fact is that the river Conca is not even really important locally, whereas when we got to the more important Marecchia river, the curtains were opened to some glorious surprises.

We started off in Pennabilli. Right up in the foothills of the Apennines, the city has a colourful history. It's changed hands (and ruling families and regions) again and again – the Malatestas of Romagna owned it, then the Montefeltros of Marche's Urbino and vice versa and now it boasts its own cathedral, a couple of monasteries, an array of piazzas, a bunch of quirky museums, and a hilltop garden complete with prayer-wheels inaugurated by the Dalai Lama. And of course, its own magnificent castle!

Down the road we saw a classic chocolate-box castle – Petrella Guidi. Stunningly beautiful, from the battlements of this pocket-sized Malatesta castle it's possible to see the gorgeous backgrounds that both Piero della Francesca and, allegedly, Leonardo da Vinci used for their pictures.

And as the lovely hill road wound into a valley, we spotted, on the next hill, Sant'Agata Feltria. Like a dream this real fairytale castle appeared. Built by the Fregoso family we thought it was possibly one of the most beautiful we'd seen. And the town around it delightful – it has an antique, still-used, teeny tiny wooden theatre, some fabulous piazzas a lovely 10th-century church and a bunch of big festivals including the massive autumnal National Truffle Festival.

Just a hop, skip and jump down the very pretty winding road we found yet another jewel. San Leo, even more important, soaring and perched on a higher rock than the others, it was sensational. The heart of the Montefeltro warlord territory, the impregnable forbidding castle, designed by Martini, has securely housed extraordinary prisoners such as the magician and alchemist Calliostro and various doomed political prisoners until just 70 years ago.

Yet the ancient cathedral built on pagan ruins was a part of St Francis of Assisi's domain and the rest of the tiny hilltop area embodies a fabulous pocket-sized real city of art.

By now we were only half way down the valley, still to come were the lovely castle of Montebello with its legend of Azzurina the albino fairy; the daunting castle of Torriana where prisoners such as Gianciotto Malatesta, who killed his wife and brother Francesca and Paolo (remember Dante?) were held in deep pits – and the castle of Maiolo which was pushed down the hill by the almighty when the inhabitants performed the 'Dance of the Angels'; naturally we couldn't miss Talamello where hundreds of cheeses were busily maturing in pits, ready to be taken out in November!

I just couldn't believe that there was much more to come, but then we were halted in our tracks by the sight of Verruchio, the Malatesta eyrie, the fabulous walled town created by the robber-baron family with views all over their territory.

Getting back to urban civilisation we were confronted by yet another massive Malatesta citadel dominating the sophisticated medieval city of Santarcangelo di Romagna.

Then the mountaintop republic of San Marino became visible. The triangular peak, a maze of rock-hewn streets, houses, shops, churches cathedrals and grand government buildings. And no less than three amazing gothic castles. This should have been the zenith of our journey but the best was yet to come.

Down on the plain Rimini was originally created as Ariminum, the port where the Marecchia met the sea. It was a completely new Roman city, prosperous, on a major Roman crossroads and powerful with an ampitheatre, even. Its riches only slightly reduced after the Romans left, the Malatestas must have lusted after it from their mountain base. And, of course, they got it, built their biggest castle and their own temple and heralded in a glorious era of art fuelled by their massive ill-gotten gains.

What a couple of days of castles! And who would have believed that this road all the way along the Marecchia was less than 50 kilometres long?

After this delightful assault on my senses a bit of a rest was in order, but soon my Romagna year came into full swing on Mayday...

The first time I saw the fireflies, I was spellbound. Returning to my rented apartment late at night, I thought that I had become intoxicated with the warmth and the scent of jasmine and that these little flying pulsating lights in the garden were another part of a beautiful waking dream.

"No dream" said Roberta Sama the next morning "We call them 'lucciole' and we are having a walk tonight to see them in my village, Castiglione di Roncofreddo – please wear walking boots"

Anyway, I had somewhere else to go over the valley first – I was off to nearby Montecodruzzo (with my walking boots) because I'd been invited on another walk, a walk for landscapes and for my well-being.

Montecodruzzo ranks pretty high in my personal hierarchy of great Romagna places for two reasons. One is the spectacular view of the surrounding countryside – all the way from the Adriatic Sea to the Apennine mountains and Tuscany. And the second is the best place to see this amazing vista – from a window table in the fabulous, unpretentious Osteria di Montecodruzzo. Here, Massimo Monti uses his family's local farm to deliver sensational 'Zero kilometre' food – at extraordinary prices.

The Gurkha squad who liberated the hill in 1945 were amply rewarded too by Massimo – 70 years later they enjoyed a great celebration in his restaurant.

But now I was here on a walk to understand another reason why Montecodruzzo was so great – because of the hill's healing properties and the opportunities for 'Benessere' or wellbeing tourism.

Donatella Onofri had designed a walk around the hill both to see the unbelievably splendid views outwards for hundreds of kilometers towards the Tuscan hills – and inwards to understand the healing power of the massive edifice.

I'd been introduced to Donatella by Daniela Corrente who ran a strange little studio in Cesena and by Vittorio Belli a local wildlife specialist.

Equipped with two dowsing rods each – one for water the other for power in the form of ley lines – we walked around the hill (and its amazing views) through its hawthorns and oak trees and in and out of its power sites. As we walked we talked about the history of the area, all the way from the Etruscans, through where Caesar crossed the Rubicon to the last war, the Ghurkas and the present day. And, of course – because this is Romagna, ruminated about the best places for mushrooms and other edible goodies.

An afternoon full of food for thought.

Later, properly prepared as instructed by Roberta, at dusk, I found myself a few kilometers from Montecodruzzo, a part of a happy crowd of over a hundred in the tiny village of Castiglione di Roncofreddo in the Rigossa river valley.

A field had been requisitioned as a car park, complete with high-vis-coated attendants. The lovely little church had been opened and decorated for the occasion, was full of families enjoying a guitarist leading children singing and an actor reading poetry. On the lawns outside there was a picnic stand loaded with donated delicious cakes, tarts, fruit juices and wine. Excited groups talked as it got dark enough to start.

And, as a bemused English family of tourists were brought out of their rented villa to join in the walk, an excited hush fell over the crowd. Short instructions and calls to enjoy the walk were given by Roberta and we started into the woods.

Are there woods in Paradise? If so these were they! Great hedges and trees and ferns were illuminated by fireflies performing their mating dance. Lovely valleys took on an otherworld air as sparkling fields came to twinkling life in the dark. The five-kilometer path was muddy after the recent rains but helping hands were always ready.

So the satisfied, chattering crowd enjoyed a truly enchanting walk. As we returned to the village, we were reminded that life was not always so pleasant in Castiglione. The village was under siege in the last world war and our happy group took advantage of the British Army-built Bailey Bridge to get to our penultimate stop – a garden lovingly created by a local resident.

Not just a garden but Mr Calandrini's life's work – everything created by his hands and called 'Fred Flintstone's Home' by locals. A stunning, and very otherworldly setting – particularly under the dark, star-filled night sky.

The guitarist was now sitting in a woodland glade in Mr Calandrini's garden and accompanying the beautiful young Samanta Balzani singing medieval songs and playing an otherworldly, and very different glass harp made of crystal and metal bowls. And all totally in keeping with the dreamy air of the evening.

But the happy end of the evening was eating tart and cake and cookies accompanied by local wine and fruit juices as we all came back to reality. Sad really.

And the next evening was to take all the sadness away. Still in the parish of Roncofreddo stands yet another soaring hillside – Sorrivoli (my translation – 'smiling flights'!) is another stunning castellated hill where lots of good things happen.

Resident Ilario Fioravanti (1922-2012) was an extremely prolific and well-known Romagnolo sculptor, but first he was a great architect. And judging by his house in Sorrivoli he had a magnificent eye for a magnificent view, and a great vision for a wonderful home.

Here, in the garden of his house and studio – Casa Dell'Upupa (the hoopoe garden) another event was taking place – an evening in his memory, hosted by his wife Adele. Aptly entitled "Food for the body, food for the mind and food for JOY" and 100 or so locals were joining in the celebration.

A harpsichord and a flute provided the music, local people provided the food and the wine, Adele and her friends provided the warm hospitality and the views were provided by a generous divinity!

Full of divine food and drink and music, we were treated to yet more divinity in the shape of Ilario's massive treasure-chest of sculptures still living in his house. Covering subjects from crucifixion to sensuality and ranging from satire to religion, the sculptures are a remaining memory of a wide-ranging mind.

Back in Longiano a few days later, another celebration was taking place – the unveiling of a new postage stamp with a picture of the castle. First day postmark will include a castle stamp and third day cover will include a cherry stamp!

Because it's cherry time on the hill of Longiano – and its ancient valley of cherry trees. At 9am at least a hundred locals were ready for the walk to celebrate the glorious fruit and enjoy the stunning valley –

before they send their postcards with the new stamps. And I'm joining the walk, nearly-fit as I am.

After a briefing by our guide, out-of-uniform local police chief Maurizio Sartini, and by local culture and tourism boss Cristina Minotti, we make our way down into the ultra-fecund valley

More amazing views, delightful walks and a happy crowd gorging themselves for 10 kilometres of apricots, peaches, sweet, sweet peas, grapes – and, of course, fabulous, big, ripe, red, succulent cherries.

It's no wonder that when we get back, the Longiano Cherry Feast is getting ready to rock.

The streets are lined with colourful stalls and much more. Vendors are selling sweets, local olive oils, local wines, kitchen equipment, local honey and local sausage, local meat and local fruit and veg, local handicrafts and local artisan work. And, of course great baskets of local cherries and cherry-related things are on sale – like cherry beer and cherry wood. There are cherries everywhere – even the delicious ice-creams on sale in the local gelateria have cherries on top.

The warm jasmine-scented nights are full of song and dance and entertainment – comedians speaking local Romagnolo dialect take the stage, alongside rock bands and country-and-western singers.

The feast-days are full of entertainment too – from the local historical group through the enthusiastically enjoined tug-of-war to the greasy pole with a great whole local prosciutto hanging from the top as an enticing prize. And, to make sure there is order throughout – Maurizio the police chief is back in uniform!

Three days full of merrymaking in Longiano – and all in honour of plump, ripe delicious cherries!

And, just a few weeks before, we'd celebrated Mayday when what seemed to be the whole population plus a bunch of multi-national cyclists were sitting around in the main square in the sun, waiting to be entertained.

Mayday is worker's day and all the workers around here are farmers ready to show off all they have worked hard for. Tractors of all sorts, big and small, green and red, make the parade, driven by proud owners, garlanded with leaves, often pulling carts – some full of merrymaking groups and one with a blow-up doll – chug their way through the square and beyond in what seems a never-ending bucolic traffic jam.

The strains of "Romagna Mia" fill the air as the politicians on the podium fight a losing battle in their pontifications.

What could be better than a Mayday lunch with some locals at their house in the valley, in the sun with views of the Adriatic some 10km away. Men and women are competing with each other rolling Strozzapreti ('Strangled Priest' – the local pasta), and we've already hacked our way into some local hard cheese and olives. Cooked in five minutes, sauced and eaten in less – the Strozzapreti are delicious – one savoury, the other sweet. Then come strawberries with custard and finally the egg whites not used in the custard have made meringues to go with our coffee.

From the house you can see the Leonardo da Vinci port of Cesenatico so it's a very short journey.

Of course, it's still Mayday in the port and here the workers are fishermen (Cesenatico has the biggest fishing fleet in the Adriatic just now). So naturally everybody was celebrating FISH.

The festa is called Azzuro come il Pesce (Blue like the fish!) and there are thousands cramming the port and the restaurants and at 10pm they're still piling in. Why? Because there is great food here and happy crowds and because the prices are little short of miraculous. Fritto misto of fish, risotto of fish, all sorts of pasta with all sorts of Adriatic fish – there are even perfect fish burgers.

And the May Day weekend still is not over, the next day in Longiano, around the towering castle there is an artisan and craft fair where local workers come to share their talents and their products with locals and visitors. It's called 'Mestieri'. It even includes workshops to learn crafts – not forgetting the major local craft of making pasta – an opportunity to try archery and a whole demonstration about the history of radio.

The event was set up by local tourism boss Cristina Minotti together with the extraordinary Folk Museum which is crammed full of local stuff – pictures, looms, Vespas, film posters, books, kitchen equipment, tools, tractors, furniture – everything that was treasured by local households and found no modern use.

The sunset was going to be great and yet another mountain had to be visited.

Naturally back at the top of Montecodruzzo there was a well-attended local Mayday dinner festival at Massimo's Osteria di Montecodruzzo.

The artichokes are just in season, so today we started with a little frittata, followed by a salad of raw baby artichoke, aged parmesan and rocket before we ate a fabulous Cappellacci (little local pasta hats!) stuffed with fresh local cream cheese and covered with pancetta, artichoke, and parmesan. Followed by Osso Buco of Massimo's white Romagnolo beef and portions of his grilled rare breed Moro Romagnolo pork, sausages, back rib and bacon.

Plus the best courgettes, aubergines and rosemary roast potatoes and gratin tomatoes that you are ever likely to eat.

And what's on next week!

The Mutoids (or Mutoidi as they're known here) are loved and cherished by the citizens of Santarcangelo. Even though they are largely Brits, this avante-garde collective appear to have been granted honorary Romagnolo status.

About as sustainable as it gets, the Mutoids take scrap metal and alchemise it into great, smack-you-in-they-eye-and-the-laughter-gland art.

Finding it difficult to live in a Thatcherite England, these Acid-House influence travellers first gelled in Berlin creating a massive MIG-based sculpture whilst the wall was being pulled down in 1989.

To cut a long story short, they arrived in Santarcangelo via London, Amsterdam, Barcelona, Berlin and, of course the Glastonbury Festival.

The Mutoidi originally visited to perform at the Santarcangelo Street Theatre Festival in 1990 and liked it so much they wanted to stay. Luckily the local lady Mayor liked them too and offered them an ideal site – a disused gravel quarry beside the Marecchia River.

Here they worked happily for ages, creating their full metal monsters, giving trouble to no-one until one distant neighbour complained and an eviction order was delivered from Rome.

Now, Santarcangelo is a funny place and apart from the fact that they really like the Mutoidi, they certainly don't like to be told what to do by any bunch of time-serving civil servants. So the citizens of Santarcangelo (pop. 22,000) rose up in their thousands and raised over 12,000 signatures for the petition to keep the Mutoidi.

And now the Mutoid Waste Company has become Mutonia – The Tourism Attraction. Already work is appearing in nearby (and just as vigorously independent) San Marino.

The big event this week was the exhilarating Mille Miglia – the thousand-mile drive for classic cars paraded near to Santarcangelo, then over the 2,000 year-old Tiberius Bridge in nearby Rimini. Pity any car broken down and left for dead as Mutoids would certainly pick it up and transform it!

Dozens of purring top-class Mercedes led the parade followed by every kind of Ferrari growling across the bridge. Then… well over 400 classic cars mounted the bridge to the cheers of the spectators. Participation is limited to cars, produced no later than 1957, which had attended (or were registered) to the original race. So Porsches, Jaguars, Bentleys, Alfa Romeos, Bugattis, Mercedes, Aston Martins, BMWs, Maseratis, Fiats, Abarths, and the rest of a multi-billion dollar parade of classic cars participated – a true feast of engineering beauty.

Although the entry fee is €10,000 per car, you do get a free pair of Chopard watches to remember the occasion.

And, for free, onlookers get a truly incredible spectacle. It is described as "A demented and indulgent road race around Italy – the fulfilment of so many pleasures at once – speed, gluttony, bravado – all crammed into three days."

Whereas on the other hand the Motogiro d'Italia, although showcasing classic motorbikes and passing through Romagna the weekend after, is a different thing entirely. Yes, it is also run over 1,000 miles (1500km) and yes, it showcases classic bikes – but no – it's not expensive to enter.

So, the amateurs say it's much more fun – even if they come from the other end of the world to take part.

On the day I visited San Marino to see the Motogiro – it was like motorcycle city – beautiful bikes everywhere, and the enthusiasm of the owners and the spectators is infectious.

Something like all the rest but less noisy (if you exclude the wild cheers of the spectators) was the Giro d'Italia. Naturally this massive cycling event comes down the Via Emilia in force so that all the Romagnoli can crowd the streets to watch.

While first the advance guard of smart cars zooms down, then the police and ambulances, then the dozen or so lorries selling pink souvenirs. And finally the competitors – a massive colourful bunch.

From the sublime to the ridiculous, the same week there was a MASSIVE metal sale. Mostrascambio – just 20km from Rimini) Over 800 stallholders take over the pretty little town of Gambettola selling scrap, antiques and items related to cars and vintage bikes and motorcycles.

It takes hours to pick through the maze of streets and the amazing exhibits and offers for sale.

Time to pick up a bargain to enter in the Mille Miglia or the Motogiro d'Italia or the Giro d'Italia or for Mutoidi to cart it away and make it into art.

Time for a party? In Romagna it's always time for a party! And at the tiny picturesque hilltop settlement of Pennabilli (pop 1,500) a massive party had just kicked off. 'Artisti in Piazza' plays host each year to 64 international theatre, music, circus and street art companies. This festival attracts no less that 40,000 guests from all over the world who enjoy great music and entertainment, fabulous food and wine and astonishing hospitality.

Asked "Why do you do this festival?" – Tonino Guerra, Romagnolo hero, replied "To have fun, of course!"

As you may imagine I was partied and dinnered out for a while and it was lucky the big food festival was a whole week away. Time for a little rest and relaxation on the balmy coast before a final two events before I left.

Forlimpopoli, Romagna has held an annual gastronomic event dedicated to Pellegrino Artusi "Father of Italian Cookery" and that year was its 18th birthday. For over a week every night between 7pm and midnight, the historical centre of this small town came alive as a 'City of Taste' for the Festa Artusiana.

Streets, alleys, courtyards and squares become stages for food stands featuring Artusi's dishes, exhibitions, performances, multimedia productions, tastings and gastronomic tours, concerts, children's events, cultural events, art displays, and more.

And, that week foodies from all over the world swarmed to Forlimpopoli to eat, drink, buy, learn and be merry! And with free entrance for everybody, there was fun and tastes, music and conversation for all.

Music was a melodious background around the town's citadel where more than 150 stalls opened up for business together with 40 open-air restaurants, which together with the 11 local ones, served massive portions of amazing food and wine every evening for 9 warm edible nights.

Everywhere you were able to buy and consume delicious specialities from the Artusi cookbook – listed by recipe number AND at extraordinarily low prices.

Pride of place was given to really local seasonal foods and great wines such as the Mora Romagna pork, the Squacquerone di Romagna cheese, Romagna peach and nectarine, the Romagna shallot, Volpina pears and the amazing wines including DOC Sangiovese di Romagna, DOCG Albana di Romagna and DOC Trebbiano di Romagna.

Finally, just down the road at the serene city of Cesena, another more ancient festival took place – the three-day celebration of St John the Baptist – Cesena's patron saint – has been taking place regularly for hundreds of years.

The city of Cesena was endowed by the rich and powerful Malatesta warrior family with both a soaring citadel overlooking the city and the world's first public library. But the thing that most Cesenate know best how to do is to celebrate, traditionally and, it must be said, rather stylishly.

The cobbled alleyways, elegant streets and delightfully paved squares are all festooned with stalls helping the inhabitants to drink, and eat and buy all they need to have a good time.

In pride of place were the red sugar cockerels, symbols of Romagna. The idea is that you resist eating these succulent delights until the eve of St John's Day and you whistle through them to get rid of all your sins! It's no wonder that all the stalls with cockerels on display (I counted a dozen at least!) were sell-outs.

Other stalls included even more traditional bits of St John's ware – beautiful hand-made sprays of lavender and garlic – the garlic to ward off witches and the lavender to ward off the smell of garlic! These bouquets were made by a daunting group of women numbering at least 20 who were creating them to fund the Red Cross. Special icecream (gelato) made of milk from the local 0-kilometer dairy was also on offer.

One of the traditions of the St John's Day festa is to buy something for your house – and (given that this is in Romagna) to get it at the very best price. All manner of stalls were doing great business – around 500 of them throughout the city centre!

Plus, a big fair, plus the usual outside summer culture that is Cesena.

And to cap it all, my friend Cristina Ambrosini finally let go of the reins of her publication for a few days and came from Rome to stay with me in Longiano.

Of course, there was a festa that weekend – a special party in the main square in celebration of the 'Streets of Taste' in the local area – in other words many opportunities to taste great local food and wine and music.

We'd also been invited to a fascinating evening called Cinema DiVino – where you watch a good film outdoors and taste great wine. As it happened very good wine indeed, organic and biodynamic wine at a stunningly beautiful boutique vineyard – Villa Venti close to Longiano with views of the castle.

Next day we did some shopping for olive oil, promised to work together on a number of projects including Cristina's first foray into the UK's World Travel Market and I put her on the train for Rome.

I went back to the UK for August to see my family. It's always a wonderful time and I feel so truly grateful and privileged to have them around.

Back to work at the end of the month, I drove to Belgium.

Professor Geoffrey Lipman, the man that I had first met in South Africa after he launched Green Globe some 20 years previously, had invited me to present at a summer school that he was holding at Hasselt University.

The summer school was a great idea. All about sustainable tourism, it was full of ambitious passionate young people from all over the world – all committed to sustainability. Plus, there were some great innovations.

In the heart of Flanders, Hasselt shows just how much Belgium has progressed socially and economically in the last 50 years.

When I went to buy shoe polish the shop-owner looked at my shoes and sold me the best and most expensive shoe polish I'd ever bought. It matched my shoes exactly, smelled wonderful and was an exclusive brand made in Paris. Not bad for a country that was practically destroyed in the First World War and emerged penniless from the second.

The lovely cobbled main square had lots of very good restaurants around it – and in the middle of the square there was a massive marquee, with a big band and singers who led the dancing every Tuesday and Thursday night. What fun!

And, being Flanders, there were dozens of great chocolate shops. But one in particular is lauded as the 'Best Chocolate Experience in Belgium' and it is. The attention to detail from the very best ingredients to superb design of shapes is meticulous. The tastes – heavenly.

All in all, a lovely, rich small town of which there are many in Flanders.

Of course, Belgium has a reputation for art and literature, architecture and learning. It also has a reputation for deep surreal quirkiness as exemplified by Magritte, Tin Tin and the Manneken Pis.

The University of Hasselt is set in a massive 17th-century city jail right in the downtown area. Its brilliant architectural design: a heavy-duty Belgian building, a cross between a convent and a castle.

The seminar inside was on the border of surrealism and futurology. It was totally ram-packed full of mind-bending questions.

OK, many of the lectures were, in fact, lectures in the formal sense of the word but if you wanted to know the future of tourism it was here in a very raw state of practically pure thought.

Geoffrey's got this project called 'SunArk' and it's more than very very futuristic. Imagine a totally zero-emission modern-day ark (a kind of Dr Who's telephone box filled with people and screens. Imagine a world (today) where everybody who enters a tourist destination is tracked on their smartphone. Imagine a computer program that feeds on big tourism data. Imagine a set of algorithms that use all this personal data to identify and direct visitors around the destination to see, to eat and drink, to sleep and spend, all in the right places and at the right times.

So, the idea is that these SunArks and their teams would be deployed in destinations all over the world to make tourism better, more sustainable and more efficient. In Geoffrey's word – 'Smart'.

Geoffrey had lined up some superb presenters to deal with some fairly unusual concepts.

The visionary Polish architect and creator of the Sun Ark, Jurek Kasperowicz, outlined the applications for this revolutionary ecological construction both as an initiative to provide desperately-needed care for refugees and as destination tourism observatories with particular applications in national parks.

The audience were treated to critical insights into the future of sustainable aviation within the European Union and on a global basis. The vision for the future of the airline industry against the background of emissions and critical agreements was delivered by world-class industry figures.

And the dramatic growth of smartphone applications in every area from crowdsourcing and tracking tourism to providing massive data were discussed and illuminated by experts.

Two global heavyweight sustainable tourism brains – Professor Harold Goodwin and Felix Dodds – delivered heavyweight presentations in the Maurice Strong 'Reflections Lectures' tracking the sustainability agenda, from 1972, its imminent outcomes and the critical need for responsible forms of tourism.

Even I gave a presentation.

But there was one event that quite blew my mind. You look at Geoffrey and listen to his presentations, remember that this man was executive director of the global airline organisation IATA, first president of the World Travel and Tourism Association, and assistant Secretary General of the UN World Tourism Organisation. Educated at a rugby-playing English grammar school. On the surface nobody could be more in tune with the hierarchy, more conformist.

And then he presents Koen Vanmechelen and his Cosmopolitan Chicken Project.

By then we were at Koen's HQ by Hasselt harbour – the "Open University of Diversity".

"This is a global, transdisciplinary and transtemporal examination of the themes of biocultural diversity and identity through the interplay of art, science and beauty." Says Koen

Koen crossbreeds chickens from different countries. His ultimate goal is the creation of a Cosmopolitan Chicken carrying the genes of all the planet's chicken breeds. In his view, much more than a mere domesticated animal, the chicken is art in itself.

Well, here, it is. There are vast tracts of exhibition space with videos, artworks, living and dead things, sounds and sights – all related to ...chickens.

My mind was totally blown by the sheer surreal audacity of it all – introduced to me by Geoffrey – a palpably middle-class, normal Englishman.

But not so much so as to not be floored by a text message I got later in the day from Cristina's sister to say that she'd had an accident and was dead. I simply didn't believe it but after some hours of investigating its truth was proved and I was totally gutted.

The event was over, I'd have to find out more about Koen's chicken project and its surreal opportunities later. Saddened, I drove back to Italy.

I had a job to do which involved hosting a few American travel agents checking out us and Romagna, looking after Angelo on a periodic visit and checking out three big Romagna festivals.

The first job would have been easier without Angelo as he had taken a dislike to the agents and spent most of his time complaining about them. This was a bit difficult as he had agreed to show them Florence and Venice. In normal circumstances there is nobody in the world who knows these two cities like Angelo. Going with him can be an extraordinary and sublime experience – but not this time, it was a nightmare.

I guess the problem was that although they were very large people, they were picky with their food so every mealtime was an Angelo nightmare.

Anyway, one day after the agents had gone back to America, I took Angelo to Dozza so he could see the fabulous painted town and the regional wine museum in the Sforza castle and we got separated amongst the museum's thousands of wine bottles. "Hello, where are you from?" Said Valentina, the young and beautiful elfin German girl engaging me in conversation. I told her exactly what I was doing in Italy, she sounded interested and told me that she was "As free as a bird" and she'd like to find out more. Quickly we started a correspondence that was to lead to much more.

I knew where Santarcangelo di Romagna was because I'd been there one evening for an astonishing performance in the main square of film music, with great light effects. At about €100 a ticket it wasn't cheap but there were at least 2000 paying punters. And the performances were superb.

So, when I went back for the annual Bird Fair Santarcangelo, I was no stranger. Bird Fair? Well they still sell a few cage birds but birds have become less important over the last thousand years or so and everything else – mainly food and drink – has become more important. A thousand stalls more important in fact. Held on the feast of St Michael, this must be the mother of all harvest festivals!

Piazza after piazza was crammed with people and food and all the stuff that goes with festas, basically food and drink and music. Naturally locals are keen to try new things too so stallholders come from all over Italy with their wares. For sale at the Bird Fair there were lots of sweet things from Sicily, lots of breads and oils from Tuscany, lots of cheeses and hams from Emilia, lots of special and interesting things from everywhere; pretty much every region in Italy has its own cuisine and its own speciality and Italians are a curious bunch interested in trying everything. Obviously, the aroma of food and drink is heady and the idea of plenty is very comforting.

But, big as it was, the Bird FaIr was only really a rehearsal for things to come. The truffle season heralded in two massive festivals in Romagna. The first was the aptly named National Festival of White Truffles in Sant'Agata Feltria the second the truly massive Festival of Saint Martin (more commonly known as the Cuckolds festival) in Santarcangelo.

Sant'Agata Feltria is truly beautiful and it has many assets that make it even more attractive. It has a historic soaring medieval castle, a pretty wooden working theatre, lots of lovely restaurants and a complete range of cobbled piazzas. It is quite spacious but even then there are so many people that want to attend the festival that it has to run over four ram-cram-packed weekends rather than just one. In the event hundreds of thousands of visitors flock to Sant'Agata in October.

And all these visitors get great value. There are hundreds of stalls selling truffle-related things from dried ceps to truffle sauces and oils to the real McCoy – little truffles protected from the air in little glass domes. And because it's the end of the season everything else is on sale too – there are dozens of stalls selling forgotten fruit and veg (plus the remembered ones as well). There are rows of stalls selling sweets, chocolates and sweet things generally – cakes, sweeties, spun sugar etc – winter is on the way! And there are many stalls selling cheese and butter and other dairy products. Plus of course the local fast food – piadina – flat bread stuffed with anything you want, mainly prosciutto, squacquerone and rucola, always warm and delicious. Performing bands strolled around to accompany singing and dancing and the 17th-century little theatre opened its doors. It was lovely.

Obviously, this was autumn after harvest so there were festivals cropping up everywhere and, as the truffle festival closed and the town swept up, Santarcangelo was preparing for the Biggie. I'd heard about the Cuckold Festival but this was the first time I would see it. Luckily, I had a couple of chaperone/interpreters in the shape of Daniela and Chiara.

The rain was just letting up and the clouds clearing a little as we got to an out-of-town parking place where we were to get the bus into the city. There were such massive crowds that the city itself was closed to cars. The bus dropped us off about half a kilometre from the main square but even there it was heaving.

Santarcangelo is a fairly substantial place but the whole city was crammed. I would not have been surprised if there were over a hundred thousand visitors that day.

Why? To eat and drink and buy and chat and watch and laugh and joke and hug and kiss and walk just like their forefathers had been doing for at least the last thousand years or so at the Fair of San Martino here in the heart of Romagna.

First we fought our way through to the main square where we could see the ceremonial arch now surrounded by heaving crowds and dozens of colourful stalls. As is usual at San Martino, many stalls display great bulls' heads and suspended from the arch itself is a magnificent pair of bull's horns. The idea? Men who are brave enough walk under the arch – and if the horns wobble – the cry of "Becchi" goes up as the man is accused of being a cuckold – his woman has given herself to another!

That emotional challenge over, we wander (or to be more exact push ourselves) around. Today Santarcangelo truly is the harvest land of plenty. Around the main square many stalls have joined together to create great tented emporia stuffed full of autumn delicacies – mushrooms and truffles, great sausages and cheeses, enormous mountains of sweets and other sugary treats, cakes and jams and chutneys. And, of course there are gallons and gallons of great wines, olive oils and vinegars – from all over Italy, and in particular from the local area – fertile Romagna. And each emporium was stuffed full of local people too, great extended families, young couples arm-in-arm and loads of kids – buying, feeding, laughing, cavorting often all at once – after all the harvest is in!

Of course, there are fruit and vegetables too, food-packed stalls, great heaving tables, trays and plates, baskets and boxes, crates and crates of it. Gleaming fruits and vegetables I recognised and local speciality exotic fruits and vegetables I didn't. Here in Santarcangelo you can find anything you want at the Cuckolds Festival – succulent Cardoons of course, volpina pears for pickling of course, perfect lumpy yellow quinces, of course, piquant medlars, of course, plus dozens and dozens of forgotten varieties of apples and pears and berries. All beautifully presented and delicious.

Here there is everything you need for your home and everything you need for your wardrobe and everything you need for your kitchen and your garden plus many, many things that you never knew you needed.

So the Cuckolds Fair was enormous and amazing, gargantuan and packed with local people walking and talking and eating and falling out of cafés and restaurants and bars and gelateries obviously set to eat and drink the city dry.

But as I was to learn, all this too was just a rehearsal for a region-wide festival that would start in just a few weeks – on the festival of the Immaculate Conception on the 8th of December, panettone would be baked and the Nativity would be ushered in.

In Romagna I found out that Christmas festivities, fun, frolics and feasting are taken very, very, seriously. I drove around the whole area to see it.

Romagnolo people just love any celebration and Christmas is the big one, so in Romagna, all the fun and the magic of Christmas is of enormous importance! Villages, towns, cities and seaside resorts enthusiastically compete with each other with the quality of their Christmas markets, Christmas lights, decorations, and Christmas music – but above all they take great pride in their nativity scenes.

Artistic nativity scenes that involve whole towns; nativity scenes on the water or on boats; live representations with hundreds of figures; delicately made in sand or salt; small mechanical moving masterpieces; multi-ethnic nativities and scenes in grottoes. Everywhere in Romagna local people treasure their own evocation of the traditional Christmas story

All along the coast, and up in the hills, historic townships were vying with each other to create the most outstanding traditional (and non-traditional) Nativity scenes and Christmas Markets. Schools and families and local church groups were making all the little figures, the cribs the shepherds, the angels and the stars – painstakingly putting them all together and making little scenes everywhere and out of anything! There were pottery nativity scenes, ones made of wool and cotton and glass – everything!

I saw the Holy Family up on hilltops, inside castle cloisters, on beaches and in harbours – made of simply every material you can imagine – and often animated, both acted and mechanical. Here in Romagna Christmas was not Christmas without a Nativity Scene and pretty much every Nativity Scene has its own little Christmas Market, where locals could buy Christmas presents and stock up on Christmas delicacies, decorations and other delights.

So, in the historic Leonardo da Vinci-designed sea harbour of Cesenatico, the ancient ships in the open air maritime museum had Nativity Scenes on each; in the historic Pope's salt-port of Cervia, there were harbourside and beachside nativity scenes; in the hilltop vine-coated wine and olive oil townships of Bertinoro, Brisighella and Longiano there were hilltop and castle court nativity scenes. And in the important cities such as Cesena and Forli, Rimini and Ravenna – massive acted Nativities in the historic centres.

Rimini hosted two spectacular nativities made of sand and in the heart of glitzy Milano Marittima there was a stunning work of art using modern animation techniques. Created using glass fibre, the one hundred elements in this setting glow at any time of day or night.

Top of the pops for many – close to home for me – were the magical mechanical nativity scenes in the local pilgrimage site – the convent of the SS. Crocifisso, in Longiano. It was full of complex and fascinating mechanical movements, lights and sounds. From here, I did the nativity walk to different nativities throughout the entire historic centre, the museums and many other surprising and beautiful settings.

Santarcangelo was showing a mechanical nativity scene inside its labyrinthine grottoes, this featured a 200-metre underground nativity walk. Animations, lighting and special effects dance over one hundred statues, created by hand by a local sculptor, Davide Santandrea.

Another original representation along a spectacular underground pathway winds through the Solfatara grottoes, the old sulphur mine in Predappio Alta, near Forli.

And in the mountains, in soaring Montefiore Conca, the entire centre of this medieval village became a natural stage for the nativity scene. More than 150 figures and thirty episodes are represented along a path winding through the streets of the town and it ends with the Nativity set up in the magnificent Arena.

My favourite – Pennabilli's starry scene winds around a picturesque hilltop from its ancient cathedral.

But the knockout big jobs were San Marino and Sant'Agata Feltria. There were many more of course that I didn't see, but to be honest wherever you were in the world Christmas wouldn't get any more full-on than San Marino.

High on the top of Mount Titano, soaring above the Adriatic coast, are the ramparts of a unique World Heritage Site – the tiny, atmospheric Republic of San Marino.

The quirky mountaintop state that refused to join Italy, that kept itself aloof from the European Union (and that scored the fastest-ever goal in the World Cup!) creates possibly the most magical Christmastime event in the world – rightly called "The Christmas of Marvels"

Naturally there is an ice-skating rink; naturally Santa Claus sets up his village (with lots of elf helpers) to help lots of kiddies – of all ages – make Christmas delicacies and wrap presents; naturally there are stunningly beautiful nativity scenes, naturally there are traditional carol concerts in the atmospheric churches, naturally there is a vast array of duty-free and branded outlet shopping in the pretty boutiques. naturally there are Christmas shops stuffed full of Christmas goods from decorations to cuckoo clocks to electronic Santas – everything – and naturally there is a fabulous Christmas Farmers' Market full of glorious local produce.

Everyone can Christmas shop to their heart's content (and often to their wallet's benefit!). From a vast range of world-famous designer brands to great Christmas decorations – and authentic cuckoo clocks! There is even a superb local Farmers' Market selling local panettone (naturally), local honey, local preserved fruits, local salamis and prosciuttos, local nougats and sweets and much, much more.

Plus, Christmas music, plus Christmas lights, plus stalls selling hot Christmas drinks, sweet Christmas confections and delicious stuffed piadina flatbread, plus the aromas and sounds of Christmastime everywhere.

Exhausted by it all, I returned to the UK for a really quiet Christmas in Bath and a few winter months with my family.

CHAPTER 10

The Best of Romagna

By the next year, I was pretty much ready to knock Best of Romagna on the head. I felt that I was getting nowhere fast.

However, I had been in touch with Valentina over the winter months since we met in Dozza, and she seemed pretty enthusiastic about the project. Anyway, she said that she was prepared to do some work with me and see what happened.

As it happened, her blend of rather caustic wit, Teutonic concentration on detail and bursts of determined energy looked like it would keep me in order for a while plus I was desperately in need of her energy if I was to continue.

One other asset that Valentina had was her language. She was a joy to talk with in English, her range of words, phrases and constructions was enormous and she played her instrument of words with enormous flair. Usually her language was colourful but that added to the impact and the fun. So Valentina was fun to work with, plus I have never known anyone who could eat more pasta as quickly and I could depend on her, so life became a bit of a ball.

Quickly we got to work creating a team of friendly locals and preparing to show Romagna to travel agents from the USA.

The idea was simple, we would choose such brilliant co-operators with such brilliant products and services and full of such passion for what they did that what we created with them would shine out as the real Best of Romagna. Naturally we chose people that we liked and could have fun with too. After all what we did had to be happy and it had to infect our clients with joy or it wouldn't work.

So, we ate great food at super restaurants, Valentina tasted wine at great vineyards, we inspected lovely small hotels, we talked to artists and guides and lots of other people.

Finally, we had our initial team of 20 – all people we really liked and that were full of passion and professionalism. And they were full of fun. Our dream team in fact.

We had three great vineyard owners: one historic, one organic and one biodynamic. We had five great restaurateurs, all offering different twists on great Romagnolo cuisine and all making their pasta fresh by hand every day. We had five hoteliers all with different styles of hotel but all giving warm hospitality with superb service, we had a master cheese affinateur, an olive grove owner and oil producer whose family had been doing the same thing in the same place, wonderfully, for seventeen generations.

As this is the land of Federico Fellini we had a couple of great film-makers and philosophers. Naturally we had an organic piadina maker. We had a bunch of artists in metal and fire and other unusual stuff. Above all Casa Artusi had become a partner too – here our clients could experience the culture of Romagnolo food started by the "Father of Italian Home Cooking" – Pellegrino Artusi.

Then we put together our offers and created our website.

Our customers would get what we considered was the very best of Romagna food and wine, history and culture sights and hospitality. They would stay not in five-star chain hotels, but lovely local country houses with warm hospitality, they would visit beautiful ancient historical places with local people and they would enjoy wonderful local food and wine.

And then we welcomed our American travel agents. The idea was that these travel agents would just love Romagna, our choices, our offers and our ambience so much that they would tell all their customers about it and come back with groups of nice Americans.

So, half a dozen at a time, Valentina and I showed our travel agents our Best of Romagna. They stayed in delightful country house bed-and-breakfasts, they tasted delicious wine in lovely vineyards, we fed them fabulous food in happy restaurants, and our guide Cinzia introduced them to fifteen hundred years of colourful stories where they happened – in Ravenna. Of course there was much, much more – and they loved it!

They loved too the performance that Valentina and I put on. Our relationship was pretty relaxed and witty. I trusted Valentina enough to act as her straight man and our travel agents found their experiences not only deliciously informative but a great deal of loving fun too. They all went back home happy and enthused knowing that our initiative was something really special really authentic and certainly not mass-produced. We hoped that now they would spread the word in at least the twenty states that they'd come from. We hoped that they would enthuse their clients who we were sure wanted something more fulfilling than today's commodity tourism.

Andrea Nicholas was the boss of Green Tourism, a world leader in checking out and certifying sustainable tourism businesses. Their inspectors visited hotels and tourism businesses around the world and checked that they were really sustainable and if so, they awarded them Green Tourism badges for their websites and brochures and plaques to put up above their doors. Simply said a Green Tourism-awarded establishment bought as locally and organically as possible, it managed its waste, energy and emissions and trained its staff in green initiatives. The idea is that this would benefit the business' suppliers, its staff, its customers and, indeed, the world.

Ever since I'd started writing Sustainable Tourism Reports Andrea had been both a customer and a supporter and over the years I'd also helped her with marketing for Green Tourism. So when she decided to expand into Italy, specifically Emilia Romagna it was natural that I would help her set it up.

The initial set-up had started very successfully but in quite a small way and a year or so later she asked Valentina and me to check out the Green Tourism-awarded businesses in Romagna and help them with marketing.

The job was fascinating, there were over forty hotels to visit. Not only were we able to help them but also expand our own knowledge and the potential for more cooperators.

And visiting the Green Hotels for me was like a journey back in time to Ostend in the 1960s. The area that Andrea had chosen to start her project was around Cervia and Milano Marittima, a twin seaside town on the Adriatic south of Ravenna and north of Rimini.

Cervia is an ancient port famous for its salt pans which were owned by the Pope in the seventeenth century and still now produce their famous sweet salt. It started its tourism in the early nineteenth century and has developed into a lovely little family seaside destination. Lots of small family hotels providing great food for breakfast, sometimes lunch and always dinner. In the season they are full up with Italians from the cities. It's clearly a lovely holiday, there's the beach full of activities, of course, with literally hundreds of beach bars keeping their bit of sand clean all the way to the sea, hiring out sunbeds and umbrellas. But apart from the beach there's always something to do family-style.

From an economic perspective the destination is totally unsustainable. A season that starts in June, doesn't really get into full swing until August and then closes down in September can never work without enormous pressures on the local social structure. Of course, families take the brunt of the work but, even then, it's really a waste of potential. But that's the way it's always worked and Italians are slaves to tradition.

The food, though, for two- and three-star hotels, is unbelievably good and the efforts hoteliers and their families make to keep their clients year after year are gargantuan. And its not just the quality – the commitment to healthy, local, fresh, seasonal menus would be astonishing anywhere else. And given that there are no hotel chains here cutting costs by delivering mass-produced crap to keep prices down, the minimal charges these little hotels make is astonishing. It's just a pity it will have to change as the global march to sameness takes over.

But for the moment just imagine a basic family-run 30-bedroom two- or three-star hotel producing great breakfasts, massive buffet lunches and dinners comprising a good antipasto, two or three different pastas made that morning from flour and eggs, with sauces, a range of main courses, desserts, good coffee and acceptable wines – all locally sourced and seasonal, all for an Italian clientele who understand food and expect the very best.

I went back to the UK for the summer and then in the autumn Valentina and I started showing off our cooperators' offers to our visiting American travel agents.

We had become so proud of them all and all of them had fascinating stories, which we understood better and better in the telling.

For many years I'd known that travel loses its true value when it becomes just a formula of accommodation, transport and price.

By now I had come to understand the level of thick necks that the Romagnolo people sported. Every small entrepreneur I met had a deep conviction on exactly how everything should be done. And our cooperators were no different.

Take our vineyards. At Villa Venti, Mauro was so sure that he needed to own his own vineyard and produce obviously perfect wine that after a short career in the rubber industry, he studied to be a sommelier, worked in a top restaurant, persuaded his wife and his family to work with him tearing down an old fruit farm, planting the perfect grapes for the terrain and lived on little more than fresh air for 5 years before his (perfect) organic, biodynamic wine appeared, while his wife Manuela slogged away in the kitchen and the terrace creating breads and jams and chutneys by hand from their own raw materials.

On the other hand, Augusto at Zuffa wine had the responsibility to carry on his grandfather's work. Nonno had not become organic because he was part of any green movement. To him it was simple, his family deserved the best, they weren't going to have to drink any old chemical rubbish – they would drink pure wine just like their forefathers had. Augusto had to get a degree in chemistry so he knew what to avoid and why, and on the way he created organic wines so good that they got noticed by the Italian Ministry of Health and chosen to represent Italy at the World Expo. Obviously, Augusto is just as determined as his granddad was.

And at Fattoria Paradiso as we arrived there was always a noisy and colourful argument going on behind the scenes – reminded me of my days at Saintseal with Nanni shouting at Dr Fabbri in my early days in the industry.

God knows why they were shouting at each other. But this fourth-generation vineyard had a colourful history with superb wines and a superb wine library to prove it. The founder, great wine character Mario Pezzi, had created a truly noble vineyard in a truly noble medieval estate. He had re-introduced great indigenous grapes to the area, grown and matured world-beating rich sangioveses when everybody else had said they would not mature.

Poor American travel agents. Finally, they got it and loved it but, for the day after they arrived, they were totally fazed. When we said we were going to take them to a restaurant and its own farm they thought they were going to see a big homogenous establishment like they would in the USA.

In fact we'd take them to a campsite, with some chalets and a big restaurant full of local workers eating their lunches. And the Americans had no idea of sizes. I'd order some stuff and the waiter would bring some carafes of their own good wine and then troll up with a massive platter of assorted meats and cheeses for everyone. Plus a few baskets of their hot, just cooked piadina flatbread.

The platter would be piled high with the family's own prosciuttos, salamis, collar, head and cheek of their own cured pork, ultra-fresh squacquerone cheese, and dozens of fabulous crostini topped with exquisite delicacies. Delving into the food and the wine they finished practically every morsel and sat back, sated. The nice waiter (they all were) cleared away. They thought it was all over.

Until the waiter reappeared with another even more enormous platter – this time loaded with three different sorts of pasta, hand made that morning. Usually there were tortellini stuffed with cheese and covered with sage and crispy prosciutto; there were strozzapreti (strangled priest pasta without egg) covered with vegetables, and always the family pasta speciality – tagliatelle with a fabulously rich sauce of pork, beef and sangiovese wine. Our guests were not quite so hungry for this course although the food was always miraculous, the Americans would try to finish. The waiter would clear away.

And then he would reappear. Now he would bring the main course! Usually great spicy pork sausages, big juicy meat patties, enormous pork chops, great long thick slices of bacon, beef and veal steaks, all grilled to perfection on a roaring open fire and all from their own animals.

Plus, the grilled vegetables – fat deep red tomatoes, courgettes, aubergines and red peppers – also grilled, also their own produce – plus superb potatoes, crisply roasted with rosemary and Cervia sea salt. Delectable. A hush would descend over the table, draughts of wine would be quaffed as energies were recouped to deal with this feast... and of course, more hot piadina would be brought.

Done with everything they could eat, our guests would sit back in their chairs – full warm and happy. When the desserts and the dessert wines were brought.

One dessert was always Zuppa Inglese – what? English soup? Well, a very traditional Romagnolo dessert actually. It's a concoction of sponge soaked in Alchermes – an ancient cochineal liqueur – covered in a rich egg custard and melted chocolate.

Or, if you couldn't eat a dessert, there was always the option of dipping rich eggy Ciambella sponge into sweet late harvest Vin Santo.

Coffee of course, naturally with a range of home-made 'digestivos' – usually including Limoncello, Banane and Licquorice.

Done? It's time to go and walk off lunch usually with a tour around Ravenna and its amazing Byzantine heritage of glorious glistening mosaics. The imperial Roman Capital of Galla Placidia was always a highlight of the visit for our American travel agents. How could they resist a little time travel? Back 8 centuries to where Dante's bones were buried then back 9 centuries to the Franciscan monastery – then straight back nearly 17 centuries to the Ravenna of Empress Galla and 21 centuries to the Roman port begun by Emperor Augustus.

Hot and hungry work this time travelling – lucky that Ravenna provides a home for the gelateria that currently occupies number 1 spot on my list of great gelaterias! This one is on the outskirts of town and is simply amazing, so it should be if it's top of my list. Anyway, its gelato is organic (not as unusual as you may think but a big plus nonetheless – at least you know that there is no messing around with the ingredients). But the killer issue here is the family's quirky tastes like beetroot gelato and blackberry and sage, arabica coffee gelato is amazing and for texture, just try the ricotta gelato: light and fluffy and totally yummy!

The American travel agents had amazing times in Romagna. So much so that they were more than happy to tell everybody about this new (actually old!) place to go.

Finally, before the real clients came I needed to check it all out personally, to do a full-on tourism stocktake of the area, as it were, so that at least I knew what it was all about... beginning with the power road which cuts Romagna in two as people rush from northern Italy to the Adriatic Sea.

Still a major route and the way that most tourists arrive, the Via Emilia was built by the Romans a couple of thousand years ago. The idea was that it would connect their new city port Ariminum (modern day Rimini) with Piacenza so they could whip armies up to the north in double quick time when revolts were threatened.

As the centuries unfolded the road proved useful for anybody who wanted to move fast for whatever reason. Naturally that attracted an assortment of travellers – and because the Romans had built their road with the mountains on one side and the fertile plain on the other, and they wanted to keep it as secure as possible, it was in their interest to foster the growth of settlements along the way.

Well known cities that have sprung up along the Via Emilia, and have grown prosperous and famous because of their positions, are Parma, Modena and Bologna. These are all in the western half of the road, but the bit in Romagna – the eastern half of the Via Emilia – has its treasure cities too, not so famous perhaps but equally intriguing.

The eastern part of the highway starts at Bologna so I thought it was a good idea to start there and work my way down. I knew too well the seductive power of Bologna's food, and I was hoping that I'd be able to tear myself away from the city after only a twenty-four hour stay.

Naturally, though, such a massive undertaking as my whistle-stop tourism stocktake needed fuel in the tank to start – in other words a good meal. Where else in the world could you be a hundred percent certain of a good meal than in Bologna where for years I had been searching for a bad one to no avail! And the red city was an ideal starting point situated just on the border of Romagna halfway down the Via Emilia.

I'm totally attached to the concept of sustainability because it answers a great many of my internal questions. OK there are a great many practical issues like the world will be uninhabitable if we keep screwing it up, but the thing that really drives me is the potential gloriousness of now. I was taught to really appreciate and revere what we have, to use it to deliver the best results and to try not to waste a bit of it. And in cookery that concept of no-waste, to me, is fundamental.

So to dinner in Bologna for which Angelo had arrived. Sat down at a local osteria, we discussed what to eat. First some ham and cheese – as usual, Angelo asked the waiter what the difference was between normal very expensive Culatello (the bit of air-dried ham from the pig's bottom) and Culatello di Zibello which was their special starter that evening. The waiter said, "Fifteen kilometres sir!" As Zibello is the epicentre of Culatello production and it benefits particularly from the air in the Po valley – it is thought to be the best of the best. We were of course overdoing it a bit to have some sensational unpasteurised mountain-milk aged parmesan with the culatello but after all Angelo had lived in England for fifty years.

Both cheese and ham were extraordinary, served with care and concern for their preciousness, and totally, totally delicious.

Ready for our second course! We shared a tureen of the local speciality. As legend has it, an innkeeper in Bologna viewed beautiful Lucrezia Borgia through the keyhole in a door. All he could make out was her navel, so he created this pasta in commemoration. Tortellini are small pieces of ring-shaped pasta that have been wrapped around a filling, in our case a mix of Parma ham and pork loin. This pasta was made fresh that day and the little belly-buttons were swimming in a delicious broth made of Bollito. Bollito? The word just means "boiled" but actually it involves a whole capon (fattened cockerel), lumps of veal, beef and pork boiled for a few hours to produce the most delicious liquid to warm all your senses.

And our main course, and my favourite, roasted Faraona (guinea fowl) melt-in-the-mouth juiciness with crispy skin – Italians are so good at roasting! Sitting on a bed of hot spicy cabbage, with garlic and fresh chilli.

There's a lot of discussion about Zuppa Inglese apart from its name – not English, not soup. For instance, which ancient licquer should you use to spice it? Rosolio or Alchermes? Anyway, this combination of molten chocolate, spiced Ciambella or sponge and custard is delizioso and we had it for our dessert.

It's summer and it's Bologna and in this city packed full of students (the world's oldest university is still going strong and is probably the biggest in Europe) there is always something happening. Tonight's event is a free film show in the gorgeous main square – the Piazza Maggiore. Not any old film but THE Romagna classic – Amarcord, the film by Romagna-born director Federico Fellini that truly encapsulated his homeland and his people. Although it won an Oscar it never got worldwide fame. I adore it.

Back to the little quirky hotel for the night, big Via Emilia day tomorrow.

Early breakfast in the hotel garden and Angelo and I talk about hotels. Personally I think that Romagna's great strength is that there are no chains of hospitality enterprises. So, no chain hotels, restaurants, coffee shops or burger shops. Of course there are a few McDonalds and Holiday Inns dotted about but that's about it. What, after all, would be the point in someone like Starbucks opening up in Italy where you have a million choices of bars all making and serving the kind of perfect coffee that Starbuck's "baristas" could only dream of and at less than half the price? This, of course, is the same story for hotels and restaurants – every one in Italy is an individual establishment with an individual or a family running it with passion and always a committment to delivering something really special, something they think is a real world-beater. To someone who wants homogeneity and manageable standards it's a nightmare, to me it's heaven, and it always delivers wonderful, memorable surprises to tourists who want real, warm heartfelt hospitality.

In a world where everybody wants something different, it's why I think Romagna represents the future of tourism.

So, we take the big walk around Bologna. I've been here many times and already checked out the forty kilometres of porticos and the seven-kilometre pilgrimage through 666 of those porticos to the hilltop basilica of San Luca plus the other main sights, including the two soaring towers. What I want to check now is the food market and three sights that I think are important – the fascinating seven-church complex of San Stefano which was originally the temple to the Egyptian goddess Isis, and the massive church of St Petronius with its sun calendar. Plus, I want to know a bit more about the university. Then we need to work out where to have lunch.

The food market is sensational and quite crowded even at this early hour. I can see now how it's set to be a massive tourism attraction – it's old, it's pretty, it's fascinating, more importantly it's a fantastic setting for luscious instagram pictures. I can visualise the masses visiting for their piece of food porn – just like the Red Light district in Amsterdam herded around by flag-toting guides to keep them out of trouble. Of course, they won't buy anything, they'll just clog up the alleyways – God knows what the stallholders or their local customers think, and I'm so pleased that my groups will be smaller and encouraged to taste and buy.

Anyway walk done, it's time for coffee and I know just the right place. Zanarini is part of Bologna café society – great coffee and they'll sell you a plate of mouthwatering 'mignon' patisseries to eat with it. Sitting out in the sun, perfect coffee and perfect miniature pastry, watching the world go by, what could be better?

Let's go, it's ten o'clock already and lunch is beckoning but our first stop is Dozza. Talk about nearly tourism paradise – Dozza has a photo stop every fifty metres plus sensational views, one stunning castle and one amazing shop. The reason that it has so many photo stops? The very pretty hilltop city has murals painted by invited artists every two years – the Dozza 'Biennale' and the murals are painted on Dozza's pretty houses which makes an amazing and eclectic art exhibition of Dozza's cobbled streets. The castle is pretty much intact and still beautiful and built by Caterina Sforza, a big-time aristocrat in her own right and inside nowadays, as befits a medieval castle, is a real treasure – the wine store of Emilia Romagna plus balsamic plus lots of other edible goodies – thousands of bottles in fact. Wine lover's paradise. Angelo and I mooch, he buys, we go; he's hungry, it's nearly lunchtime.

And we (he!) needs an aperitivo. Time to drop in to see Augusto and Valentina at Zuffa organic vineyard. There's nothing like their sensational Sangiovese, selected for that showcase of Italy – the 2015 World Exhibition in Milan. With a special assessment by the Italian ministry of health – it's just the thing to put Angelo in good heart for the day.

He is now desperate for lunch so we miss out Imola, another Sforza town and a city of art in its own right, and drive to Faenza. This is ceramic central and we decide to explore after our feast. Every

Romagnolo man has a passion for food and wine and so does his wife – his 'Azdora' – and both of them know that they could make it big in restaurants, but Leonardo Spadoni has the money and the power and the knowledge to do so.

The first time I met Leonardo was in his palace in Ravenna. As he took me on a tour to see his works of art and his magnificent collection of classic cars, he explained his mission – no less than to bring Romagnolo cuisine to global prominence. Together with his partner in the enterprise, agronomist Emilio Antolini, he had put together initiatives to bring back and popularise many old local foods, wines and specialist recipes. Together they had organised special food weeks and festivals, leaflets and advertising programnes to spread the word about delicious forgotten local cuisine.

Leonardo had made his international niche as the biggest miller in the area with the most modern mill and by creating no less than 300 different speciality flours. In such an agrarian economy as Romagna where everybody had such high regard for food, this was no mean achievement.

And Leonardo's partner had achieved just as much. Emilio had invented a method of preserving grain so that it didn't go mouldy. In an area where wheat was king – Emilio was its chief consort. He'd been able to purchase his own castle on the proceeds and fill it with modern works of art. And, like with Leonardo, his kitchen was the centre of his household.

The hub of Leonardo and Emilio's empire was the piggery, and I had been privileged to be given a tour. Not, of course, the sort of piggery I had imagined, full of mud, muddy pigs and arks – the Fattoria Palazzo was palatial and totally high-tech modern. Paradise for pigs, you could say. Of course, they were able to roam in their own acorn-strewn woods, of course they got the best feed, of course they procreated well – and all of it was computer controlled to deliver the happiest, tastiest pork. Not just any pork – the local breed of pig is famous for its taste and its slow growing, nurtured and revered for its deliciousness all over Romagna on smallholdings in tiny herds – Emilio and Leonardo were trying to pull off a major coup, they had the best boars and a significant percentage of Mora Romagnola sows – their target was to produce the ultimate pork and the perfect prosciutto to compete on the world stage with the likes of Jamon Iberico the prized ultra-expensive Spanish ham.

So now Leonardo and Emilio controlled the production of the best-of-the-best staples of Romagnolo cuisine – ham and flour. Now they had started a small up-market restaurant chain to cook and serve their food in the very best conditions so naturally they'd recruited a Michelin-starred chef to manage the cooking.

Angelo and I were to eat our lunch in this first Casa Spadoni restaurant. We were excited!

The restaurant has been created out of an 18th-century silk mill on the outskirts of Faenza. It is massive and incorporates a substantial owner's residence now made into a 12-room luxury boutique hotel plus a lovely garden with pergolas. Leonardo and his assistant Beatrice have obviously spared no expense to make a substantial – about four hundred covers in three separate restaurants – and unique environment. The overwhelming design ethos is fun, rustic, piggy and very retro-chic! Big oak tables, a massive, specially made cast-iron barbeque, kitchens and big ladies making fresh pasta by hand all on display.

We started our lunch with a selection of meats, relishes and cheeses. There were the most amazing Mora Romagnolo prosciuttos, salamis, tiny sausages and other bits of the sweet little pigs, plus fresh squacquerone, other local cheeses and fig relish.

For our second course, the pasta ladies had made us something special – a "bis" – two different pastas. Tortelli di ricotta a spinaci (pasta packets with ricotta and spinach) and naturally tagliatelle covered with a rich sauce of their own Mora Romagnola.

And our mains came from the fantastic, massive, specially-made barbeque – bits of Mora – chops, steaks, sausages, a beef steak thrown in for good luck plus the most delicious, perfectly cooked pork liver.

Of course, there were grilled vegetables, and, of course warm just-cooked piadina flatbread, naturally stamped with the Spadoni pig logo.

There were white and red wines to accompany our feast – a sangiovese and a dry albana both from the Spadoni estate. Dessert? Of course, with the classic sweet albana dessert wine we had the ubiquitous Zuppa Inglese and little pannacottas and semifreddos.

Just down the road lay the erstwhile hub of ultra-exquisite European ceramics. After a thousand years of high-class production, Faenza is still big in pottery. There was a time when any European royal family simply had to have their Faience-ware to entertain their guests – and that was when there were hundreds of royal courts in Europe. And Faenza grew rich on the proceeds. Even now the main squares are stunning and the artisan workshops fascinating. Faenza's position on the Via Emilia still helps in transporting its beautiful wares around the world. No time for gelato unfortunately even though Faenza houses one of my top dozen gelaterias.

I'd never heard of Forli until low-cost airline Ryanair called its airport Bologna-Forli and I flew into it on a visit to Bologna. Now I know the city for what it is. A rich and beautiful city of art with a deeply dark recent history.

Dusk is just falling in the beautiful main square, the piazza Saffi, and I'm just explaining to Angelo that the fine eagle-headed cast-iron lamp posts that surround the ornate square have been dual-purpose in their time. With its history of fascism, Forli can be quite a dark city.

During the Second World War, local anti-fascist partisans were hung from the lamp-posts and after the war they provided a hanging-place for fascist collaborators. So apart from emitting light these lovely tall eagle-headed sculptures also emitted shadow.

So, we went for a stroll – in a quite different Via Emilia city of art – Cesena, I think, has the most lovely main square I have ever seen. On one side is the big bold golden-stone Malatesta fort with its wide opening for medieval horse-mounted troops to emerge, opposite the fort there is a row of pretty shops, cafés and good restaurants, on the other side a lovely park and finally a tiny road to a sweet little piazza. Everything in Cesena is pretty, authentic and comfortable. There is lots of interest and simply nothing threatening – plus it has a fabulous five-hundred-year-old library and the best gelateria ever.

But Angelo reminds me, it's time for dinner. We're off to the spiritual home of Romagna food and drink, culture and history – Santarcangelo di Romagna.

The moment I return to Santarcangelo I am filled with memories – about my visits to the great millennia-old fairs the city holds; the Bird Fair each September and the Cuckolds fair in November both draw thousands from all over Romagna for fun and food and wine-packed merrymaking. Great hordes jostle to buy and talk and sing. But also I remember my involvement in the International street (or in Santarcangelo's case piazza) theatre festival – an open-hearted event if ever there was one.

Everybody I bring to Santarcangelo loves this city of medieval terraces on a hill so I always study them to see if they've got it – Angelo certainly had.

But I had a problem. There are two sensational restaurants in Santarcangelo and a half a dozen amazing ones, but we only had time for one.

There's just two of us and there is going to be a lot of food so we had to recruit a willing partner – the lovely Ofelia – a local girl who loved food and could certainly eat! We started with the pork platter – prosciutto, salami, dried sausage, seasoned coppa (head), flat pancetta, seasoned lardo (fat), goletta (cheek and throat), and testarda with pickles and squacquerone and ricotta cheeses. Then we had three pastas – the passatelli (made of breadcrumbs, parmesan, nutmeg and lemon zest bound by egg yolk and swimming in a rich chicken and pork stock), strozzapreti (strangled priest pasta – in a sauce of rabbit and artichoke) and gnocchi made of semolina and ricotta with a sauce of pit-aged sheep cheese, green beans and black truffle.

So, we got to the main course with little trouble and shared veal cheek on a bed of cooked mixed wild herbs, veal tripe in a rich tomato and herb sauce and slow cooked veal with mashed potatoes and black truffle.

Phew! But that wasn't all. Apart from the pasta station that created our fresh pastas and the piadina station sending us baskets of warm freshly cooked flatbread from time to time, there was also a gelato station and one for totally yummy desserts.

Fresh squacquerone cheesecake with candied figs and almond crumble, ricotta cake with chocolate sauce, another Zuppa Inglese and an almond gelato with a pistachio cream.

That was certainly a big end to our day on the Via Emilia.

On day two after our exertions on the Via Emilia, we needed to get some sea air.

Those Romans had an eye for a good thing. As I said they needed roads to transport their troops to keep the locals in order. So, when they conquered up north – that is up to the Apennine mountains, they had to build a road over their newly-conquered territory. Obviously before the Via Emilia was built, they had to have a road to its beginning. But where? They naturally built a starting point – a city of course. At the end of the Via Flaminia, the road which took them from Rome to the coast at the end of the mountains, they built a city to be the start of the Via Emilia.

And not just any old town, they built a brand spanking new Roman one on the shores of the Adriatic Sea. Ariminum was complete with its Grand Forum, its two central streets the Cardo Maximus and the Decumanus Maximus and its triumphal monument (an arch to the emperor Augustus). On top of all that there was the beautiful Tiberius bridge and the biggest amphitheatre outside of Rome which held twelve thousand spectators. So Ariminum was big stuff – a worthy stop for any of Rome's armies, diplomats, merchants – anybody, in fact.

Here the Via Flaminia stopped after leaving Rome's Aurelian walls and wending its three hundred kilometres through the Apennines arriving in Ariminum in time for tea, or whatever.

Ariminum was the crossroads – at the Arch of Augustus you could choose either the Via Emilia to Bologna and Milan or the Via Popilia to Ravenna and (later) Venice.

For the next couple of thousand years it remained important and historic. In the middle ages Rimini, as it came to be called by then, was the home of the enormously wealthy and powerful Malatesta family who ushered in a glorious era of art and architecture.

And massive amounts of all this wonderful heritage from the Romans until now is still here for all to see. Roman and medieval Rimini is a real treasure chest.

But it wasn't heritage that attracted Angelo and me to Rimini in the 1980s. It was the fact that the coastal bit of the city with its vast beaches, the birthplace of Federico Fellini of Dolce Vita fame had become Europe's biggest, glitziest fullest-on mass tourism destination in about 1965 and since then its progress was mainly downhill. This meant that the over a hundred and fifty thousand hotel beds were available as cheap as chips and we wanted them to make and sell cheap holidays.

Rimini is a tale of two cities and now the bit we overlooked for years – ie the bit without a beach had become more interesting and we needed to re-explore the Roman bits, and the Malatesta heritage. A sensational and historic walk.

Just down the road from Rimini is the rather smaller and prettier resort of Cesenatico – our lunch stop.

The beach runs pretty much all the way from Cattolica in the south right up the Po Valley in the north. There are dozens of resorts from big to small, from really pretty to quite ugly – but the beach is the beach.

Cesenatico is unexceptional apart from two things: it has one of the biggest fishing fleets in the Adriatic and a port that was re-designed by Leonardo da Vinci. The port is fabulous, every metre is a photo opportunity and the restaurants, supplied by the fleet, are sensational.

I have a favourite restaurant and a favourite meal, which we sit down to share. Angelo and I have a long history of eating spaghetti alla vongole – possibly the simplest and most delicious and most more-ish pasta that exists. Added to the sight and smell of the sea those little cockles tossed into hot fresh spaghetti with a teeny bit of chilli, parsley, garlic, and a slug of white wine – sensational! In this little harbourside restaurant our massive helpings are served in big copper bowls – they always look like there's enough for five at least.

There is no argument about the second course. It's fritto misto for him and mixed grill for me. The key to deep-frying little Adriatic fishes is the batter – it must be light and dry not heavy and oily so you get the taste of the shells, the bones and the fresh, fresh, fish combined with the sweet airy batter – in Angelo's massive bowl go little prawns, baby squid, fresh anchovies and small sardines plus a few fat shrimp. I try one – remarkable. And my simple mixed grill – skewers of grilled squid and prawns, a lovely little Adriatic Sole, grilled Branzino – what more could you want? A coffee and a rest after all that eating exertion.

It's about an hour's walk over the beach and through the pinewoods to Cervia – the walk is a delight and Cervia itself is a gem.

Time to rest for the evening; it's going to be a long day tomorrow.

I love Pennabilli, not just because it's a beautiful ancient town at the top of a hill with a fab cathedral, a lovely piazza or two and amazing views but also because it has a personality.

That personality was Tonino Guerra the 20th century renaissance man who chose to retire there.

Angelo doesn't think much of Tonino – well he wasn't Venetian was he? Tonino was one hundred percent Romagnolo. Mosaicist, screenwriter with dozens of films and three Oscars to his credit, poet, artist, musician and dynamic spirit.

But my memories of Pennabilli were wilder. Once a year this beautiful town absolutely comes alive, really alive. There is something happening on every street corner, every park, simply every nook and cranny. In May for four days beautiful Pennabilli plays host to the International Street Theatre Festival – hundreds of brilliant buskers, dance groups, bands, mime artists, comedians and conjurers, high wire artists, singers, musicians, mystics and more perform and thousands come to enjoy. On any street corner you can hear jazz or country and western, klesma or soul, rock-and-roll or hip-hop. Wild for this festival is too tame a word – once I stood aghast as a mechanical dragon plodded his way through the crowds grunting and moaning as he breathed out great gusts of flame. Naturally there was food and drink and dancing and gelato, naturally there are pretty artisan markets selling everything from leather masks to perfumes and sweets – after all this is Romagna!

And walking Angelo around the hilly parks, the local monasteries and churches, the piazzas and the viewpoints, I tried to explain about Tonino Guerra and the fab festival but to no avail. He was more interested in our next stop – Sant'Agata Feltria.

Just twenty or so kilometres down river from Pennabilli, Sant'Agata Feltria is also stunning. It has a real fairytale castle, a magnificent piazza, the prettiest little wooden theatre you've ever seen and a lovely staircase with guiderails made like a long colourful snail by Tonino Guerra. But Angelo wasn't interested in any of that his mind was set on truffles!

Sant'Agata Feltria has a big Italian claim to fame – every weekend in October the National Truffle Festival is held here. It is MASSIVE. Of course, you can't eat truffles by themselves so everything else is on sale too. All over the place. There are hundreds of stalls selling absolutely everything – from dustpans to beautiful butter, from great hunks of meats and sausages to a hundred different types of cheeses, from lipsticks and shoes to every possible kind of local fruit, from sweets and chocs to dozens of types of dried mushrooms. And the stars of the show, the little beauties to which the main square of Sant'Agata Feltria is devoted and whose musky scent suffuses the whole town – truffles.

Angelo was in his element, tasting truffle oils and truffle paste in the piazza stalls just added to his appetite for more. Naturally tagliolini con tartufo was to be our lunch.

And the afternoon was spent doing a bit more sampling and shopping before we drove down the Marecchia river valley, hills studded with castles, to the biggest one of all – a whole republic with three soaring castles on a hillside, more a mountain really – the pocket-sized republic of San Marino up at the top of Mount Titano.

In my view San Marino really is a tale of two cities – one sacred, the other profane. Sacred San Marino is a beautiful, spiritual ancient UNESCO world heritage site with castles, cathedral, churches and cobbled streets, like Saint Marinus with high social aspirations and Roman law. The profane San Marino is too commercial to be true; its major industries were banking, gambling and selling stuff to tourists, lately, in particular, Russian tourists. As a result, many shopkeepers have taken Russian brides who now run their shops and stand outside grabbing passing visitors. Nonetheless San Marino is definitely the place to buy cut-price Ray Bans. And the views, on the one side to the hills of Romagna and the Apennine mountains, and on the other to the plain and the sea, are truly spectacular.

Before dinner, I just had to take Angelo to see San Leo, as different from San Marino as chalk and cheese. San Leo is also a spectacular mountaintop community but almost totally sacred and not a bit profane. It's strange because the tale is that Saint Marinus and Saint Leo were buddies: both stonemasons, both coming from Dalmatia to help build Ariminum and both Christian mystic hermits. Be that as it may, both the cathedral built on a pagan site and the old, old community church are unbelievably beautiful, and spiritual. And the impregnable soaring, gaunt citadel prison is fearful.

There are too many good restaurants in San Leo, though, so I needed to shake Angelo out of his reverie before he noticed them. Into the car and off to dinner. At the top of another big hill.

I had been hoping to take Angelo to Gradara but he hadn't had a good meal for hours and it was probably just an hour away from his bitching time. However, on our way to our dinner on another mountaintop I told him about it. The story is in Dante's Inferno, which is part of the Divine Comedy – strange title because there is nothing funny about it at all.

Poor, beautiful Francesca da Rimini, I always think, falling in love with the wrong Malatesta!

By now we were up another mountain in Verucchio the birthplace of the Malatesta clan. And pretty beautiful it is too with amazing views and the mandatory castle plus a very, very splendid restaurant. It's called the restaurant della Rocca – which means castle or fort so it's pretty Malatestian and while you're eating you can practically see all the way over the Adriatic to Croatia.

Angelo isn't interested in the view, though, his head is immersed in the menu.

And he chose a splendid meal for us – a big plate of starters, two sorts of freshly-made pastas – cappelletti stuffed with ricotta and tagliatelle with their sensational ragu, then everything that they had that they could cook over their log fire – meat, veg, the lot. Obviously Angelo was hungry. I even risked a Zuppa Inglese for my dessert. And then it was home to Longiano, which I'll tell you about tomorrow!

Longiano is where I came when I was ill and it's where I stay now. The kindness of its people made me better when I was very sickl. I didn't realise then that the town was well known for its miracles and a pilgrimage place for centuries. Once this hilltop town of about a thousand souls had seventeen churches!

Nowadays there is still the massive convent with its miraculous crucifix and a much-depleted family of monks and just one other operating church. The rest have been converted – one church has become a fabulous bar, another convent is now a theatre, yet another, a row of shops and a bar, an exquisite chapel has become a museum of cast iron another has become an amazing art space, another lovely church has become a museum of sacred arts and yet another church has become a public space and a special place for Christmas where every year there are dozens of nativity scenes on display.

Quick whistle-stop tour of the churches for Angelo and I tell him that at least two of the churches have miraculous objects in them. That's enough to make him hungry again.

We walk up the hill to one of my most favourite museums in the world – Longiano's Museum of the Territory. Basically, the idea is that when anybody dies or clears out their house all the 'junk' goes to this museum. This has been happening since the last war and the museum is now crammed full of fascinating items from 1950's Lambrettas to film posters. It's a complete history of ordinary people and full of faces of the past that peppered our bedrooms like Sophia Loren and lovely Gina Lollobrigida and difficult to tear ourselves away from it. I tell Angelo to stop playing the table football machine – we need to see Longiano's castle.

The quite beautiful edifice which dominates Longiano and has extraordinary views to the hills and the sea brings a story to life. What happened here is sheer conjecture but the castle was actually built for Gianciotto Malatesta, and it's sure that he lived here for a while. Until, that is, he was dragged away to his own private hell one of the hideous dungeons at Torriana castle, 20 kilometres away, where he met his slow death.

Anyway, this castle, apart from being beautiful, has a great art collection – said to be the best of modern art in the province. Here you can see Kandinski, Renoir, Cézanne, Degas and others of that ilk, not perhaps at their million-dollar best but certainly very good. Plus, a bunch of superb modern Italian painters of the 40s and 50s which Angelo loves. And a great collection of modern etchings...

The collection was started by a local poet who had little money but lots of words, which he swapped for pictures. Obviously a very effective ploy.

Time for lunch! And a Michelin-listed restaurant is in the castle grounds. Dei Cantoni restaurant is one of the main reasons I chose Longiano that October when things were going wrong: they were so incredibly kind, plus they did an amazing spread for my birthday. Today Angelo and I go for the no-nonsense lunch – two courses on one plate, a 'Piat Unico' each. Today's set lunch includes Garganelli – short lengths of tube pasta – with a rich sauce of Formaggio di Fossa – piquant pit-matured goat's cheese – and roasted leg of pork in a lovely rosemary sauce with rich mashed potatoes. Naturally there was freshly/baked bread and piadina. Naturally I had a teeny, tiny chocolate mousse with my coffee. Now off to another hill with a story for the afternoon.

Legend has it that the Empress Galla Placidia, on a tour of her local province, stopped at a hill for refreshments. She was given a cup of the local albana wine in a rough terracotta vessel. After having drunk it she pronounced "This wine is so good it should be drunk in gold!" Hence the local community took the name 'Drunk in Gold' or "Bert in Oro" in local dialect.

Angelo and I were on our way to Bertinoro to check out just a few of the hundred-odd vineyards growing mainly the golden albana, the rich red sangiovese and the fizzy white Pagadebit – all delicious fragrant local wines.

Of course, although Bertinoro is not only famous for its great wines, it is a stunningly beautiful place too. The soaring Bishop's castle which once dominated the whole area is now a conference centre dedicated to ecumenism and peace, and the pretty town itself is focused on hospitality, even has a festival dedicated to the pursuit of welcoming visitors.

It's always nice to have a walk on a hill taking in lovely sites, but it certainly improves your appetite and Angelo was dreaming about dinner. I had a nice surprise in store for him.

Just 15 minutes down the road from Bertinoro is an old Via Emilia town called Forlimpopoli. It's had a bit of an up-and-down ride, rebelling against the papacy and getting pillaged etc. But now things are calmer and Forlimpopoli has re-invented itself as a centre of excellence in cookery, food and wine. This new life has been made possible because of Pellegrino Artusi who was born here. Nowadays Pellegrino is not as well known as he was although he is still famous in culinary circles as the 'Father of Italian Ccokery'. His fame and influence stem from the fact that during the 19th century he travelled the length and breadth of the territory that was to become Italy, collected recipes, tested them, categorised them and in 1870, as the country of Italy was born, published a book called "Science in the Kitchen and the Art of Eating Well" – in Florentine Italian, the language of the new country – Italy. It was a sellout, reprinted many times and and as floods of Italians emigrated, was carried with them to remind them of home.

As a result of Artusi's influence, a foundation has been established in his birthplace, complete with a few restaurants following the same delicious recipes printed in the book.

This was to be Angelo's surprise dinner. We were to have recipe no 117 to start, followed by recipe no 69, followed by recipe 324 and then we were to have a 675 for dessert!

The flowers and herbs on tiny toasts with anchovy were delicious, freshly-made tagliatelli with the prosciutto sauce amazing, the stew of veal breast with fennel sensational and of course the Zuppa Inglese unbelievably good. Not only did we get a great meal but we were transported back a hundred and fifty years to an age of real cooking.

There was nothing for it other than to go back to Longiano quietly for a great sleep.

I still can't believe what Angelo was obsessing about the next morning – Nodino di Vitello. He knew that today we were to take the train to Florence to check it out and he has this favourite trattoria there. By the time we left Longiano to get the train to Florence, he'd mapped out exactly what we were going to have for lunch. But first we had to get there.

The little train from Faenza takes a heart-stoppingly picturesque route over the Apennines with just amazing views. On a good day it's simply unbelievable, roaring rivers, high mountain passes, pretty little villages and it was a very good clear day. So when we arrived at Florence Santa Maria Novella station we were satiated with beautiful sights. Naturally we did all the tourist stuff and more, the Ponte Vecchio, Boboli Gardens, the amazing panoramic Belvedere, the palaces and the piazzas.

Everywhere, though, there were crowds. Angelo had little fits of rage as he spotted the enormous lines of tourists in shorts and sneakers ringing the delicate duomo, eating snacks as they shuffled forward before they were herded in. He reached boiling point as he was nearly run over by groups of tourists whipping past us riding segways. And when he spotted tourists on fat-wheeled bicycles screeching to a halt and circling their tour guide beside the glorious statue of David he nearly reached breaking point. "They are vandals" he said "I brutti! It's terrible"

So, we were in desperate need of some light entertainent – the glorious three-floor central market – food porn and more. It has everything perfectly displayed. Anything you can eat – the very, very best of all foods, it's here. Our tongues were hanging out. We bought enough amazing food for an army, to take back with us.

And now for lunch in Angelo's chosen trattoria. Of course we had to start with those little Florentine specialities – bits of toast covered with chicken livers, then, in Angelo's words "Pappardelle, suco di lepre is one of God's own creations" and so it was, the rich wild hare sauce the perfect complement to the large flat freshly made eggy pasta. And then, of course, the veal saddle meat in its stew – the "Nodino di Vitello" was stunning. What could we have for dessert other than reviving lemon sorbets?

Now we just had to walk off the food as another dinner was ordered in Faenza at Casa Spadoni. Luckily we made it back to Longiano without exploding!

The next night we were to be in Ravenna exactly where this adventure had started some five years previously and we got there via our pit-stop in Bagnacavallo.

Bagnacavallo is a country town that was pretty much surrounded by reeds and waterways. At least it was a few hundred years ago when it established its reed-weaving industry. Chairs, handbags, baskets, once upon a time they were all the rage. Maybe that's why Lord Byron chose it to escape to with his latest love Teresa. Anyway, he brought his daughter Allegra to Bagnacavallo and it was here that she died aged just five .

Probably Byron would have enjoyed the local market in the Piazza Nuova – one of Europe's most perfect piazzas. To be honest it's not so perfect – rather than being perfectly round or perfectly square, it's elliptical – but stunningly beautiful nonetheless. Built in the mid-18th century as a local trade centre it now hosts all sorts of little festivals. And it's got a couple of brilliant restaurants. In one of which we were to have our lunch... and our entertainment from Maurizio the proprietor, who's been everywhere. Top of the list of his stories are his escapades working on the Orient Express. Anyway, his food and presentation is impeccable, and its mainly fish so we could have a lovely light fish lunch in delectable al fresco surroundings in stunning architecture before we followed the canal to Ravenna.

I want to take Angelo to Sant'Apollinare in Classe en route. It shakes me to the core – always.

You get to the outside of this classic 6th century basilica with its campanile and it looks great and serene. All around there is flat land. And then you remember that here was the second biggest port in the Roman Empire and maybe the most important one as it was facing east. Here usually 500 Roman ships were moored; at one time it was a bustling polyglot port with thousands of Egyptians and Greeks, Libyans, Africans and others working and milling around eating and drinking. At night there was a mighty Pharos flame to keep the port lit and guide ships. It was big and noisy and dramatic. Sant'Apollinare was the port's church and now it's all that is left; there is not even water as the sea has receded ten kilometres.

But inside the church is amazing. I've seen all the other local Byzantine churches, but to me Sant'Apollinare is special. The others are dark. This is always full of light and very special light it is.

Mosaics and a little fish dinner for Angelo before we go to bed in the cosy palace in the city wall. Tomorrow, I'm taking him home.

It's difficult to tear ourselves away from breakfast and all the home-made goodies on display. But we must – we are taking the Via Popilia towards the north. It's a lovely journey through the enormous watery Po Valley park with great lagoons on both sides of the road and we've got two little Venices to see before we get to the big one.

First stop is kind of a second breakfast, early lunch sort of thing. We're in pretty little Comacchio, a lovely pocket Venice complete with canals, pretty Venetian houses and good restaurants. It is truly delightful and here they have one speciality that Angelo and I desire. Eels.

Naturally our second breakfast by the waterside includes the local speciality – delicious, tender, fragrant eels, marinated, grilled, barbequed and in a delicious risotto with local rice too. Unbelievably wonderful.

Set up for our journey we are off to another, but bigger, little Venice: Chioggia. Of course, beautiful little Chioggia is not Venice but it is as Venetian as it could be and it was rich too. It also has the lion of St Mark as its emblem but it's a bit smaller and not quite as beautiful. Angelo describes it as a cat, but that's going a little too far in my view. And it's on the side of Venice's fabulous lagoon, just the place to eat a lunch of small deep-fried Adriatic fishes before we ditch the car and get the boat across to the place of Angelo's birth – Venice's famous Lido. He's promised to give me another tour of Venice, better than the one he gave me in 1966. We'll see.

Couple of boat stops en route and we get off at Palestrina's little island cemetery, catch the bus to the end of the island, get another boat to the end of the Lido then the bus to the posh bit – Santa Margherita, home for Angelo. Now we're in the heart of the Lido, home to the fabulous Grand Hotel des Bains, the scene for 'Death in Venice', now no longer, having given up its place to the even more plush Excelsior. Here was, and still is to some extent, grand tourism for the wealthy of the world. There still are no shortcuts taken in providing each and every need for their pampered guests. The fact is that they've been doing it for generations and wouldn't know how to do anything different. Angelo and I attested to this fact by having a wonderful aperitif with all the trimmings.

Then we got the boat across the lagoon to St Mark's square. Venice's magnificent skyline appeared while the boat scudded through the waves. There is always a frisson as I see the Biennale gardens, then the Arsenal and finally the Bridge of Sighs, the Campanile, the glorious basilica and San Giorgio Maggiore.

We are off the boat and everything has changed. Not the buildings and obviously not the water and not the appearance of the streets, cafés, restaurants or shops. But between the Lido and St Marks and between my first wonderful visit in 1966 and now. This is not the same place at all.

The Venetians are a gruff and punchy lot but proud, big hearted and brave, and Angelo is typical of his race. But in the past, they have been courteous to a fault. Now they are short-tempered and angry. Why would they not be? Venetians believe in form, it characterises the style with which they live their lives. Rich or poor, good form impregnates each and every day. There are rules in Venice, hundreds of them, which dictate every aspect of life; what sort of coffee you have, and when; which colours you wear together; the care you take to dress; where and when you eat; which pasta you can have parmesan or pepper with and which you can't; how you stand on your boat etc., etc., etc. And, of course there is Venetian – the language of Venice, not Italian as you may have presumed, and as like Italian as Dutch is to German. Venetian is not a dead language and every true Venetian, like Angelo, speaks it.

Of course, if you're not Venetian, you're entitled to break the rules – have a cappuccino after 11am for instance. But if you break the rules you have to pay like a foreigner and you will be treated with less respect. Not knowing the rules, after all, means that you are not a civilised person and not due the respect of any Venetian.

For centuries the Venetians put up with people who didn't know the rules in their city and they made a great deal of money out of them. These foreigners came, the Venetians showed them their glorious romantic jewel of a city, sold them fabulous Murano glass, gave them the ultimate in hospitality, built the grandest of grand hotels, prepared the best foods and most amazing wines and... charged them vast amounts of money. The foreigners paid up with grace and, grateful for the life-changing experience that Venice and Venetians had given them, went home, or bought a canal-side palazzo, or both. And often the foreigners even tried to learn the rules because it added to the value that they had got from their visit. Everybody was happy.

Tourism has increased nearly a hundredfold since I first visited Venice with Angelo and now this beautiful city is on the front line of a global battle.

The millions of new visitors don't know the rules, they don't even know there are rules and if they did they wouldn't care, after all they've paid to be there, it's their right to do as they wish. So, they clog everything up including shops, streets, cafés and restaurants that locals feel they have a right to visit unimpeded. On top of that they put cheese on their seafood, drink cappuccinos after lunch and wear shorts and sneakers. And as they don't spend real money, the local thinking goes, they're not entitled to real things. When the life and soul of your city is dying and you're overrun, what can you do but sell your shop to a Chinese person who changes it into a Venetian mask shop selling Venetian masks made in China?

You take the money and buy a home in Thailand and a flat in Mestre. And Venice changes a little more and you are sad and angry.

Venetians are angry, their beautiful life in their beautiful city has been stolen from them to display to people who they feel have little understanding and no respect. And they are not even paying a fraction of what it's worth and they are not even showing respect. Neither, of course, are they getting the real thing; eventually they'll realise it and stop coming. What will happen then?

So, as we barge our way through the crowds to see Venice's treasures and we see Angelo's old friends, we hear them recount with resignation and amazement the latest stories of tourists and their unknowing stupidities.

We've seen them come and we've seen them go. The last fifty years or so has been a real education for both Angelo and me. During that time many destinations have become fashionable and like comets risen in glory and fallen into disrepair and unpopularity. Big time destinations like The Kenya coast, the Costa Brava, Rimini, all have had to reinvent themselves. And now the world's great destinations are feeling the heat. It's not just Venice and Florence, the new discomfort of overtourism is giving pain to the citizens of Amsterdam and Paris; Barcelona and Berlin; Dubrovnik and Skye and the Inca Trail amongst dozens of other beautiful places.

It's sad, but now I realise why Romagna is so important to me and why it's immune to the tourism disease.

Angelo and I entered the travel industry over 50 years ago for many reasons, but primarily to share the love of the world's great beauty and diversity with others.

We've both had a good life on the proceeds – let's hope that somehow the same will be possible in the future. That somehow visitors will take a little time to respect the places, the cultures and the people that we are all privileged to visit.

CHAPTER 11

Yesterday, Today and Tomorrow

We've seen how the global travel and tourism industry has transformed from its fragile roots in an aristocratic pre-war infancy to a burgeoning boisterous adolescence in the course of just sixty years.

Who could have imagined that dictator Francisco Franco would have been the first to see this opportunity to transform his country's economy through the soft power of tourism?

Who would have thought that the mighty World Bank would have picked up on this idea and seeded it in precariously developing countries all over the world?

Who would have imagined that their partners in this massive enterprise would have been the entrepreneurs of the western world, soon to be the massive travel organisations, airlines and cruise companies represented by the World Travel and Tourism Council – the bosses of the world's 100 most powerful travel organisations?

And who would have believed that within 60 years China would be the world's biggest tourism source market and was poised to use its massive tourism power to wield economic and political manacles through the revived and expanded Silk Road?

I and most of my many friends in the industry didn't start out in the 1960s just to make loads of money, although that's not to say that plenty of cash wouldn't have been very welcome.

We actually believed that travel and tourism was an amazing activity with sensational benefits for everyone involved, not forgetting the constant partying, the glitz and glamour, the travelling and the fun of our industry.

If asked, I'd say that tourists coming to a destination would provide money for local people to start and expand businesses, pay taxes and create prosperous outward-looking communities. The tourists would benefit, in turn, from expanding their horizons in many ways, escape from their own realities and see someone else's for a change. Can't be bad can it?

With that simple attitude, we all believed that travel and tourism was 100% good and the more tourism the happier the whole world would be. So what happened?

Well good things, bad things and really sad things happened.

From the 1960s until 1990-ish, tourism looked relatively sustainable. In other words, thinking people thought that travel and tourism was "a good thing". We all did it with a clear conscience. OK in 1982 a hole in the ozone layer had been discovered but that wasn't anything to do with us happy people.

Then in 1992 The UN Environment Programme's Rio Earth Summit happened, led by Maurice Strong.

As a committed onlooker, it is difficult to express how much I believed that our world would change for the better as a result. 'Sustainable Development' was the key phrase, together with 'Corporate Social Responsibility'.

And it was to apply to every known activity, including the global travel and tourism industry. Henceforth tourism was to be environmentally sustainable, culturally sustainable, socially sustainable and, of course, economically sustainable.

We all thought that tourism had reached a peak at about 500 million international travellers in 1992; now was the time and the opportunity to make it really rewarding.

There was so much global activity around the sustainable tourism banner, new organisations, conferences, 'How-To guides', reports, that it was impossible to believe that we were not all now part of a responsible grown-up industry revolution.

At about the same time organisations like 'Green Tourism', 'Green Globe', The 'International Ecotourism Society', 'Global Sustainable Tourism', 'Responsible Travel' and campaigners and whistle-blowers like 'Tourism Concern' were formed to make sure it all happened.

Following the general theme of tourism doing good, a myriad of global organisations like the 'International Institute for Peace and Tourism', 'Philanthropic Tourism' and 'Voluntourism' now appeared, 'Massive Good' was to use massive air ticket revenue to do wonderful things. Even our travel-related carbon emissions were to be monetised and used to help the less-well-off through Gold Standard carbon certificates and the newly formed 'Cap and Trade' carbon market.

As far as transport was concerned, there had been pretty much untrammelled growth. Railways and coaches benefitted from the deregulation of the 1980s and the growth of passenger traffic; cruise lines benefitted from the security of home-away-from-home and the inclusive fares which reduced destination spending and made budgeting easier for customers.

Airlines, too, were growing dramatically, partly as a result of the historic Chicago Convention of 1947 which, in an effort to stimulate global trade after WW2, forbade the imposition of taxes on airline fuel or spare parts anywhere in the world. This was a dramatic tilting of the playing field to give an operating advantage to airlines over all other forms of transport. The same convention established the International Civil Aviation Organisation (a UN organisation) to protect and order international airlines.

In the last sixty years, following the increases in tourism, both domestic and international, hotel stock has naturally dramatically increased. In particular, big brands have grown, but there have also been major increases in independent hotels, guest houses and bed and breakfast establishments.

In big and small destinations all over the world (it is estimated that there are some 90,000 tourism destinations) local tourism initiatives – tourist boards and destination management organisations of one sort or another – seek to market and manage their visitor numbers.

So from 1992 – when international travellers reached half a billion, and domestic tourism reached about two-and-a-half billion – pretty much everybody was on the same page. Most organisations were vaunting their plans for economic, cultural and environmental sustainability. In destinations the big hotel groups, aware of their brand value, took the lead with green initiatives, whilst surface transport companies made the most of their environmental advantages. The airlines could only pay lip service – after all they were emitting some 80% of travel-related greenhouse gases.

Two enormous finance-packed initiatives also had tourism involved – the Millennium Development Goals and donor-funded international sustainable development supported by almost every developed country was to use sustainable tourism to develop local economies.

And in 2002, 10 years after the Rio Earth Summit, the outline of a form of tourism that would benefit all was agreed. The Cape Town Declaration on Responsible Tourism was published.

Over the next six years it was pretty much full steam ahead, by 2008 the build-up was amazing, packed full of energy and optimism for the potential of a really good tourism industry delivering benefits all over the world.

New global and local organisations and new global partnerships were formed. All with 'sustainable tourism' in their names. The world of tourism saw its future as green.

It also seemed that the world was moving towards a global cap-and-trade system whereby all sectors (in the tourism and related trade, airlines, transport and shipping organisations, energy providers etc) would be issued 'caps' on their greenhouse gas emissions. These caps would reduce over time. If any organisation failed to get down to their cap they would have to buy carbon credits from someone who had. A carbon credit is expressed in terms of tonnes of emissions.

An important feature of these credits is that it is also possible to purchase different standards of credit. For instance, the highest value credit is 'Gold Standard' carbon offset. In addition to them being verifiable and monitored, they must show a benefit to less developed communities who host the relevant renewable energy initiatives.

So, the effect would be that rich organisations who were emitting too much carbon would have to pay for this and the money would go to help poorer communities. Naturally not a great prospect for free-wheeling global organisations, or their political lobby groups. But great for the world's disempowered.

Cap-and-trade systems had started all over the world, supported by carbon markets. The biggest and the most serious of these markets was the EU carbon trading system – EU ETS (European Union Emissions Trading System) which is still operating today.

Anyway, by 2008 all eyes then were on the 15th session of the United Nations Climate Change Conference (COP15) when world leaders would meet in Copenhagen in December 2009 – this, it was thought, was where things would change. It was obviously important for tourism to become involved because it would be massively affected by climate change.

The build-up was amazing. It started in Davos in 2007 with a major conference under the World Trade Organisation. Everybody involved in travel and tourism sustainability was there. Massive scientific documents were sponsored by the World Tourism Organisation, the World Meteorological Organisation and the UN Environment Programme amongst others. Everything pointed to climate disaster if nothing was done urgently, and on the other hand, real opportunities for everybody through sustainable tourism. Adaptation to climatic change and mitigation of its effects could lead to a healthy tourism industry with benefits for all.

The conference led to the publication of major scientific reports outlining the dangers of tourism-related climate change, leading to seminars in 2008 at Oxford University to discuss and understand the Earth-shattering nature of this research.

As part of the process agreed at Davos, on the run up to the COP15, the Tourism and Travel in the Green Economy Symposium was held in September in Gothenburg, Sweden.

So, we were all ready for Copenhagen!

When President Obama took the stage at COP15 in Copenhagen on Friday, Dec. 18, the world was impatient. After nearly two weeks of negotiations, including a late night of talks on Thursday, diplomats at the Copenhagen climate summit seemed no closer to forging a practical global-warming agreement. Developed and developing nations remained far apart on emissions reductions and climate finance, and the U.S. and China were still hung up on the issue of transparency. As he began to speak, Obama took the tone of an impatient professor whose students had blown a term-paper deadline. "The question before us is no longer the nature of the [climate] challenge but our capacity to meet it," he said. "While the reality of climate change is not in doubt as the world meets today, our ability to take collective action is in doubt right now, and it hangs in the balance."

And 11 years later, it still does.

It didn't help that in 2007-2008 the biggest financial crisis since 1929 had hit the world. 'Batten down the hatches' the accountants cried. Short-term survival rather than sustainability was the watch-word.

Even so, international tourism managed an increase in numbers of 5% to 846 million in 2006, another 6.6% to over 900 million in 2007 and... astonishingly, in economically awful 2008, it even managed to grow 2% to 922 million.

However it was clear to see that the heady optimism of the 90s and the early 00s had almost completely disappeared. The soft, long-term values of sustainable tourism were no match for low prices in the tourism numbers game.

The fact is that mass tourism needs to grow to survive. And there is one fail-safe way to grow – ridiculously unsustainable cheap prices.

And cheap prices mean – low cost destinations with low wages, shoddy career prospects, low training and rubbish opportunities for local people, minimal respect for local culture, traditions, food and wine. The empty, powerful headline 'Venice for $100' says it all.

The one thing that could have changed everything – the internet – had become the World Wide Web. This had the effect of offering the best opportunities to the highest bidders, thus denying cash-strapped local tourism businesses the chance of effective low-cost global marketing.

Big money cash-register organisations such as Booking Hold-ings (previously Priceline) – who own Booking.com and others like Tripadvisor and Airbnb – came to dominate world travel marketing. The best way to make lots of money is to be asset-light – why bother with owning hotels or airlines, let someone else take the risk and do the hard work. All you need to do is to outbid the hotels on Google and you're there between the customer and the organisation that will provide their holiday. Now you're in a position of power and able to negotiate the terms with both sides.

That's how the OTAs (Online Travel Agents) have grown. To understand the revolution just look at the value of these organisations without commitment to anyone or anywhere – Booking.com's parent, Priceline, founded in 1998 (now Booking Holdings), for instance, is now worth $86 billion; Airbnb is worth $31 billion, whereas the world's biggest hotel group (IHG) with over 4,000 hotels is only worth $8 billion. And TUI, the world's biggest tour operator (now rebranding as an experience organisation), taking care of the needs of 30 million tourists a year, is worth just $6 billion.

So, the old way of booking your holiday has given way to the new one.

Once upon a time you went to your travel agent and they held your hand through the process. They booked your transport and accommodation and took responsibility for your happy travels. For this they were paid around 10% by the hotels etc.

Now you go online and take responsibility yourself – the OTA, such as Booking.com or Airbnb, rakes in up to 25% from your booking. Easy money you may think!

Anyway that's how it now works, the OTAs create the marketplace and travellers choose the 'best' deals. Invariably the cheapest and the most image/brand-powerful deals, that is to say!

Mass tourism is driven by price and perception of 'value' – it's been the same since the 1960s when it took off.

And mass tourism is no different than any other form of mass production – it depends on homogenisation and maximum repetition to make maximum cost savings and maximum efficiency. Airplanes need to be flown to their max, seats need to be sold to their max, hotel beds need to be occupied to their max. And over the last 60 years pretty much every little way of making this happen has been incorporated in the system.

The challenge is that international mass tourism has to get bigger to survive and the same applies to the airline industry.

But this frenetic activity is happening against a background of increasing emissions awareness. Gradually the world is becoming aware of what everybody was saying in 2008 – if global warming hits +2°C it's apocalypse.

Maybe by now you are wondering what's happening to the biggest emitters in the tourism world – the airlines?

Well, since 2012, to fly point-to-point in Europe, European airlines have to join the EU Emissions Trading System the EU ETS. All airlines operating within Europe, European and non-European alike, are required to monitor, report and verify their emissions, and to surrender allowances against those emissions. They receive tradeable allowances covering a certain level of emissions from their flights per year.

The European system has so far contributed to reducing the carbon footprint of the aviation sector by more than 17 million tonnes per year with compliance covering over 99.5% of emissions within Europe alone.

But of course, emissions are a global problem and need a global solution.

So... airlines flying into and out of Europe to intercontinental destinations were also meant to be part of this scheme from 2012, but as the deadline approached all hell broke loose.

Powerful lobby groups, plane-makers, airlines, governments and a range of other big-time industries objected. The US government even banned their airlines from joining the scheme, citing the Chicago Convention and the Openskies Treaty signed to foster world trade after WW2 and giving airlines major tax breaks including tax-free fuel.

Eventually the EU bowed down to this barrage of powerful opposition and conceded that international emissions should be monitored internationally and the issue was handed over to the ICAO (the Montreal-based international civil aviation organisation also set up by the Chicago Convention).

The ICAO was to come up with a valid plan to monitor and manage international airline emissions by 2016.

And it did!

The plan is called CORSIA and it is a tiny bit weaker than the EU ETS (well coming from an organisation that engineered a 70-year tax break for their members it would be, wouldn't it?).

Here are the obvious reasons: CORSIA is voluntary – not all airlines need to join until 2035 by which time emissions will most likely be at least doubled. CORSIA only covers carbon emissions rather than the broader greenhouse gas emissions. If the airlines break their emissions caps they'll have to invest in forests to mitigate the emissions. Given current forecasts of air travel growth the world will become one enormous forest – until the trees die, when all that stored carbon will be released.

Anyway, whatever the history, we have arrived at a situation in 2020 where:

The travel and tourism industry is still getting bigger – that is to say more people are travelling each year.

There is no effective control on world airline emissions and maybe there never will be.

Another massive issue is that it is clear that travel is becoming more dangerous, making it more stressful and taking away the freedom that travel once represented.

We live in a dangerous world. A number of governments are at odds with their citizens – there are still many human rights abuses. This leads to disempowered citizens, millions of climate and political refugees, and fosters the growth of both regional and international terrorism.

Add to this challenging background of the internet, 24-hour news and the fact that disasters are good press and you have very good reasons for people with grudges to use violence to get them aired internationally using tourists to do so.

Moreover in many less developed countries with human rights issues hospitality workers are very low on the food chain, it stands to reason that they do their jobs for money, not for love and see rich tourists simply as full wallets, which can often lead to resentment when they are treated with disdain.

Another issue that stirs anger is the changing of historic local culture to entertain tourists. In many cases host communities' culture is the little that they have to hold on to, and to see foreigners, who know nothing about their history, treating them as items of entertainment, photographing their families and their homes as though they were unpaid exhibits can understandably lead to irritation and bitterness.

Against this background it is easy to see how tourists can form political targets particularly in countries that are already subject to unrest.

In many countries the difference between rich and poor is insurmountable, and, naturally it is the powerful that control tourism. Foreign tourists often are just fodder for an economic machine that extends globally.

As the world becomes more unequal it is likely that tourists will become more segregated from the host community. Is this a formula for a happy relaxed holiday or would tourists get a better, more fulfilling experience in a destination that was more harmonious?

OK so it's cheaper to go to a country that cares less about human rights than the tourist dollar. Maybe it presents better 'value' but actually when the holiday is over do visitors take the 'value' home with them or their memory of the total experience?

There are exceptions – Bhutan has led the way with Its Gross National Happiness policy – a philosophy that guides its government. It includes an index which is used to measure the collective happiness and well-being of a population. And there are other countries that are also making strides to deliver holidays with real, genuine hospitality.

Furthermore global tourism is dramatically increasing – and everybody wants to go to the same places! As, gradually, the world's population becomes more prosperous, particularly in Asia, many more people will want to travel (it is forecast that the middle classes will swell by 3 billion people by 2030).

Because of the logistics of tourism (it's more efficient – cheaper – to increase flights to old destinations than to start flights to new ones) overcrowding in key iconic destinations becomes a massive unsustainable issue.

This effect is boiled to destruction by the OTAs' marketing of tourism products based on price and popularity. Why should they care? Their shareholders are naturally interested in money – they have very little real skin or responsibility in the tourism game.

That has led to the situation today where over 99% of tourists go to just 0.1% of destinations – places like Venice and Florence, Amsterdam and Paris, Angkor Wat and Machu Picchu with big drawing power.

Above all – it's a numbers, not an intelligent values game! Tourism's Achilles heel is the fact that success and failure are consistently characterised in numbers by everybody. The bigger the number the greater the success. Given our emissions problems, our overcrowding problems and our sustainability problems this cannot be healthy and will ultimately lead to disaster.

But overcrowding, unsustainable growth, the internet, and growing emissions are not the only challenges facing the world of tourism.

On the political-economic front there are two key issues that will not go away.

As world tensions increase and are dealt with in more and more sensationalism-seeking ways, the incidences of tourism-targeting by terrorists have increased. And the more tourists travel to countries with poverty and human rights issues (cheap destinations), the more they become targets.

Finally, tourism geography is changing. At one time tourists came from a relatively small number of affluent western countries. Now China has become the number 1 source market for tourists. Asia, overall is taking the lead position.

And it is clear to see that China is intent on using its tourism numbers to create a platform for economic and political soft power

The Silk Road (now rebranded by China as the 'Belt and Road Initiative') represents the biggest tourism opportunity for a generation but will the now number 1 tourism source market, China, use it to create greater global influence?

Already the power of Chinese tourism is having a major effect on the Silk Road countries on the way to the west. For instance, around Lake Baikal in Siberia there is local agitation as Chinese people buy property; near Almaty in Kazakhstan a major tourism development is taking place to attract Chinese people to gamble. High-speed trains will shortly run from Beijing to Berlin. Will they be loaded with groups of west-bound tourists?

It is a short step to Chinese-branded hotels and restaurants all along the Silk Road, even to Germany and Italy. It is an even shorter step to China's centrally organised tourism taking place from China to the Mediterranean.

The benefit to China? Wielding economic and political power.

Whereas the number of trips abroad taken by Chinese citizens was in the tens of thousands in the 1980s, the current figure is well over 150 million per year. While it may remain a marginal phenomenon in demographic or trade terms, tourism is a crucial issue in contemporary China, a major object of governmentality and a means to push soft power initiatives to receptive countries.

The Silk Road has been an important thoroughfare for centuries; for the last 20 years or so it has been developed as a tourist route with the UNWTO Silk Road initiative bringing 34 countries together to brand themselves as Silk Road Countries and to develop tourism cooperatively, an initiative that I've been proud to be a part of.

China's $1trillion-plus 'Belt and Road Initiative' which follows and extends the Silk Road looks rather more daunting. The Chinese government calls the initiative 'a bid to enhance regional connectivity and embrace a brighter future'.

Others see it as a push by China to take a larger role in global affairs with a China-centred trading network – incorporated with a powerful tourism push.

Sooner or later the massive potential of over a billion tourists had to achieve political status.

Even given these challenges, amazing opportunities are on the horizon for tourists and global tourism.

To understand the future of tourism it would seem a good start to understand the activity's fundamental purposes. In other words why do people spend their time and their money doing it? Are they after business? Escapism? Hedonism? Education? Understanding? Self-actualisation?

It is in fulfilling these needs and attempting to reconcile them with the needs of the environment and society at large that will define tourism's future direction.

So, the world, as never before, is chock-full of tourism opportunities. Here are a few that could help to establish a sustainable future over the next ten years or so:

It seems crazy that destination communities are not 100% in charge of their tourism inflows, after all they have real skin in the game: theirs is the home that is visited, with or without their permission. They could benefit most from the cultural, social, economic and environmental opportunities presented by having visitors and they could suffer most from tourism getting out of hand. Moreover, the attraction that powers the visit is their home, their history, their prettiness, their location, their community.

It would seem a small step for destination communities to assess exactly what they want from tourism, what they want to offer and how they would brand and market their tourism initiatives. These simple matters for small companies often seem out of the reach to destination community politicians.

The whole direction of global tourism could be changed for the better, and benefit many more people, if destinations were fully in charge of their own tourism rather than just reacting to price-led market demands.

Given the amount of the visitor's time, money and commitment that a simple trip takes to organise, it seems strange that few people really get the most out of their experience. This is why in the last few years new forms of travel agents have appeared and proliferated.

In particular those travel agents that assist their clients to have great experiences have become more and more successful and widespread. These agencies add value to tourism and to their clients' experience, making travel a more cherished activity rather than a simple throwaway mass tourism commodity offer. Currently there are over 100,000 small travel agents who could fulfil this role and help change tourism experiences for the better.

And, there must be a way to assess the success and failure of tourism rather than bald, featureless numbers. Some sort of value perspective that would target real benefits and dangers for all participants – tourists, destinations, transporters – could change the way we all experience, value and manage tourism.

Generally OTAs specialise in either transport (eg Skyscanner) or accommodation (eg Booking.com) or a mixture of both (eg Expedia). All of the OTAs regard their relationships with their clients as expandable. As with any relationship they are jealous of their partners. It is clear that they visualise their relationship as a bridgehead through which other offers can be added to the initial purchase. Most OTAs would like to see themselves as One-Stop Shops providing the whole range of tourism facilities and this is likely the way that they will develop.

The future for OTAs will depend on their algorithms delivering pertinent and affordable total tourism solutions to their clients. And the amount of millions that they spend with Google and Facebook. Given the nature of the web economy they will certainly change – but who knows how?

One final thought on the OTAs: there is a rather piquant irony in the story of their rise to eye-watering market valuations and quasi-monopolistic control of the world's travel industry. The very technology that has put them there could carry the seeds of their own fall from favour and the gradual dissolution of their climate-wrecking, culture-dissolving domination. An important part of the solution could be the grassroots revolution that is taking place throughout thousands of small local destination businesses and disruptor start-ups like specialist travel agencies and experience creators. The reason these cheeky revolutionaries may be capable of spreading entrepreneurial woodworm through the structural timbers of the OTAs is the very thing that brought those OTAs to power: digital media.

A bright young graduate with a great idea and the skills, originality of thought and authenticity to build a solid social media following can create a disruptor business in an astonishingly short time and with a very tiny budget. And a small local family business with a great product – an attractive destination, regional knowledge, time-tested hospitality, cooking and customs – can turn their hard-earned knowledge of what really makes their farm, vineyard, guesthouse, village or valley the centre of the civilised universe into a small fortune. Especially if that bright young graduate is a member of that very family.

Look what Greta Thunberg did to global climate awareness in just the first twelve months of her campaign, starting at fifteen years of age. Now imagine hundreds – even thousands – of Gretas everywhere making millions and millions of people all over the world aware of just what their tourism dollars could do if they became part of the climate solution. And how much more they could appreciate – and be appreciated by – their host communities. If, for instance, tourists made just two really high quality visits a year instead of half-a-dozen cut-price city breaks; if they travelled by high-speed train where possible, rather than only budget airlines; if they took time to discover the exquisite crafts, culinary delights and culture of the local families at their destinations, they could not only massively reduce the damage being done by thoughtless, volume-driven, 'mad-dash marauding' tourism – they could find out what a profoundly satisfying experience travel can provide for everyone involved – hosts and guests alike.

To achieve this, all that is required is that the customers inform themselves of where to find such destinations, hosts and experiences – and that the hosts inform themselves of just what a treasure chest they have been sitting on all this time. And digital media provide all the answers, from blogging to viral marketing, from instagram to twitter, from Facebook to WhatsApp, the grassroots movement has all the tools it needs. The authentic experiences are already there for the enjoying, the hosts are there – they have been often for many generations – and ready to share their knowledge, their history, their food, their crafts, their pride and their hard-earned wisdom on how to make the most of their land and their lives, whatever providence may offer them. All that is needed is to make the connections – and the means to do that also already exist…they are the same means that were used by the OTAs in the first place.

All this activity could create a truly sharing economy, one in which the biggest rewards go to those who can benefit most – and create a form of tourism that truly fulfils both guests and hosts.

And, while we're on the topic of digital transformation, there's also this… the gaming industry is a global phenomenon with massive investment and now with over 2 billion gamers, a figure that is increasing daily. Clearly the motivation is similar to that of tourism – escapism, fun, learning, entertainment. It will be a short step to virtual tourism, both as a small hands-off experience and as a bigger, totally immersive one.

As technological innovations have improved virtual reality capabilities and popularised the medium, virtual tours have become more commonplace. Currently, you can use VR to check out a casino or museum from your couch, visit Red Rock Canyon from your favourite recliner or take a trip to Bath while you're in your bath (just make sure you don't drop whatever device you're using).

When VR tours are done well, it almost feels like you're there — which begs the question: will people start checking destinations off their bucket lists by booting up a device instead of booking travel and actually making a real-life trip?

Both will shortly be true. It will even be possible to have real-time conversations with local people, shop for local goods, visit entertainments and (nearly) eat local meals. All without overcrowding the destination, taking a flight, emitting tourism-level emissions, or being exposed to any danger. As a learning tool and as an experience device, virtual tourism is on the way.

Travel-related carbon offsets will also change the world we live in for the better. Currently airline emissions are at least a billion tonnes of greenhouse gases a year. If this were paid for at a reasonable rate for gold standard carbon credits – say $30 a tonne – it would transfer at least $30 billion a year to less developed countries' sustainable development initiatives.

Add to this the opportunities for other industries and individual travellers and you create a major wealth transfer opportunity, plus countries that are developing into totally green sustainable economies.

Finally here are two words that are already changing the travel and tourism industry forever – the 'Experience Economy'.

Already there are half a million micro firms all over the world creating, developing and marketing experiences.

Once upon a time travel was about going there, doing stuff and coming back. The key was… Where was there? The pulling power of the destination dragged the passengers in.

Ever a leader, TUI with its 30 million or so passengers, in the search for sustainable profits, has morphed into something really interesting. No longer a tour operator, TUI has now reconstructed itself as an experience-provider.

Why? Because they can, not only make much more money out of experiences, they can also own them. If you want a TUI experience (like a TUI cruise or a TUI hotel) there's only one place you can go – that's TUI. And TUI have backed it with real money – spending over €200 million buying experience marketing companies.

However the Experience Economy offers opportunities to literally anyone with passion for a really good idea.

Just create your own unique experience, plug in the accommodation and you're on your way. Marketing is, of course, the key.

Estimates of the current annual global spend on experiences are about $200 billion and that is certain to increase.

Another major advantage of experience-based tourism is that, rather than the destination pulling in the clients, the experience does. Just think – clients could go to the 99.9% of destinations that would love them rather than the 0.1% that are over-popular. Just how many hundreds of thousands of little businesses could the Experience Economy create?

The Experience Economy, an amazing exotic Silk Road, over 80,000 destinations all over the world offering their own fabulous authentic experiences, VR tourism, emission payments helping to empower people … and more.

It looks like the next sixty years of tourism will be even more fascinating, colourful and opportunity-full than the last…

If we avoid the climate change catastrophe, that is!

Editing by Robert Barnard-Weston
www.BloomfieldGroups.com

Multi-tasking editor of this book, Rob Barnard-Weston first met Valère when he became his favourite freelance copywriter in the heady days of Land Travel at its peak. They have seen each other through many peak – and trough – experiences in the decades since that time. In addition to becoming a green marketing guru (Valère's chosen title for him, not Rob's own), Rob has also co-launched the UK Farmers' Markets movement, a sustainability consultancy, an eco-artisan bakery business, an industrial-scale composting company, a small but perfectly-formed eco-B&B, a local environmental charity and five children. Now those children are more-or-less fully fledged, he and Karen, his long-suffering wife, deliver workshops, among other things, on 'How to Run an Eco-B&B' in their ridiculously gorgeous home city of Bath, England.

Printed in Great Britain
by Amazon